POSTCARD HISTORY SERIES

Salem and Roanoke County IN VINTAGE POSTCARDS

POSTCARD HISTORY SERIES

Salem and Roanoke County in Vintage Postcards

Nelson Harris

ISBN 978-0-7385-1838-1

Published by Arcadia Publishing
Charleston, South Carolina

Printed in the United States of America

Library of Congress Catalog Card Number: 2005924321

For all general information contact Arcadia Publishing at:
Telephone 843-853-2070
Fax 843-853-0044
E-mail sales@arcadiapublishing.com
For customer service and orders:
Toll-Free 1-888-313-2665

Visit us on the Internet at www.arcadiapublishing.com

To my son, David

Contents

ACKNOWLEDGMENTS

I am most grateful to George Wade of Roanoke for allowing me access to and use of his extensive collection of Roanoke Valley postcards. All of the cards used in the book, with the exception of those from my collection in the last chapter, are from his personal collection. I most appreciated his trust in me to care for his cards while they were in my possession, and I am pleased to make his collection available to the public through this book. I am also grateful to the staff of Arcadia Publishing, especially my editor, Kathryn Korfonta.

The material for the many captions accompanying the images came from a variety of published sources, notably Raymond Barnes's *A History of the City of Roanoke* (1968), Norwood C. Middleton's *Salem: A Virginia Chronicle* (1986), Deedie Kagey's *When Past is Prologue: A History of Roanoke County* (1988), William E. Eisenberg's *The First Hundred Years of Roanoke College, 1842–1942* (1942), and Frances J. Niederer's *Hollins College: An Illustrated History* (1973). Finally, I am always indebted to my wife, Cathy, for her love and support in all of my endeavors.

INTRODUCTION

Nestled in the Blue Ridge Mountains, the Roanoke Valley embraces a rich history of commerce and culture while remaining sensitive to its natural surroundings. This tender balance produces a way of life long cherished by the valley's citizens, whose pace and spirit reflect an appreciation for the unique setting they call home.

The first residents of the Roanoke Valley arrived around 8000 B.C. Archeological evidence, uncovered at various points over time, has demonstrated the presence of several tribes of American Indians up through the middle of the 18th century. In fact, the name Roanoke comes from a Native American word for shell money. Certainly the Blue Ridge Mountains, the river and creeks, and the fertile plateaus served these valley ancestors well.

The first European visitors to the area were most likely two traders, Thomas Batts and Robert Fallam. In 1671, Batts and Fallam recorded a three-day visit in a journal they kept, during which they called upon the Tutelo Indians, in the probable vicinity of present-day Salem. It would be another 100 years before a European settlement, Fort Lewis, appeared. Around 1755, Virginia established Fort Lewis west of Salem to offer protection to frontier settlers during their tense relations with American Indian tribes in the area, including the Powhatan and the Monolan, among others. Settlers continued to move into the valley during the latter half of the 18th century.

Salem got its start when a landowner by the name of James Simpson added to his holdings with a 31-acre purchase in 1800. With that acquisition, Simpson set out to establish a town, planning a few simple roads and 40 residential lots. Within a few years, most of the lots had been purchased, and the first wood-frame houses were being built. For reasons that have escaped historians, Simpson chose to name the new community Salem in documents at Fincastle, Botetourt County, in 1802. The town grew under the guidance of a second developer, John Brugh, who plotted additional lots that gave the town a post office, taverns, shops, and a stop for stagecoaches. Salem was on its way. It eventually became, in fact, a stopover for Pres. Andrew Jackson on his trips between Washington and Tennessee. By 1820, Salem had a population of 290.

As Salem grew, so too did the Roanoke Valley with other towns and settlements. In 1828, the citizens of Franklin, Botetourt, and Montgomery Counties began petitioning the Virginia Legislature for the establishment of a new county. In 1838, their efforts proved fruitful; the Commonwealth approved the division of land from Botetourt County, thereby creating Roanoke County. Newly appointed county justices chose Salem as the county seat.

In the two centuries that have passed since the formation of Roanoke County, both the county and Salem have grown and developed in significant ways. For the past 100 of those years, the picture postcard has chronicled some of those changes. The postcard captured new buildings, special events, industry, and public spaces in an effort to promote the ideals and achievements of its many subjects. *Salem and Roanoke County* captures that visual history in over 200 cards. Tangible remainders of the vision, service, and commitment rendered by so many over the years to make the Roanoke Valley what it is today include Lakeside's two-million-gallon pool, Catawba Sanatorium, Cavern Hill Inn, Academy School, the Baptist and Lutheran Orphanages, Roanoke College, Hollins University, and Salem's Main Street. These cards remind us not only of a shared history, but of a common spirit that continues to move the valley forward.

This book concludes with a chapter of previously unpublished vintage postcards that depict structures and scenes in Roanoke City. They are included here to both compliment this volume and to supplement an earlier volume on Roanoke City postcards.

Salem and Roanoke County is, as with all previous volumes, a labor of love produced with great affection for this beautiful valley I am blessed to call home.

—Nelson Harris
Roanoke, Virginia

One

SALEM

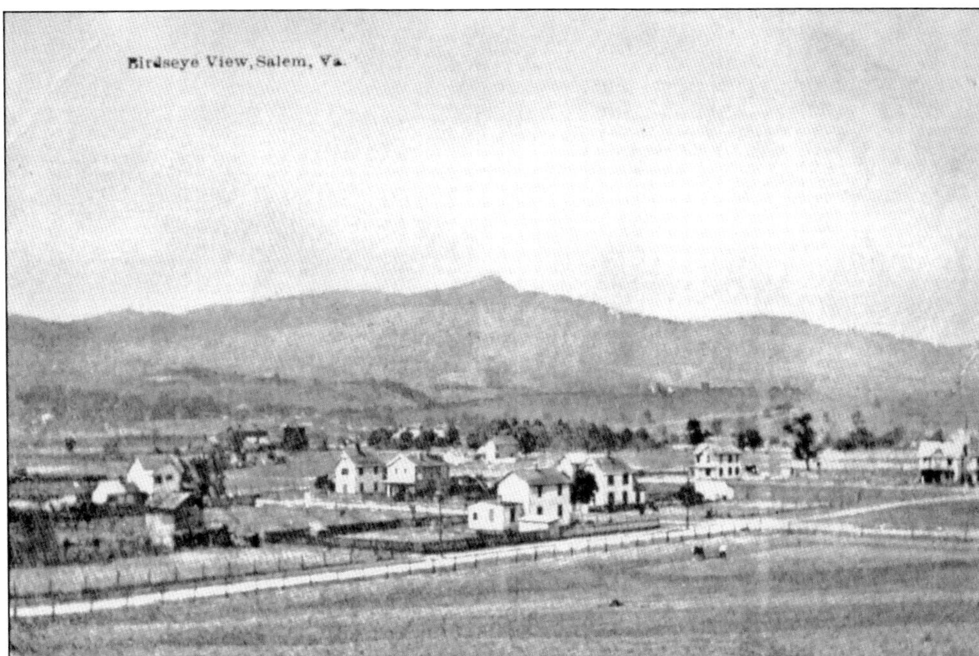

BIRD'S-EYE VIEW OF SALEM, 1910. This century-old view of Salem shows the development of the town since its inception in 1802, when James Simpson created 40 residential lots on 16 acres. The lots fronted one main road, which Simpson named "Roanoke Street." The lots were one of two sizes: rectangular (66 by 266 feet) or square (132 feet). The cross streets were originally named Limestone Street (later called Union Street), Water Street (later Broad Street), and Market Street.

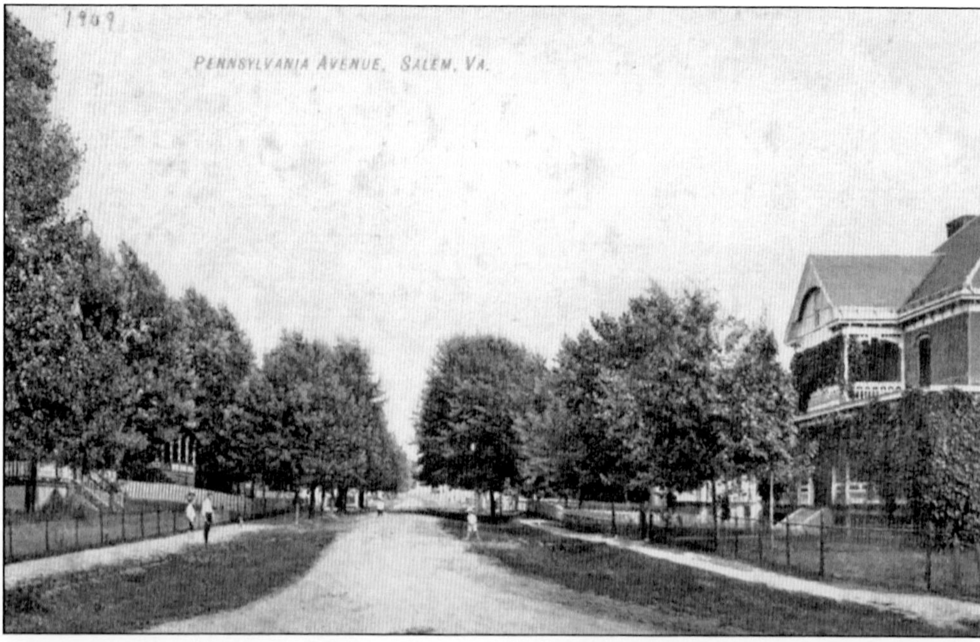

PENNSYLVANIA AVENUE, 1909. This early street scene illustrates the stately residential developments that marked Salem's development at the beginning of the 20th century.

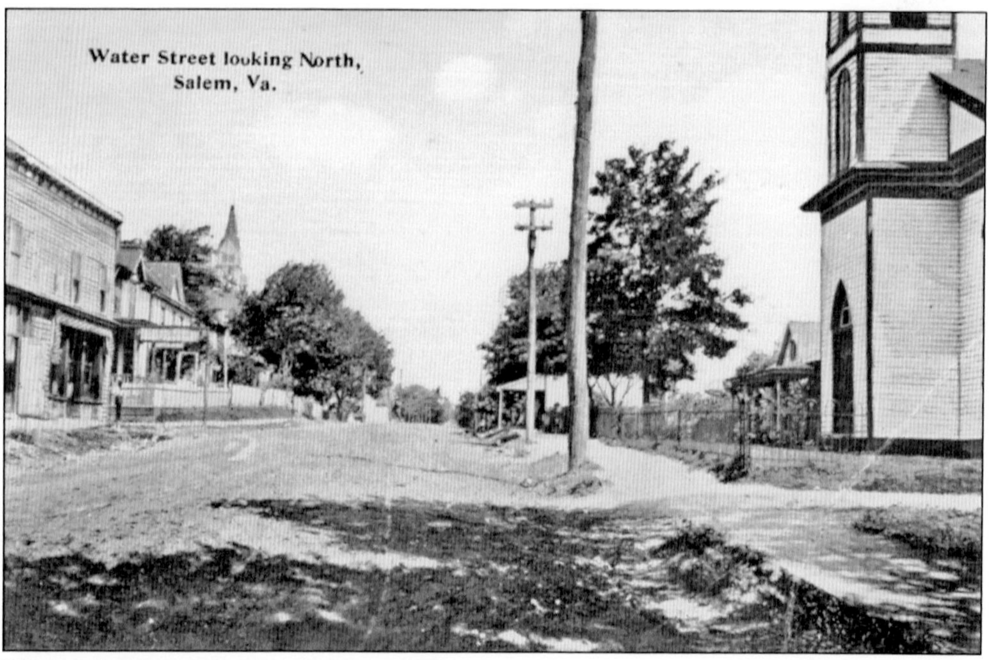

WATER STREET, LOOKING NORTH, 1910. Water Street, later South Broad Street, was one of the earliest streets laid out in the 1802 plot of Salem. Water Street became the dominant center for Salem's African American community.

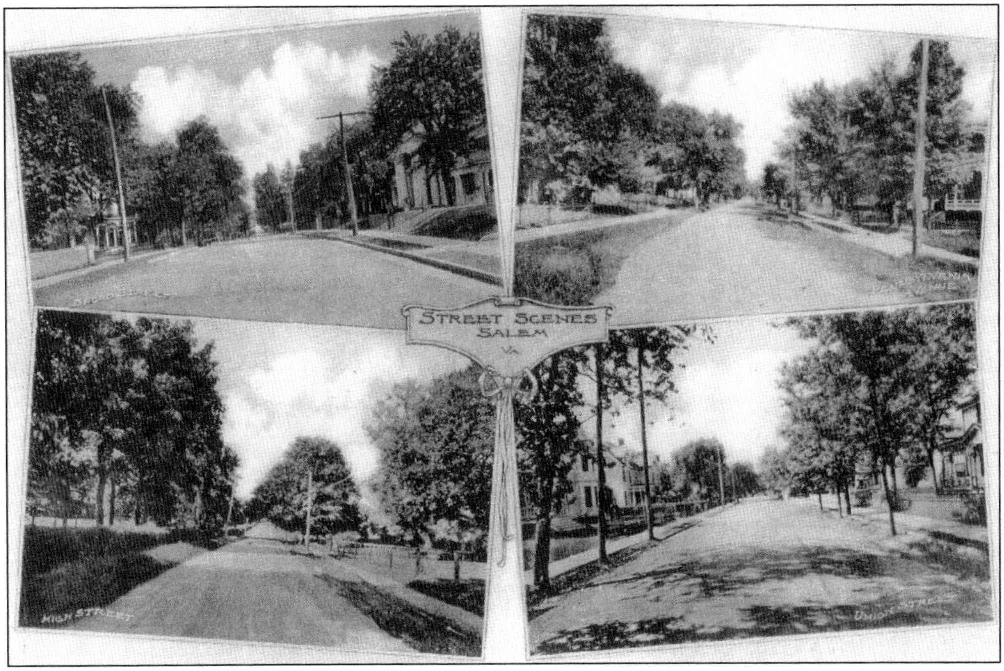

Street Scenes, 1915. Various street scenes, namely Broad Street (top left), Pennsylvania Avenue (top right), High Street (bottom left), and Union Street (bottom right), are pictured here.

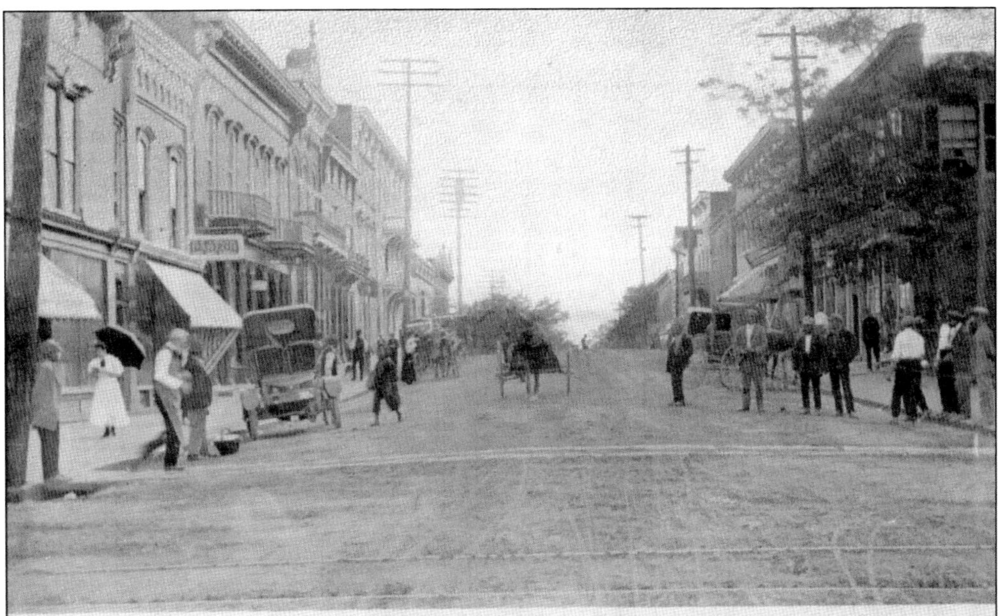

Main Street, 1910. Dirt streets and horse carriages marked town living 100 years ago. In the foreground, one can see the outline of a crosswalk (probably brick) that allowed pedestrians to maneuver across streets while avoiding the ankle-deep mud that often plagued towns after heavy rains.

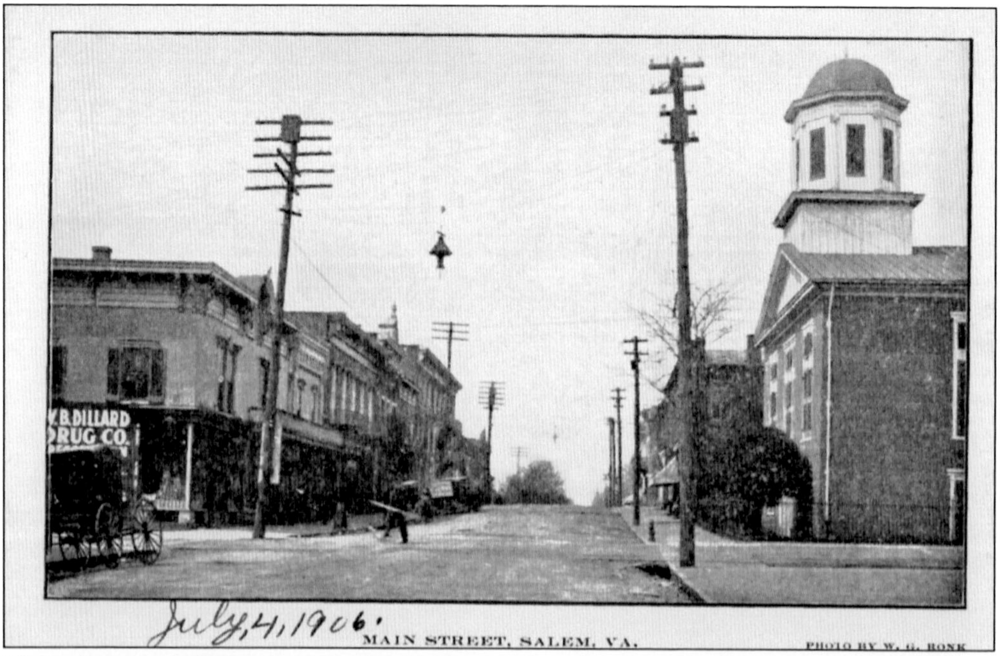

MAIN STREET, 1906. Roanoke Street was James Simpson's original name for Main Street, which is pictured here in the early 20th century. The street was only a few blocks long when it was first developed, running from present-day Colorado Street to Union Street. (Photograph by W. G. Ronk.)

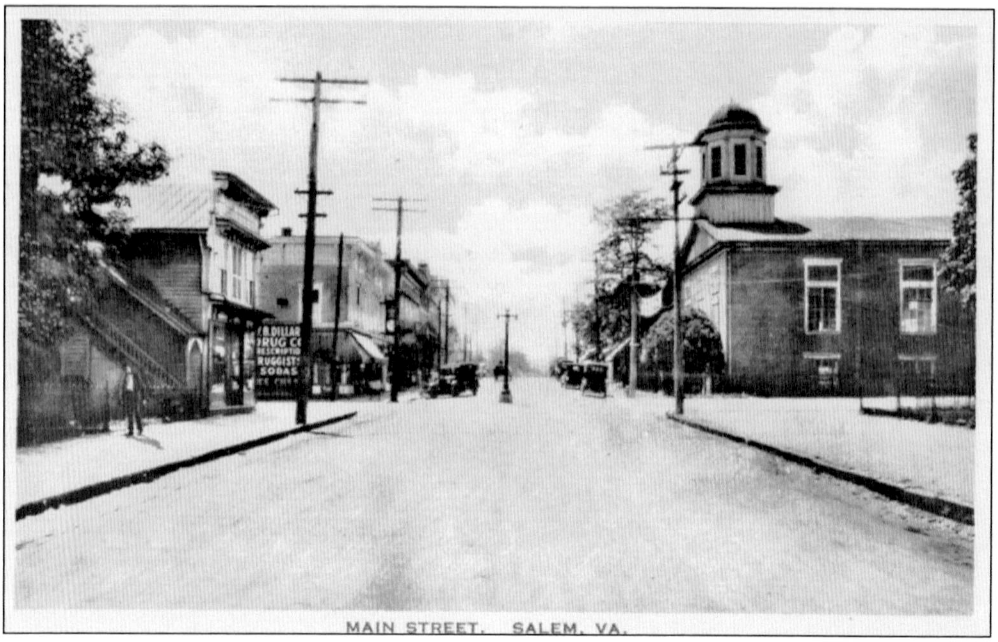

MAIN STREET, 1915. This scene is further back from the intersection pictured in the above photograph.

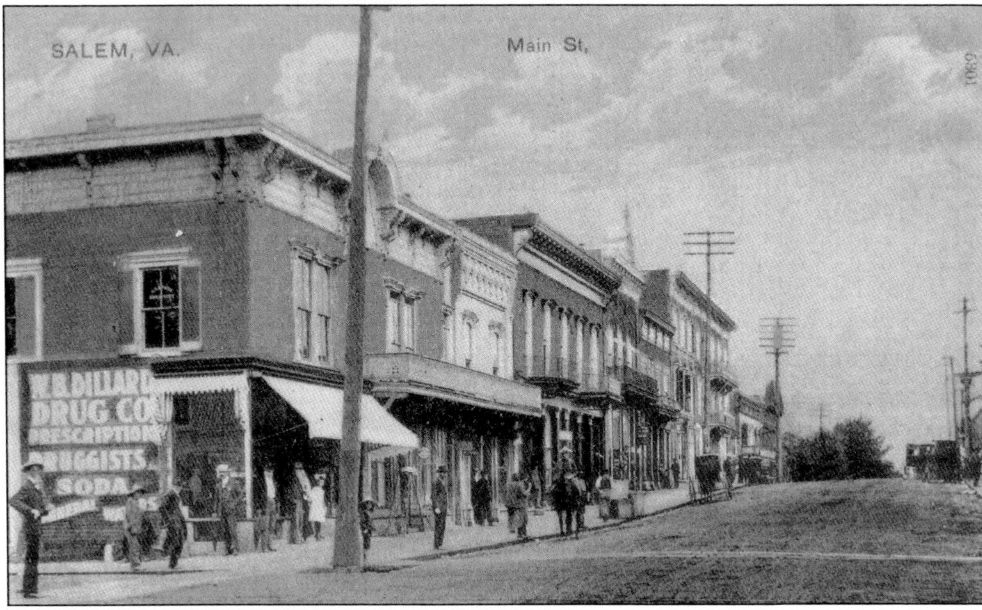

Main Street, 1910. Prominent on the left is a sign for W. B. Dillard Drug Company—Prescription Druggists, Soda, and Mineral Waters. Watts Dillard was a prominent Salem business man involved in numerous civic projects. His drugstore, at the corner of Main and College Streets, got a hot-water soda urn in 1901, which was big news. The *Salem Times* reported "both hot and cold drinks will be served in summer and winter." This same establishment had earlier turned heads with the installation of a fly brush and fan, a contraption that drove away flies from the soda fountain and kept the air stirring constantly.

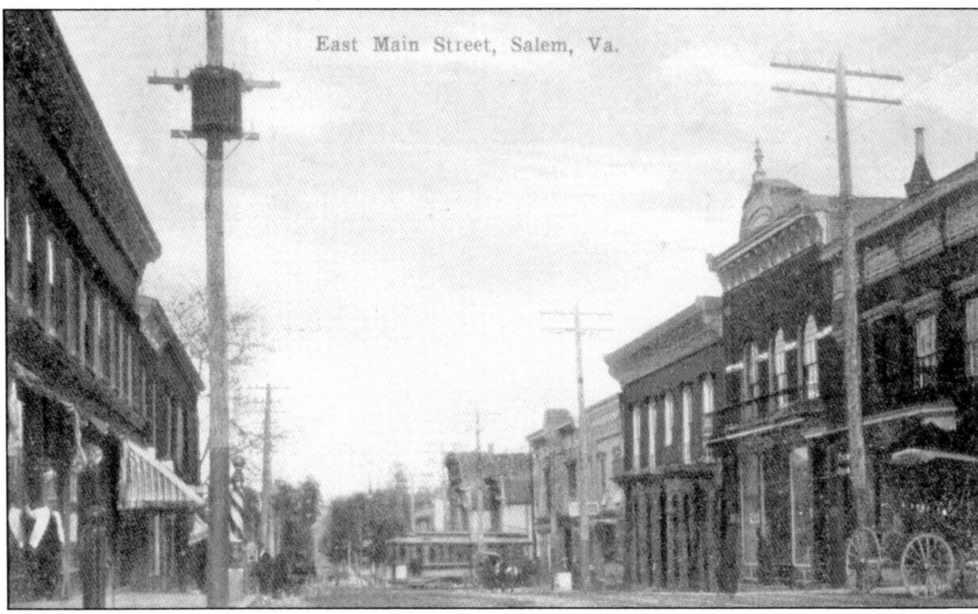

East Main Street, 1910. The following message is written on the back of this postcard: "Dear Mama. Does this look like home? Not much, I guess you would like it down here because people are so easy going and don't believe in working all the time." Home, by the way, was Dover, New Jersey.

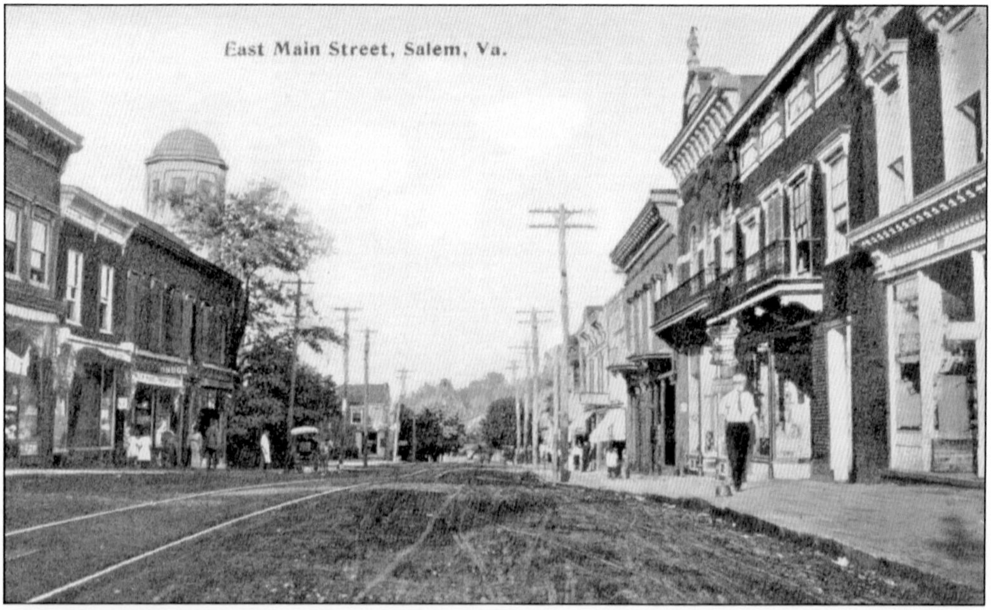

EAST MAIN STREET, 1915. After much discussion, Salem's city fathers agreed to a streetcar route on Main Street in 1894 (the tracks can be seen in this photograph). The system served Salem and connected riders to the Roanoke line that crossed over Masons Creek. The streetcars operated for many years, but they were abandoned in 1931 with the discontinuation of the Salem-Roanoke line. The trolley tracks along West Main Street were removed in 1938.

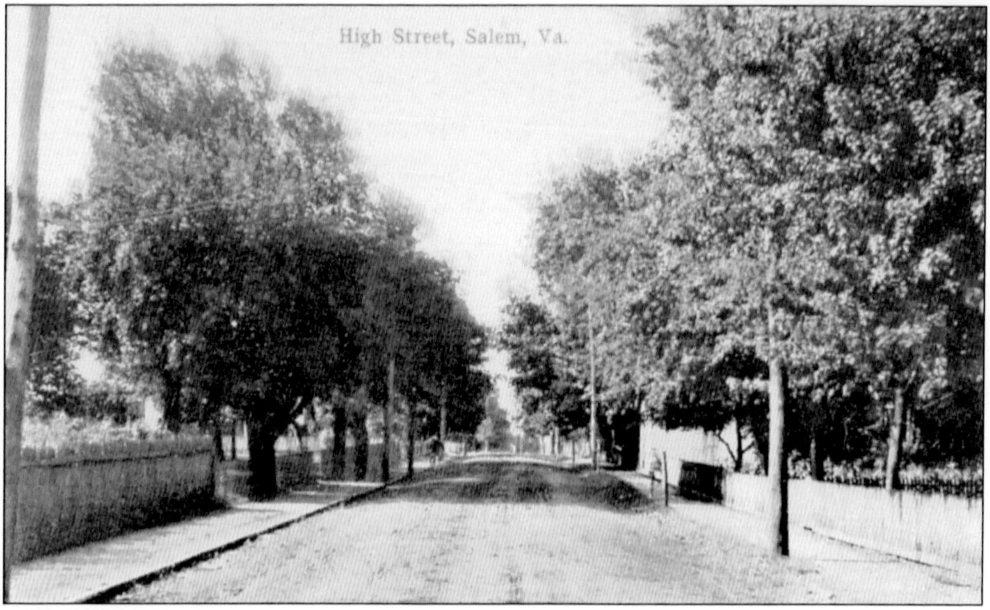

HIGH STREET, 1915. Salem's first major population and economic boom occurred between 1880 and 1890 with the development of the railroad. The population nearly doubled during that decade. In 1891, The *Roanoke Collegian* reported, "Building continues, High Street is being graded and widened, the streets are brilliant with electric lights, the laying of sewer pipes is being pursued vigorously." This card depicts the many improvements made to High Street during that time.

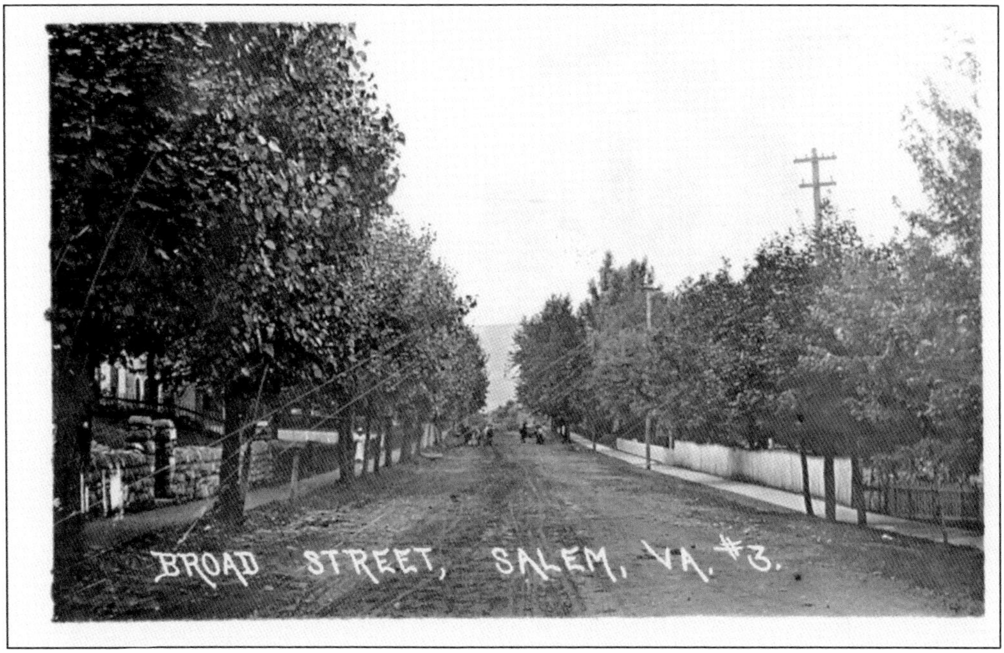

BROAD STREET, 1910. Business leaders in Salem and Roanoke sought to promote their respective communities through a variety of promotional pamphlets. Scenes like the one above were often included to demonstrate progress and prosperity. Salem was labeled the "Queen City of the Southwest" in an 1884 circular.

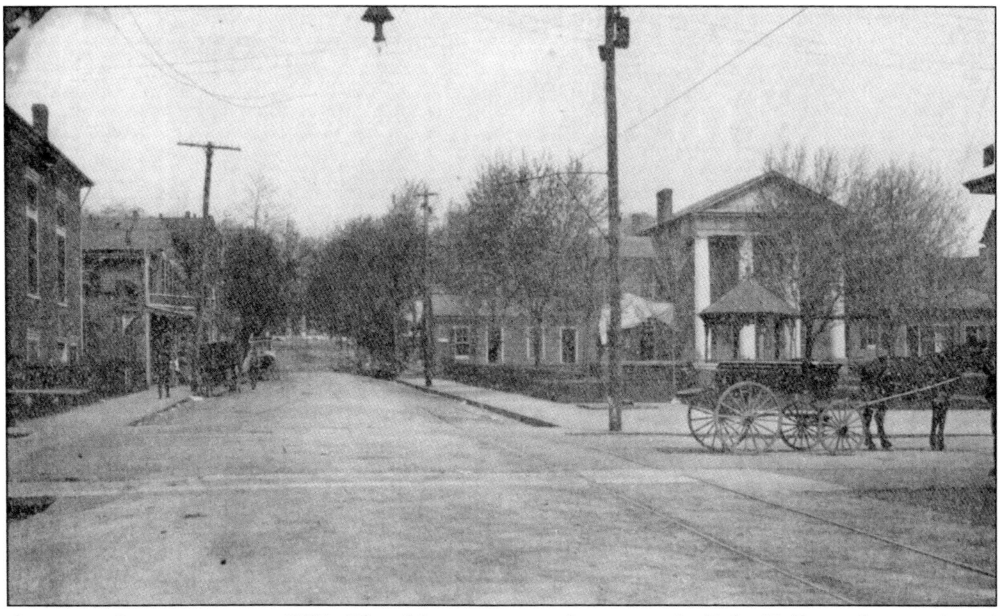

COUNTY COURTHOUSE, 1905. The old county courthouse was built in 1841 on a lot purchased by Roanoke County for $400 from John Gray of Missouri. Salem hotelier William C. Williams constructed the courthouse, which served as a hospital during the Civil War. If anyone dared to carve on the wooden interior ornamentation, they could be fined $5. The courthouse stood for 69 years before it was demolished in February 1909 due to severe structural deterioration.

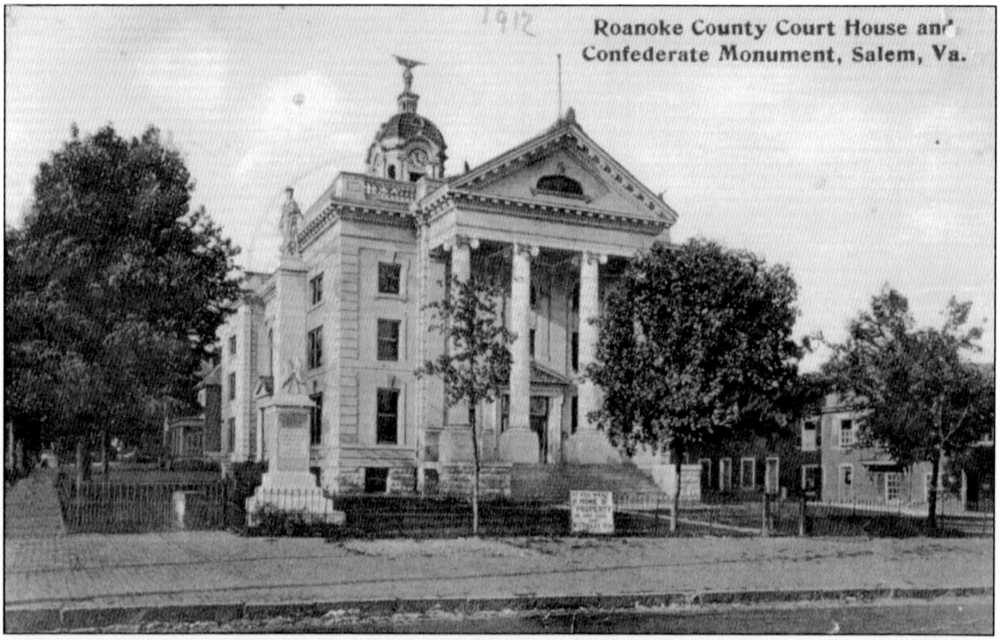

ROANOKE COUNTY COURTHOUSE AND CONFEDERATE MONUMENT, 1912. The new courthouse was built between 1909 and 1910, with the first court session occurring in the spring of 1910. The cost for the building was $43,870. The 28-foot granite Confederate monument was erected by the local chapter of the United Daughters of the Confederacy and situated where Salem's Flying Artillery Company was mustered into service in 1861.

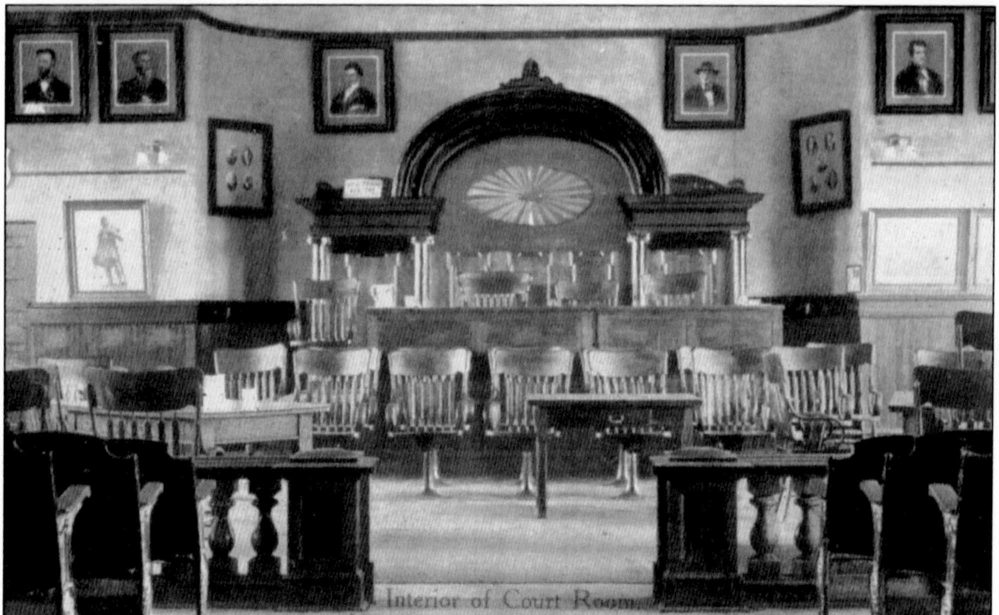

INTERIOR OF COURT ROOM, NEW COURTHOUSE, 1910. Judge William Moffett convened the first session of circuit court in the new courtroom on April 1, 1910, and dedicated the day to "the hearing of matters and reading of papers of local historical interest."

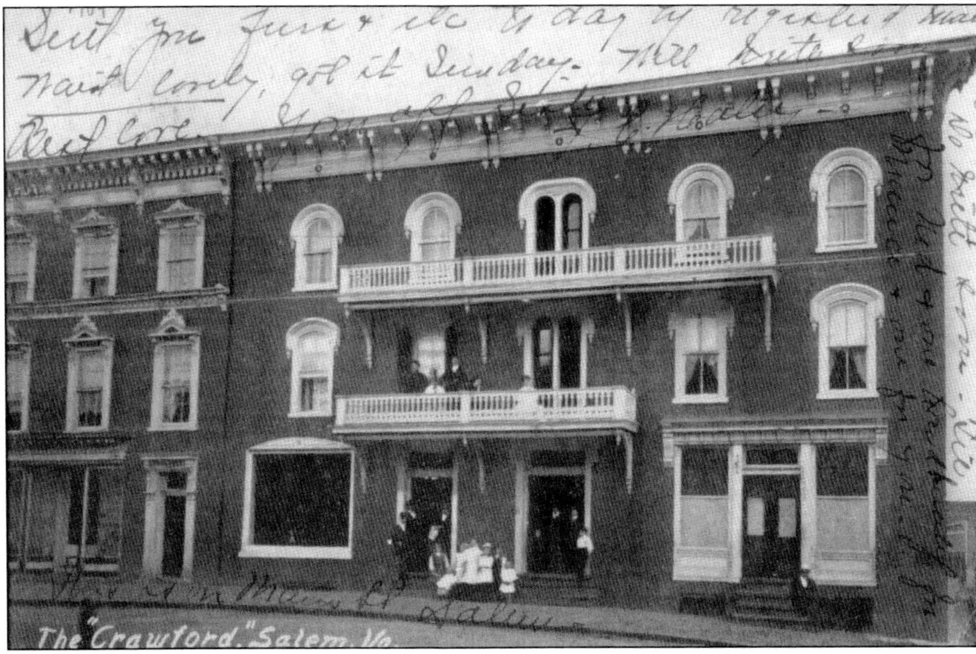

THE CRAWFORD, 1909. This hotel stood on Main Street and was erected by W. D. F. Duval in 1871. It contained 40 to 50 rooms with bath tubs and running water. For a few years, the hotel was owned by the Chapman family and renamed the Lucerne.

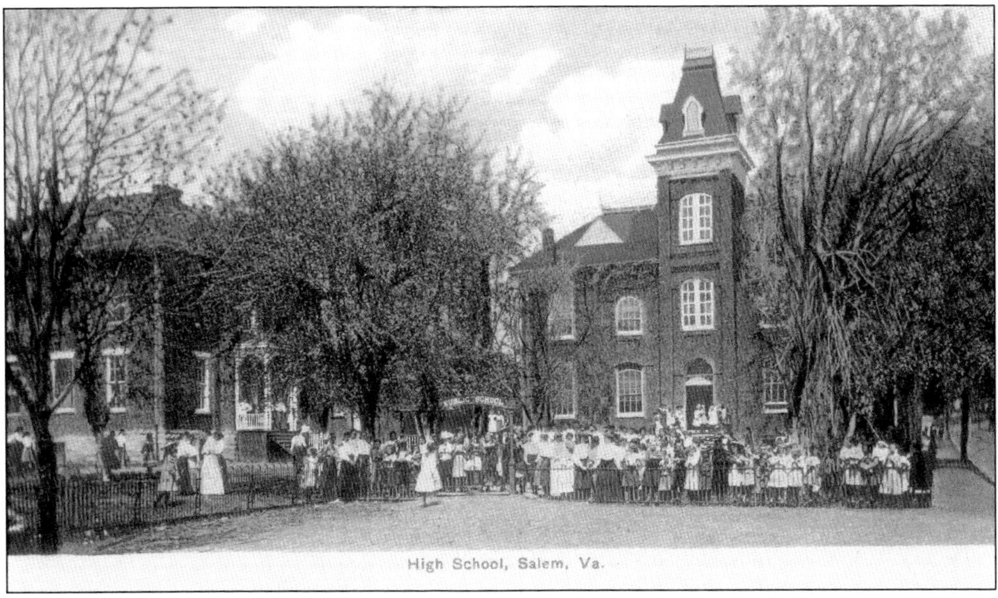

SALEM HIGH SCHOOL, 1909. What is now known as the Academy Street School served Salem's students for many years. The building on the right was constructed in 1890, with an addition (left) coming in 1895. The original portion served the lower grades, and the addition became the high school. Other additions came in 1901 and 1908. When first opened, it was known officially as Public School No. 1.

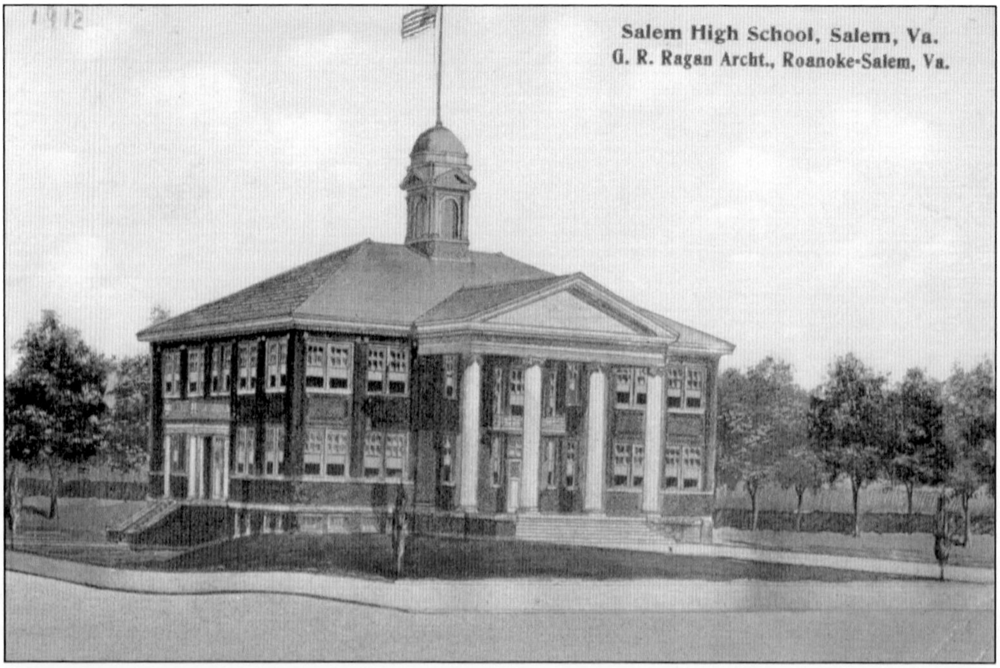

Salem High School, 1912. The new high school, built on Broad Street, opened in 1912, relieving the overcrowded Academy Street School. Additions followed in 1920 and 1923, but the school was heavily damaged by fire on January 19, 1931, forcing town leaders to consider a new high school. (Drawing by G. R. Ragan.)

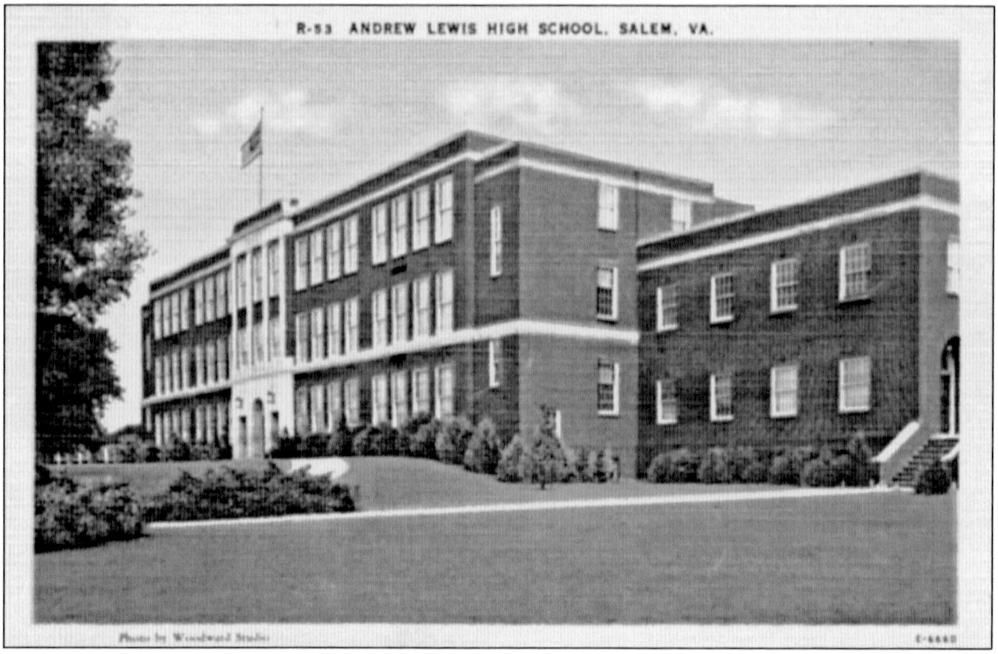

Andrew Lewis High School, c. 1940. After much political struggle with Roanoke County, Salem leaders were able to move forward in 1932 with their new high school, which was named after Gen. Andrew Lewis, a famous citizen. The school was dedicated on September 8, 1933.

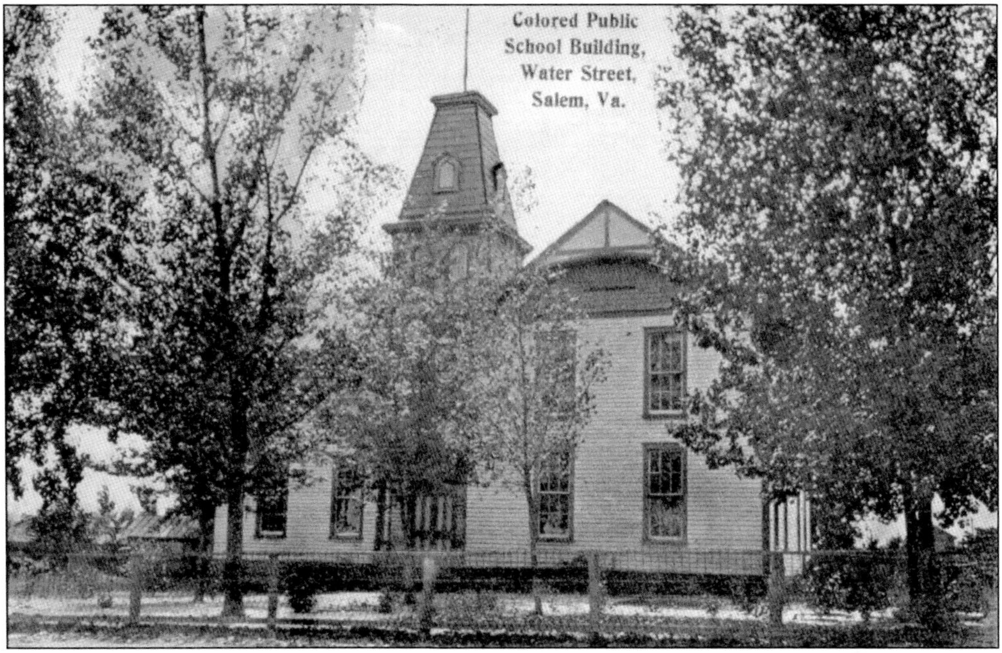

COLORED PUBLIC SCHOOL BUILDING, WATER STREET, 1918. The Graded School A was erected on Water Street as a six-room frame school between 1890 and 1891 (the same year the Academy Street School opened for white students). By 1895, the school had an enrollment of 258 under John Duckwilder, the principal.

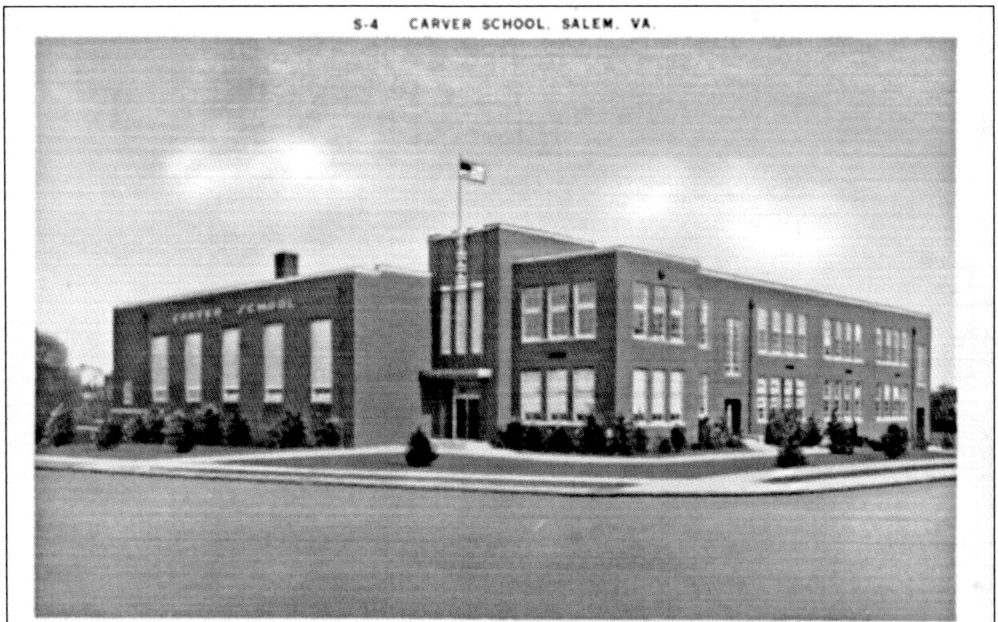

CARVER SCHOOL, "ROANOKE COUNTY CONSOLIDATED HIGH SCHOOL FOR NEGROES," C. 1940. The George Washington Carver School was opened in the fall of 1940 in response to the deterioration of the Water Street school. The construction cost was $125,000.

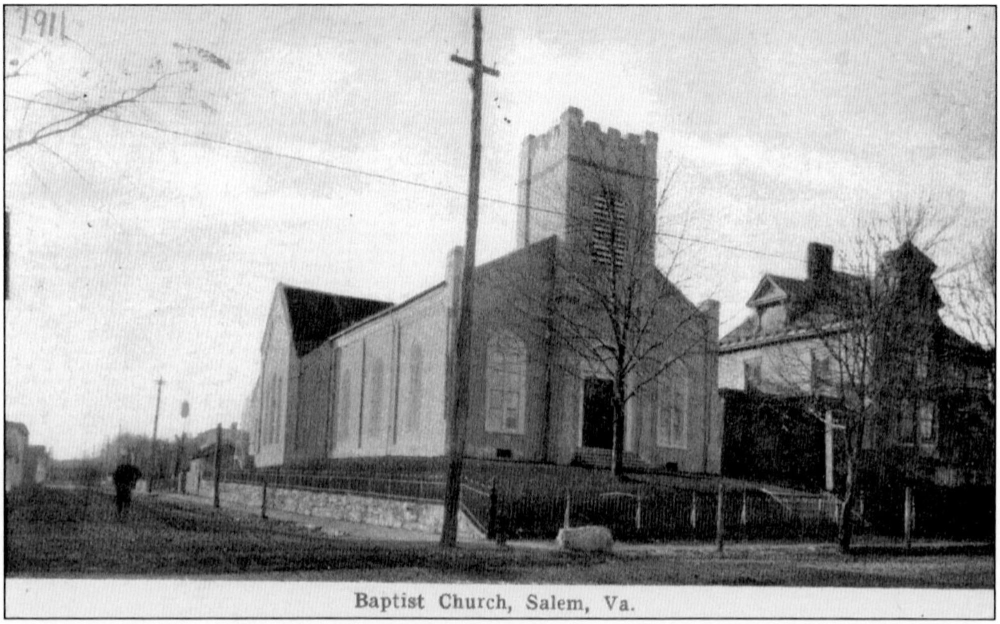

BAPTIST CHURCH, 1911. The Salem Baptist Church was organized in 1870 and dedicated its sanctuary at the corner of North Broad Street and College Street in 1873. An educational building was added in 1952. The new sanctuary, which can be seen today, was erected in 1967.

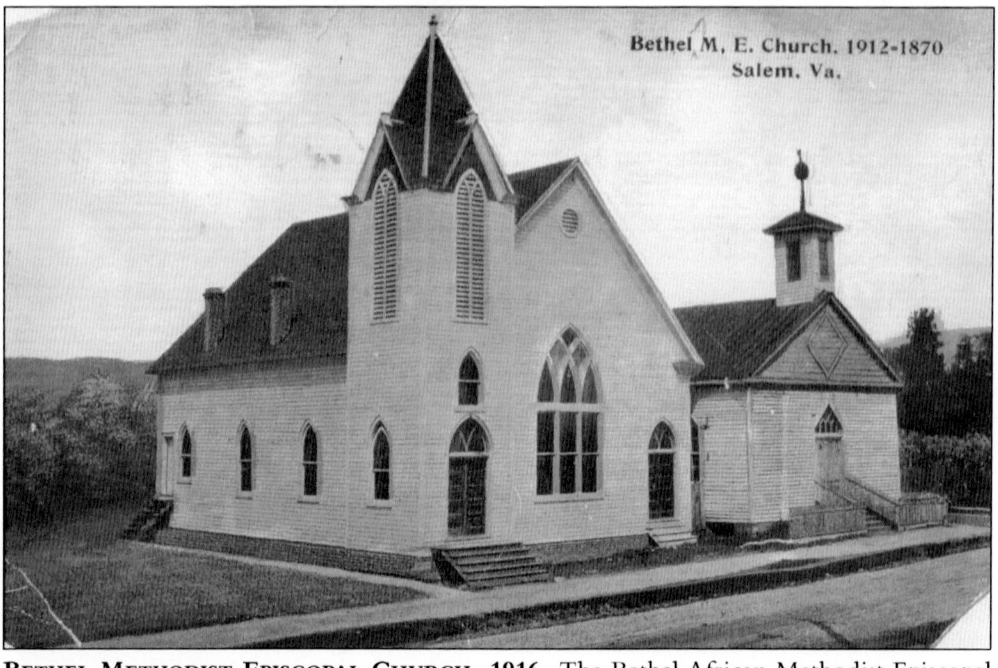

BETHEL METHODIST EPISCOPAL CHURCH, 1916. The Bethel African Methodist Episcopal Church was started in 1870. At the date of this card's printing, it stood on the corner of Water Street and Calhoun Street.

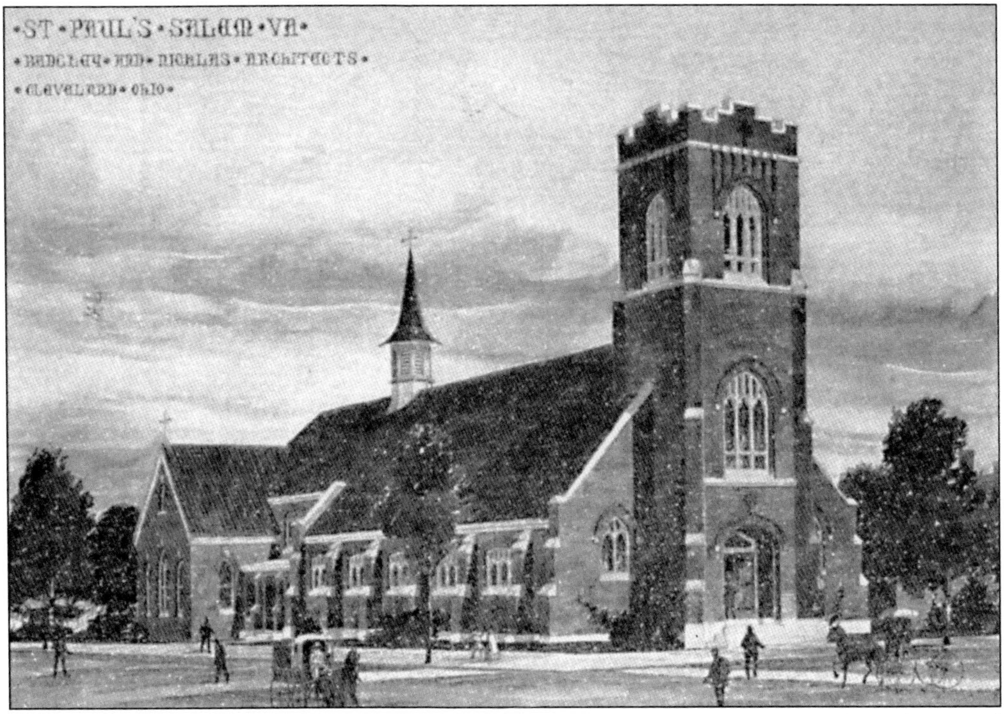

ST. PAUL'S EPISCOPAL CHURCH, ARCHITECTURAL RENDERING (NO DATE). This architectural rendering of the St. Paul's Episcopal Church is close to the actual design, but the church was altered a bit (as seen below) when finally constructed. (Rendering by Bedgley and Nichlas Architects, Cleveland, Ohio.)

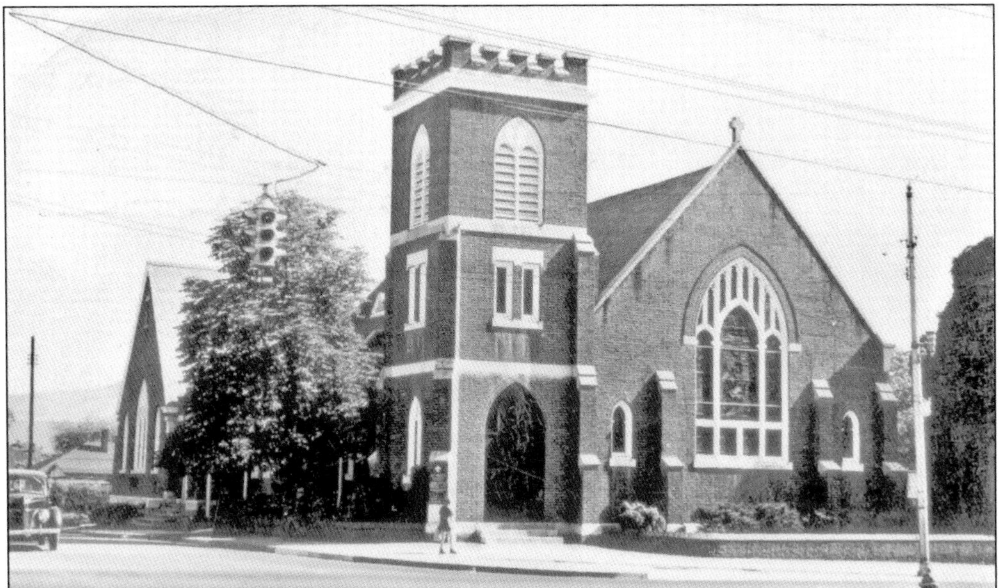

ST. PAUL'S EPISCOPAL CHURCH, 1948. The congregation was organized *c.* 1867 and moved a few times before erecting this sanctuary on Main Street in 1911. There have since been numerous acquisitions and additions to the facility.

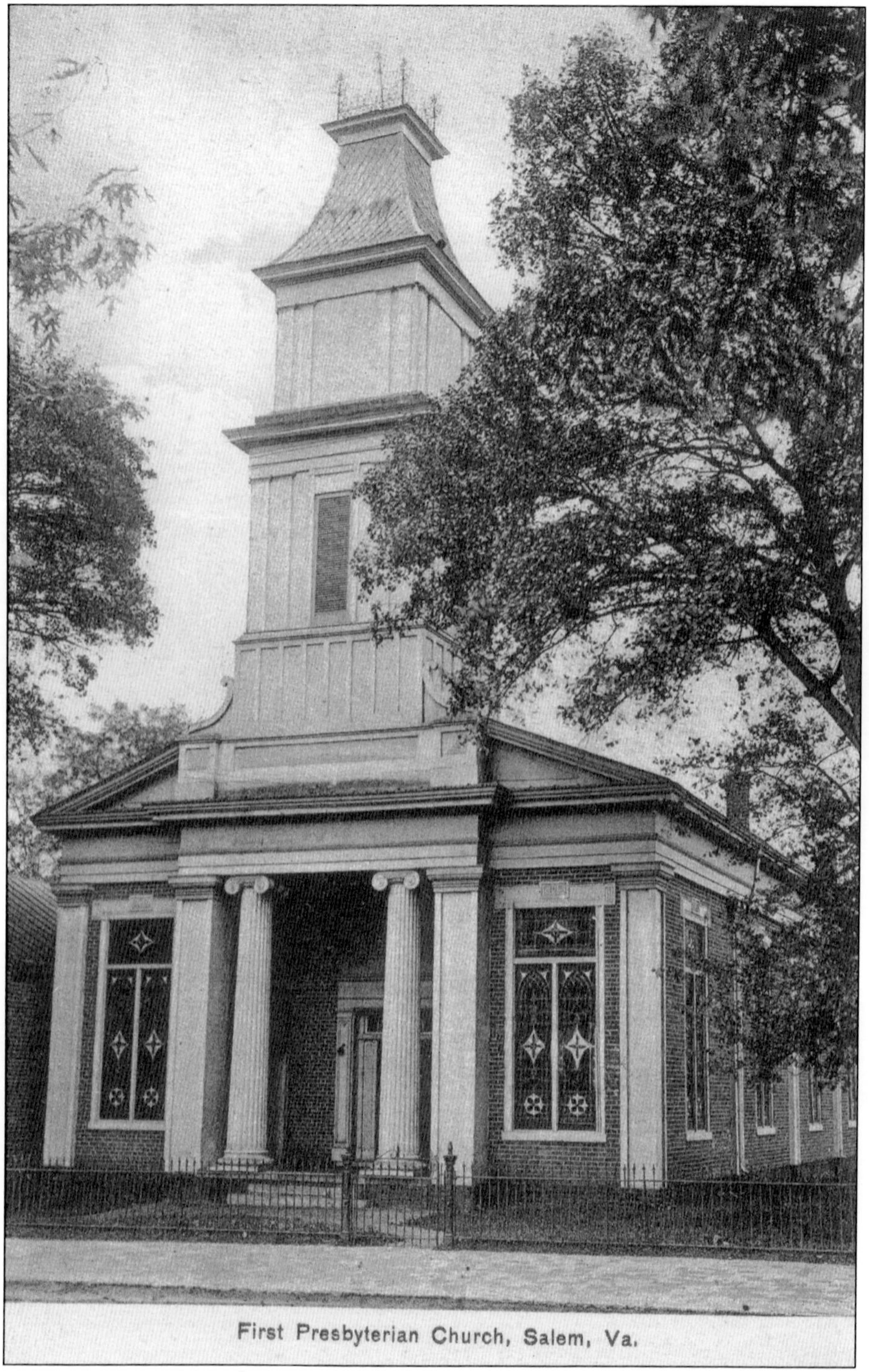

First Presbyterian Church, 1910. While termed First Presbyterian Church here, the sanctuary is known as home to the Salem Presbyterian Church located on Main Street. Salem Presbyterian was organized in 1831 and dedicated this sanctuary in 1852. Additions were made in 1914 and 1958.

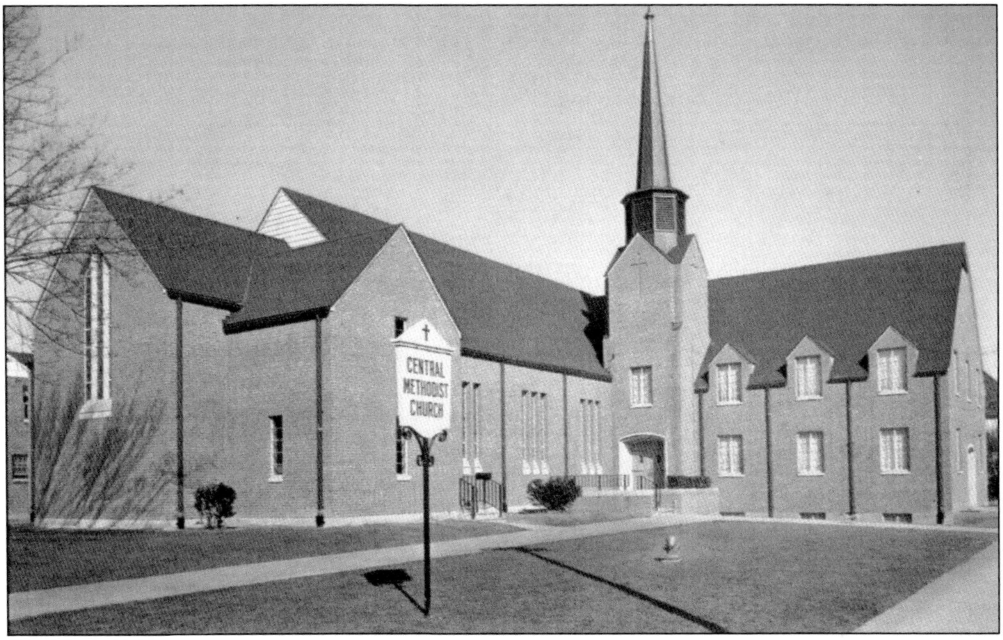

CENTRAL UNITED METHODIST CHURCH, *C.* 1960. Known originally as the First Methodist Episcopal Church when organized in 1908, the congregation later was called Second Methodist (1939) and then Central Methodist (1954). The sanctuary shown here was consecrated on June 26, 1955.

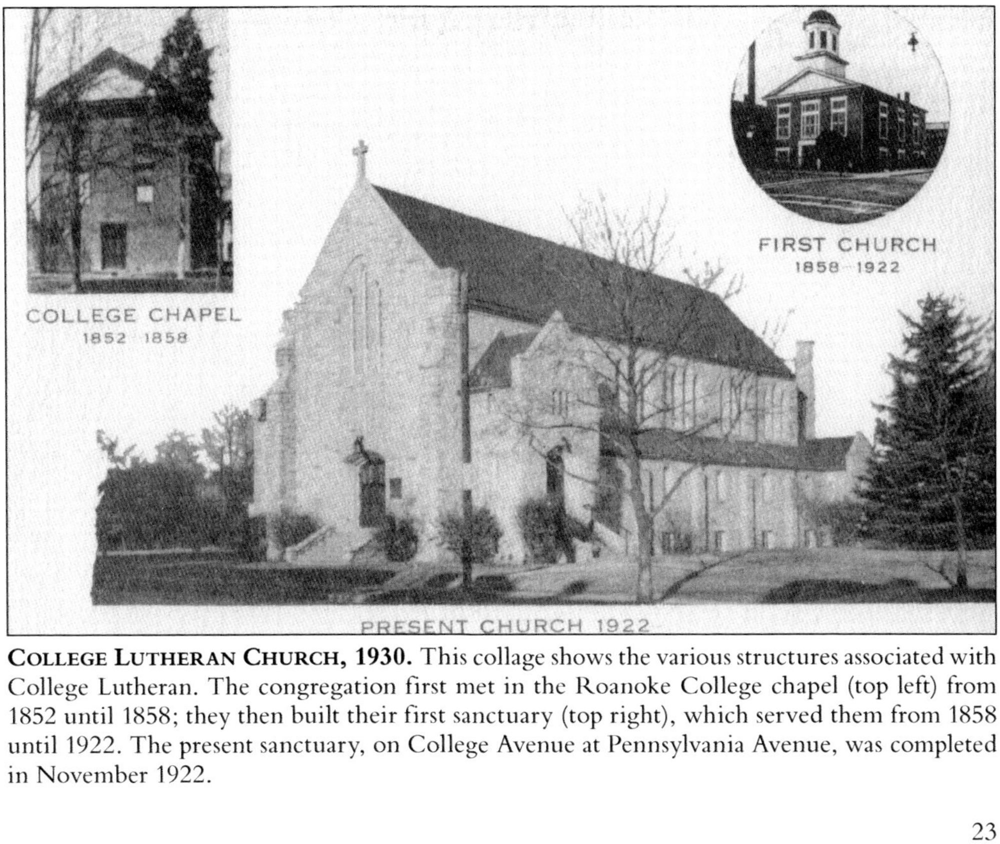

COLLEGE LUTHERAN CHURCH, 1930. This collage shows the various structures associated with College Lutheran. The congregation first met in the Roanoke College chapel (top left) from 1852 until 1858; they then built their first sanctuary (top right), which served them from 1858 until 1922. The present sanctuary, on College Avenue at Pennsylvania Avenue, was completed in November 1922.

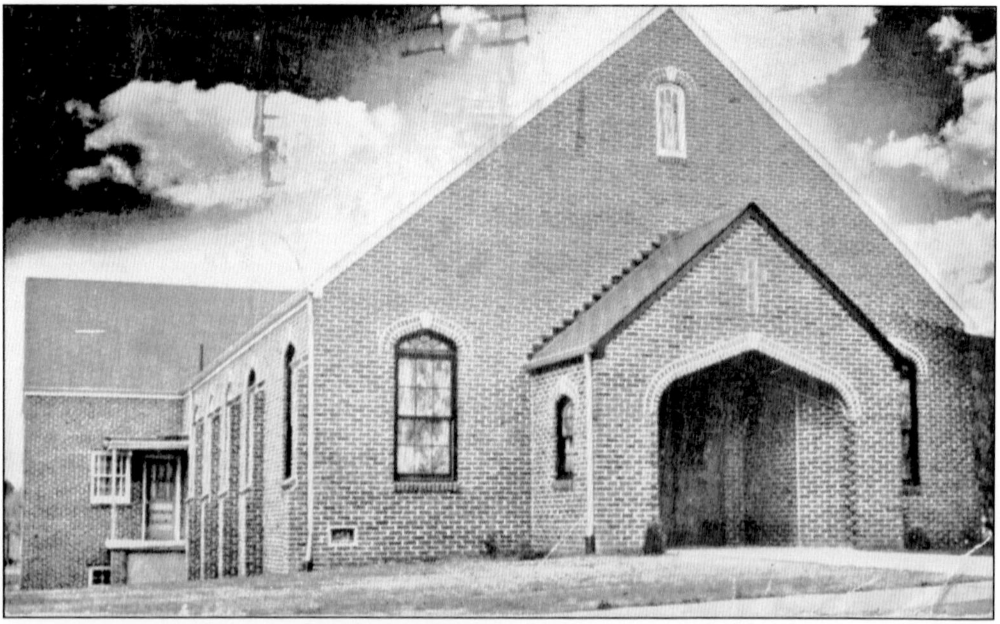

PENTECOSTAL HOLINESS CHURCH, 1957. The congregation was organized in 1915. Their present sanctuary, on North Bruffey Street (shown here), was dedicated in April 1953.

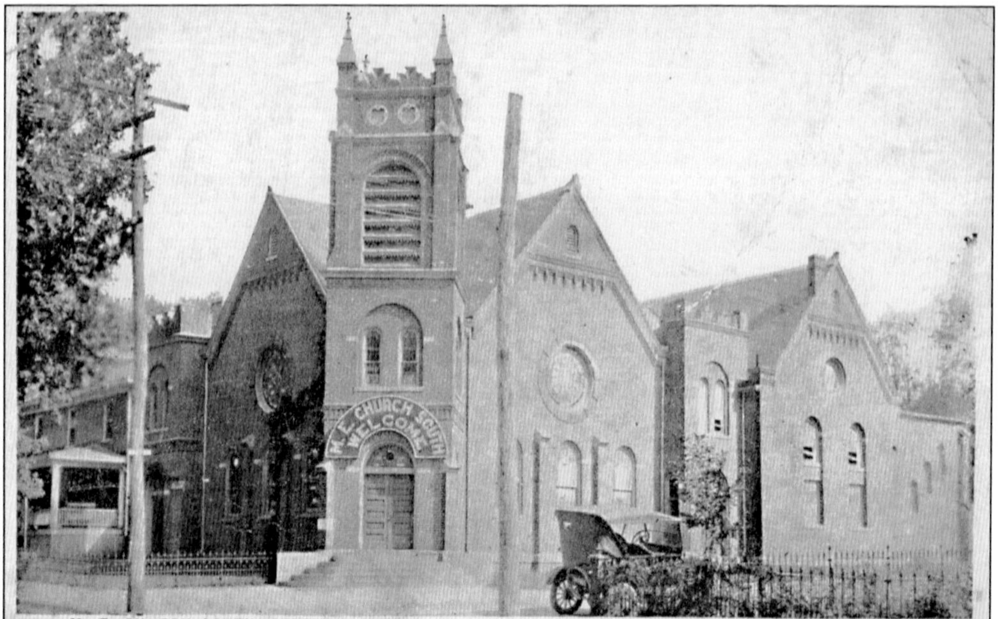

METHODIST EPISCOPAL CHURCH SOUTH, 1915. This was the sanctuary of the First United Methodist Church from 1904 until 1953. It was located on the northeast corner of College and Clay Avenues.

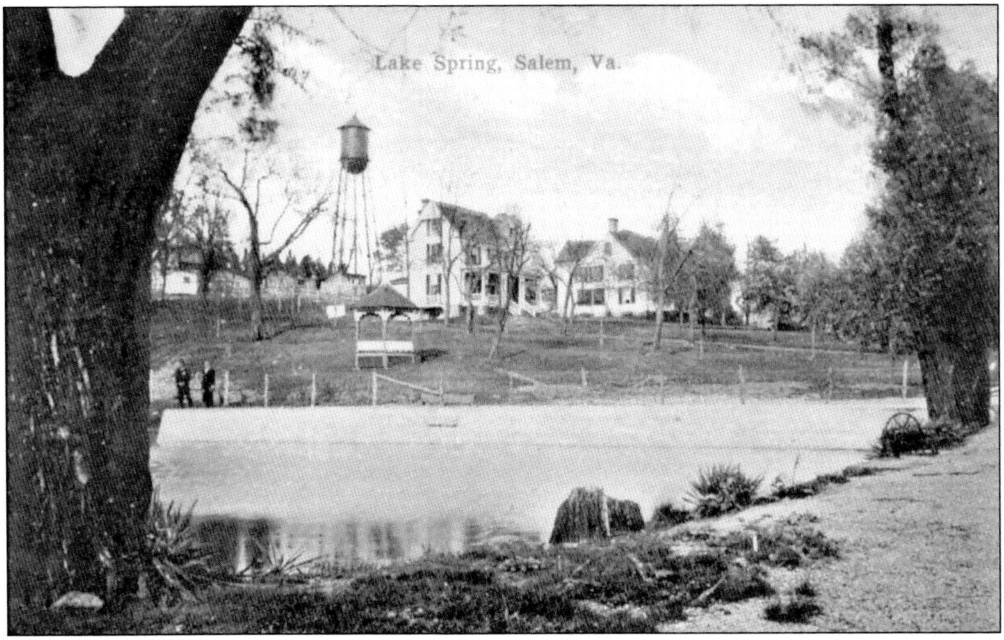

Lake Spring, 1910. The purchaser of this card sent the following message to his brothers: "Your letter received this morning. . . . Father is working for the Virginian R.R. at present. . . . I expect to take an examination for a R.R. mail clerk sometime this fall." His brothers lived in Baltimore, Maryland.

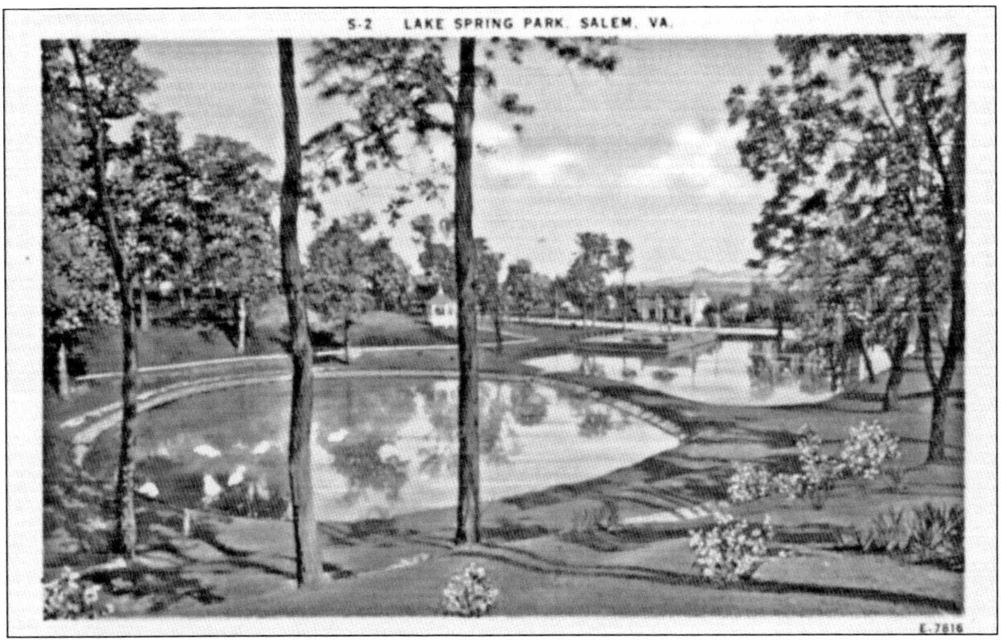

Lake Spring Park, c. 1940. In January 1901, the Lake Spring Park committee was formed to develop a park with the property the town had recently acquired. The land was already being used regularly by the citizens for various outings. The *Salem Sentinel* asserted, "This beautiful, cool and refreshing park would bring hundreds of people to Salem every year from Roanoke to visit." Lake Spring, after certain improvements, became Salem's first and most prominent park.

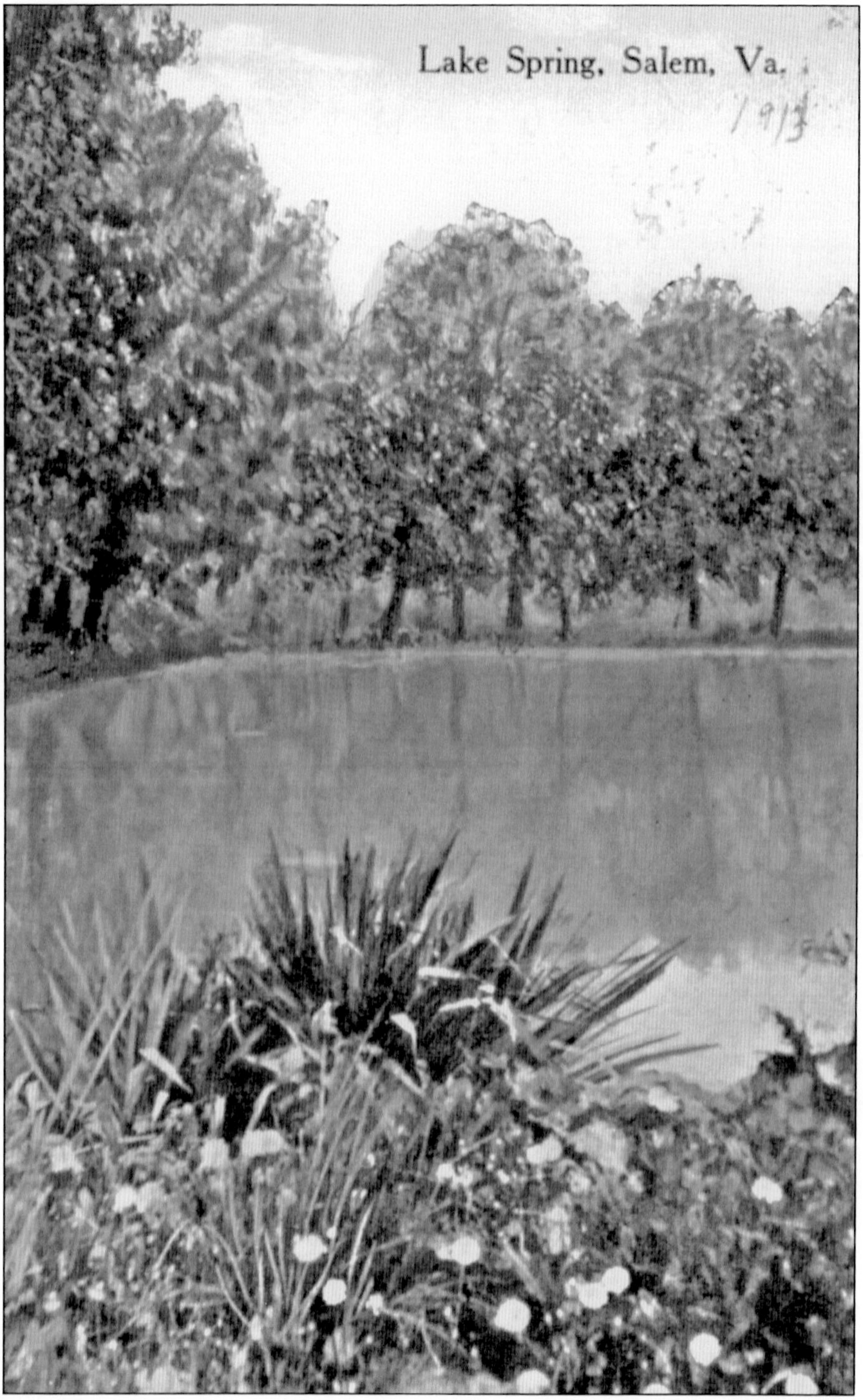

LAKE SPRING, 1913. Lake Spring had a high utilitarian value beyond providing a park setting. The lake fed water to nearby homes using pipes laid in 1876 by hotelier Joe Chapman. Chapman had also built a hotel near the site to capitalize on the lake's popularity. The hotel burned in 1892, forcing Chapman to sell the land that, a few years later, was purchased by the town itself.

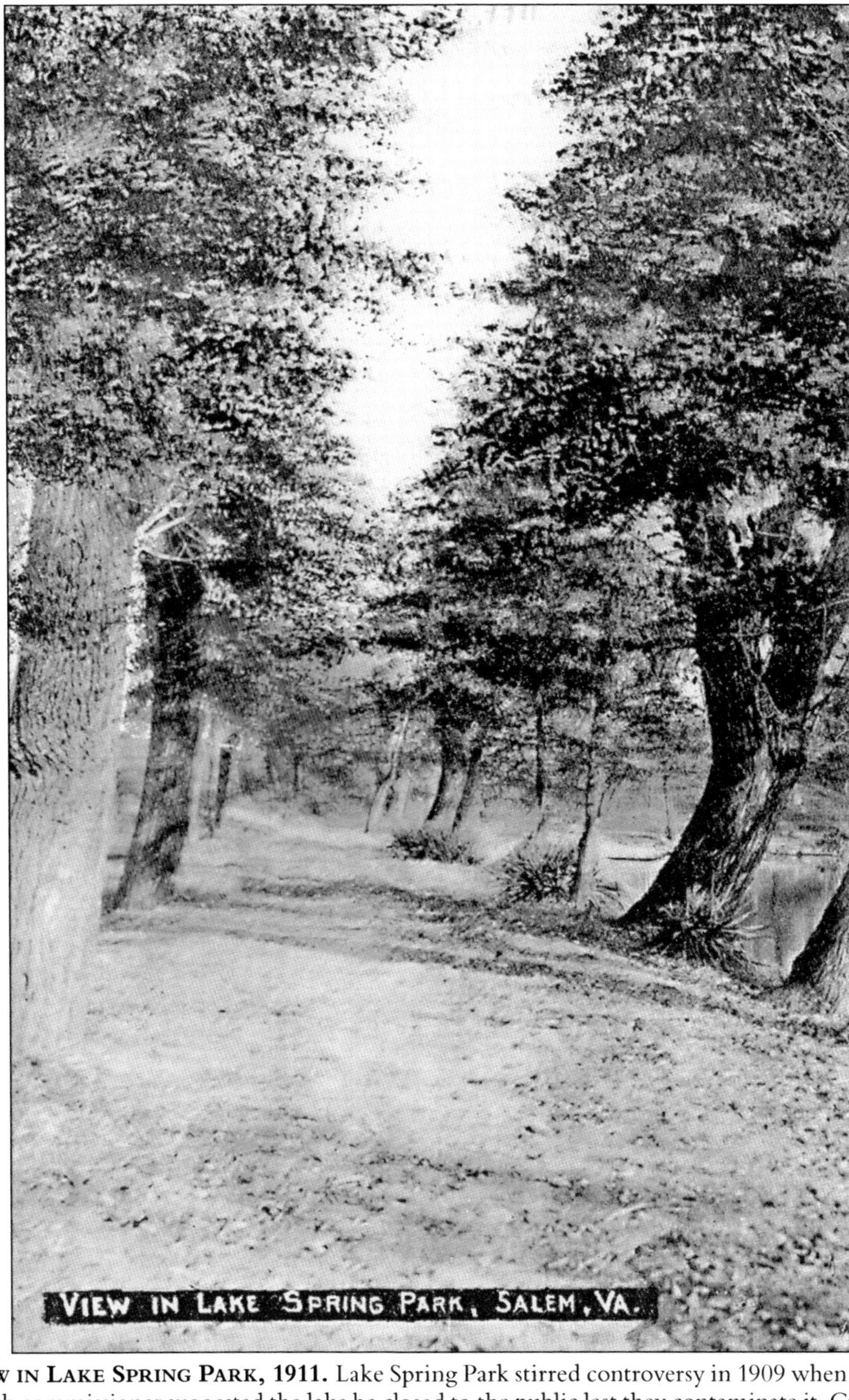

VIEW IN LAKE SPRING PARK, 1911. Lake Spring Park stirred controversy in 1909 when a state health commissioner suggested the lake be closed to the public lest they contaminate it. Citizens protested, noting that Chapman's hotel guests had fished and boated there without any problems in the past. Further, the *Salem Times* pointed out that a circus troupe had allowed their elephants to wash there, yet no one fell ill. The restrictions were soon thereafter eased.

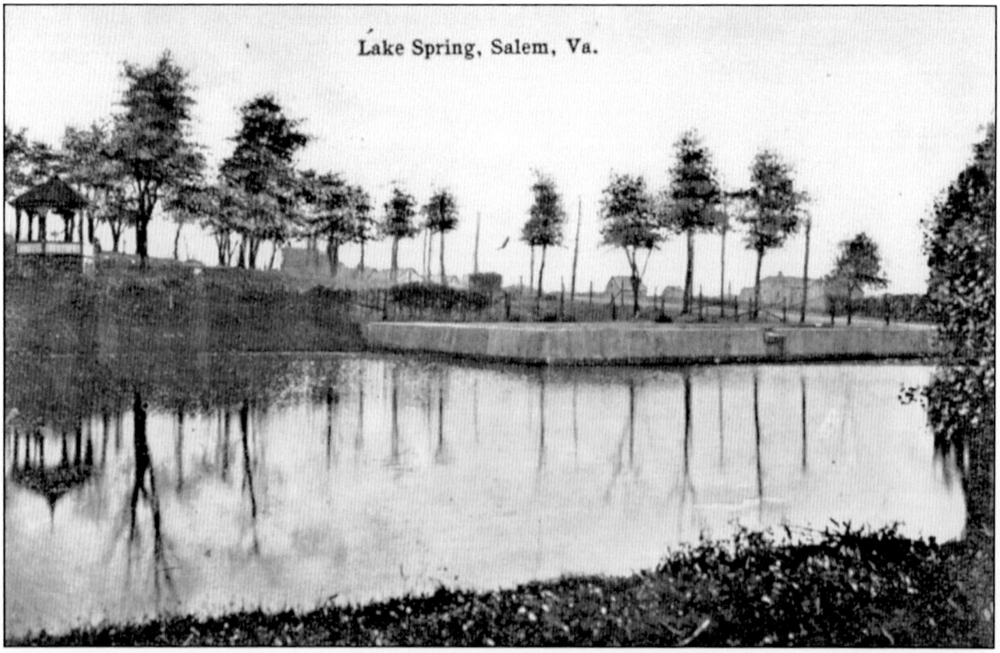

LAKE SPRING, 1915. During the 1930s, Salem put in showers at Lake Spring to help children keep cool in the summer heat. In 1931, Lake Spring was abandoned as a source for the town's water supply and was formally dedicated as a park. To mark the occasion, the Junior Women's Club staged a Spanish fiesta on a barge in the middle of the lake.

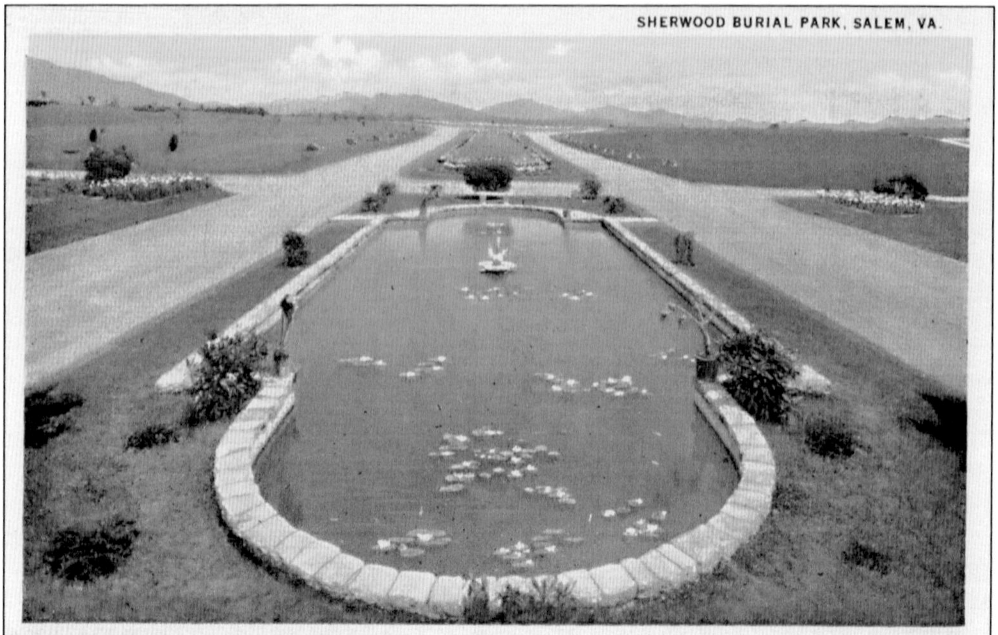

SHERWOOD BURIAL PARK, *c.* 1930. The Sherwood Burial Park, named for the old Sherwood estate that was near the property, was developed on a 35-acre tract in 1928 by C. B. Strickler.

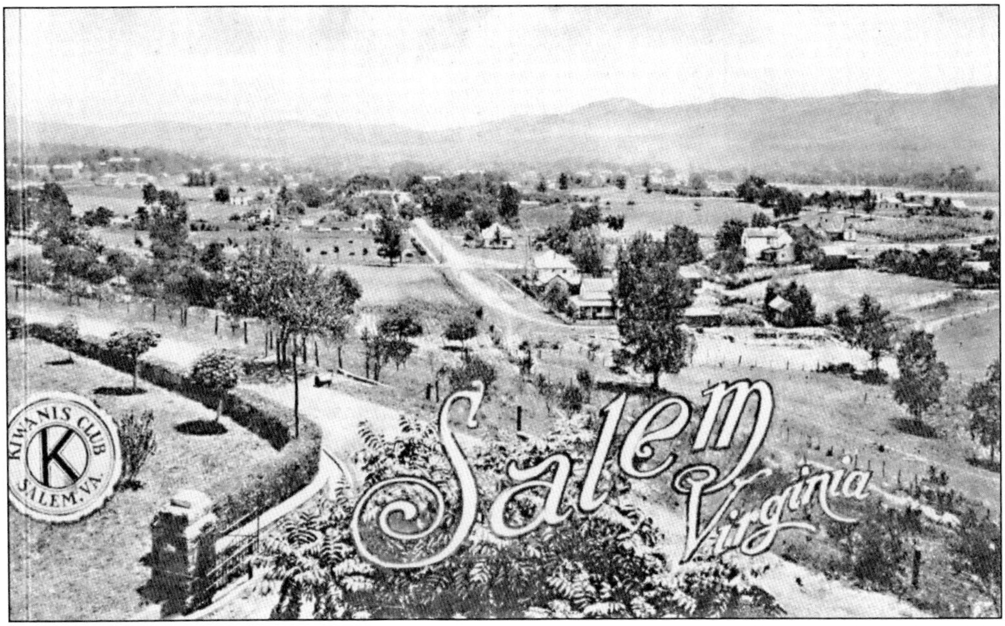

VIEW OF SALEM, C. 1920. This view of Salem was part of a series of postcards produced by the Salem Kiwanis Club to promote the town. The club was formed on March 15, 1921, and quickly assumed the initiative in a number of civic projects.

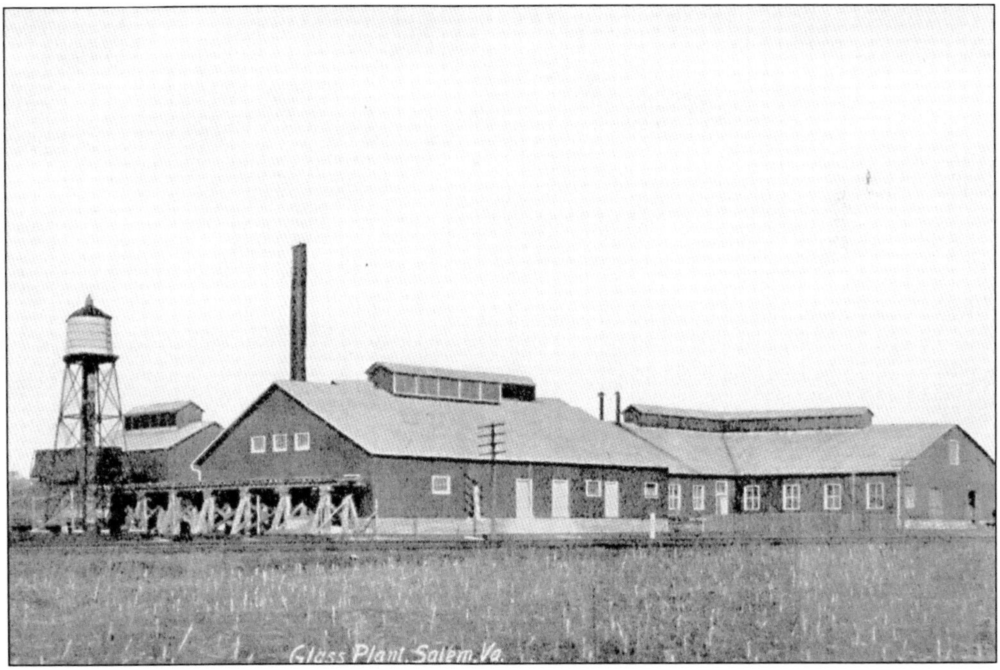

GLASS PLANT, 1920. In 1911, the Piedmont Glass Company purchased and resurrected an old glass plant. During the early years, the plant employed some 125 workers, who produced glass bottles for a variety of uses. The plant was closed for two months each summer due to the extreme heat from molten glass. In 1914, the name was changed to the Salem Glass Company.

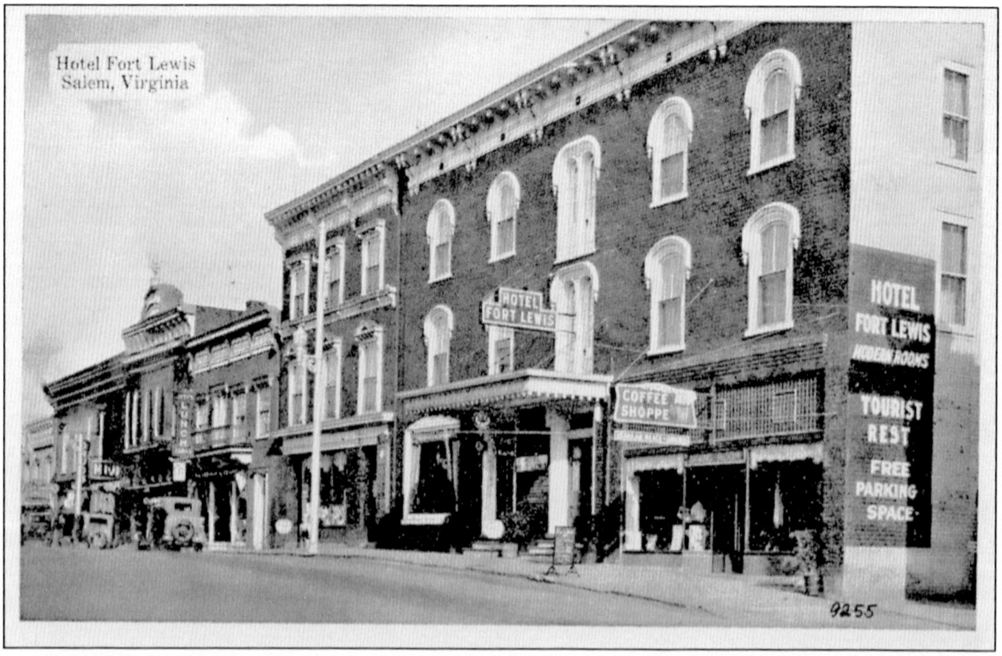

HOTEL FORT LEWIS, 1930. In 1927, Salem businessman Henry A. Oakey purchased the former Hotel Salem and changed its name to Hotel Fort Lewis. The structure was demolished in 1974.

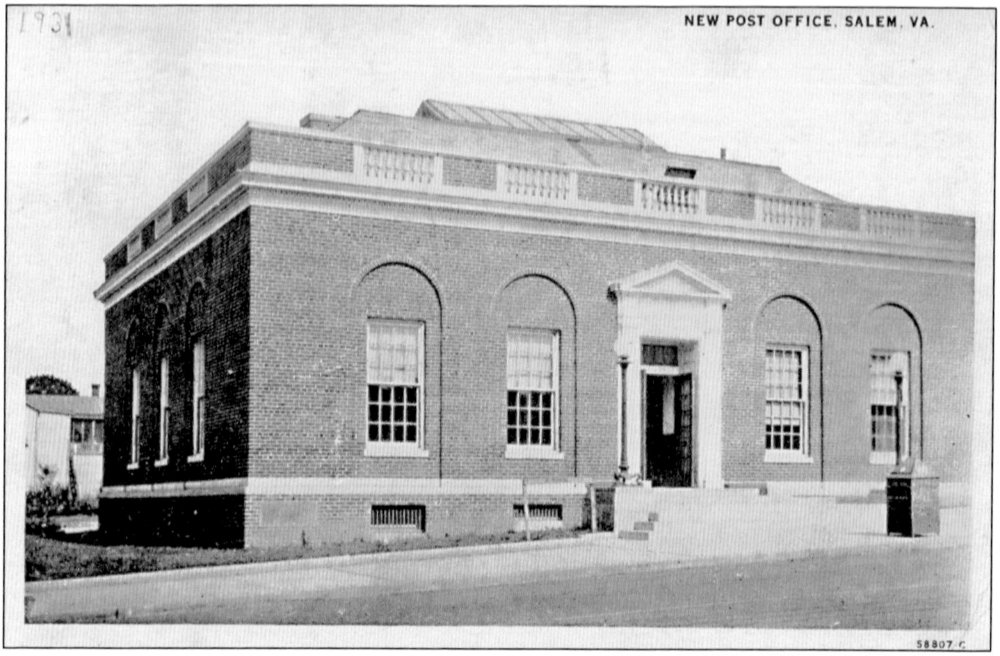

NEW POST OFFICE, 1931. The construction of a federal post office on Main Street was a saga that lasted many years. Land purchased by the government in 1917 went undeveloped until 1922, when construction finally commenced. The post office officially opened in June 1923.

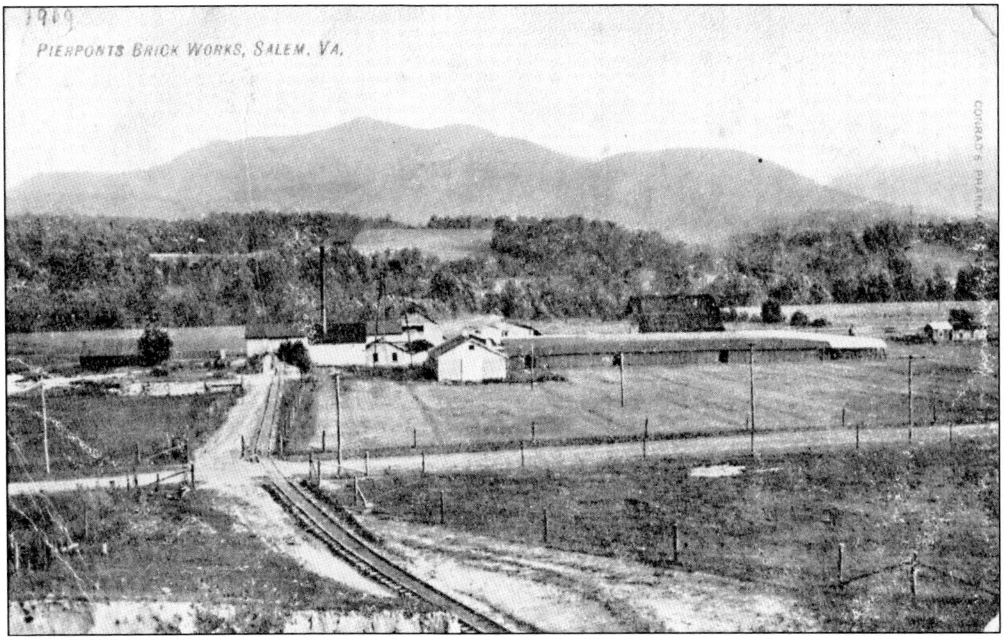

PIERPONTS BRICK WORKS, 1909. The brick works were owned and operated by Salem businessman George E. Pierpont. In 1908, Pierpont was one of the privileged few in Salem to own an automobile.

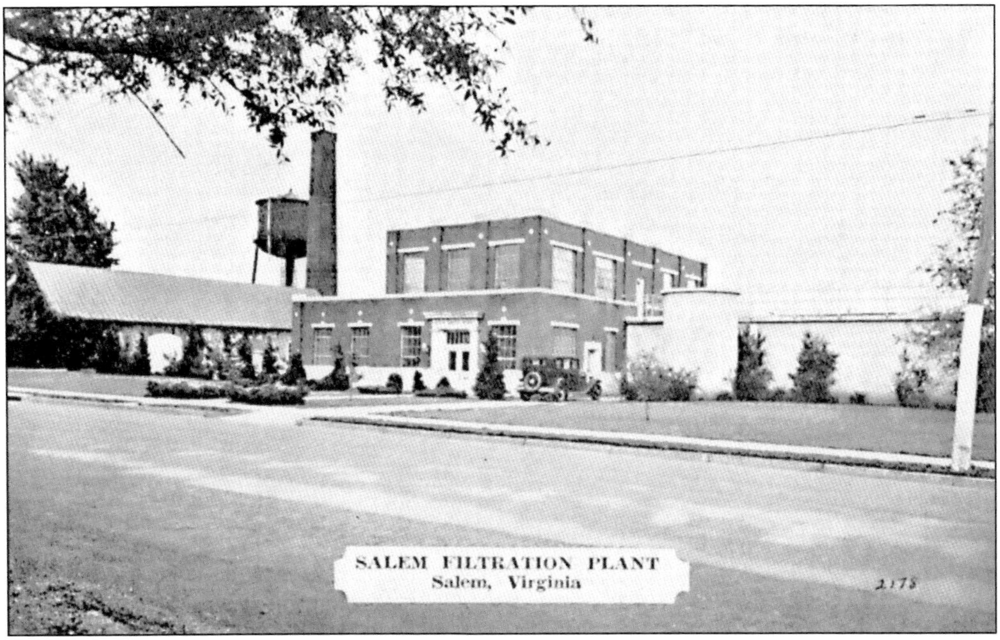

SALEM FILTRATION PLANT, C. 1920. The filtration plant was an early element in Salem's water supply infrastructure, but the water supply system itself dated to the 19th century. In 1874, the first concept for a water supply system was advanced to the town council, and in 1875 Salem citizens approved a bond to finance a reservoir and pipes. The original water rate at that time was $5 per year for five-member families, $1 per year for each hotel room, and $10 annually for bars.

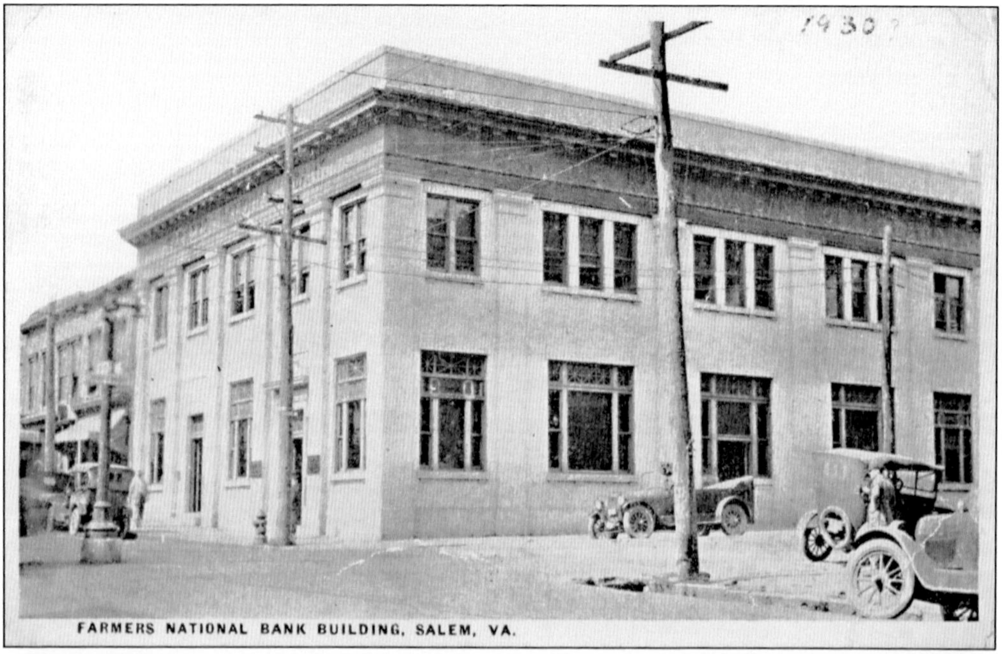

FARMERS NATIONAL BANK BUILDING, 1925. The Farmers National Bank was organized May 8, 1871, with capital of $75,000. Through the leadership of Salem's prominent businessmen, the bank successfully weathered the economic turbulence that put other banks out of business during the latter part of the 19th century.

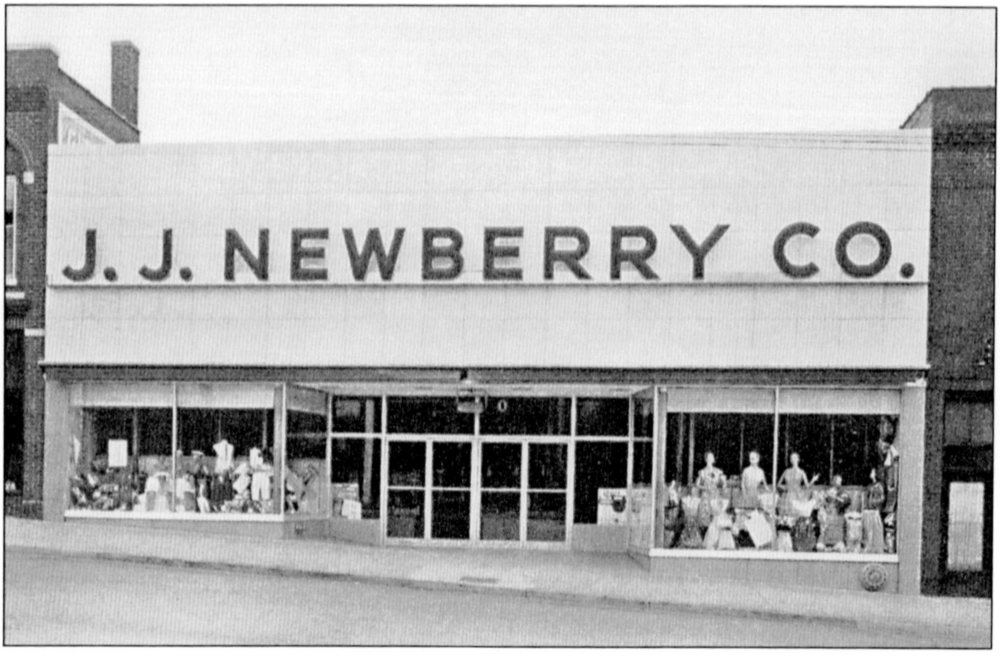

J. J. NEWBERRY COMPANY, *C.* 1960. One of the more contemporary establishments was Newberry. The postcard boasts, "Completely air-conditioned on two large selling floors, approximately ¾ mile counter space carrying over 30,000 separate items of merchandise. A modern luncheonette unit serves refreshments, a quick snack or a complete meal."

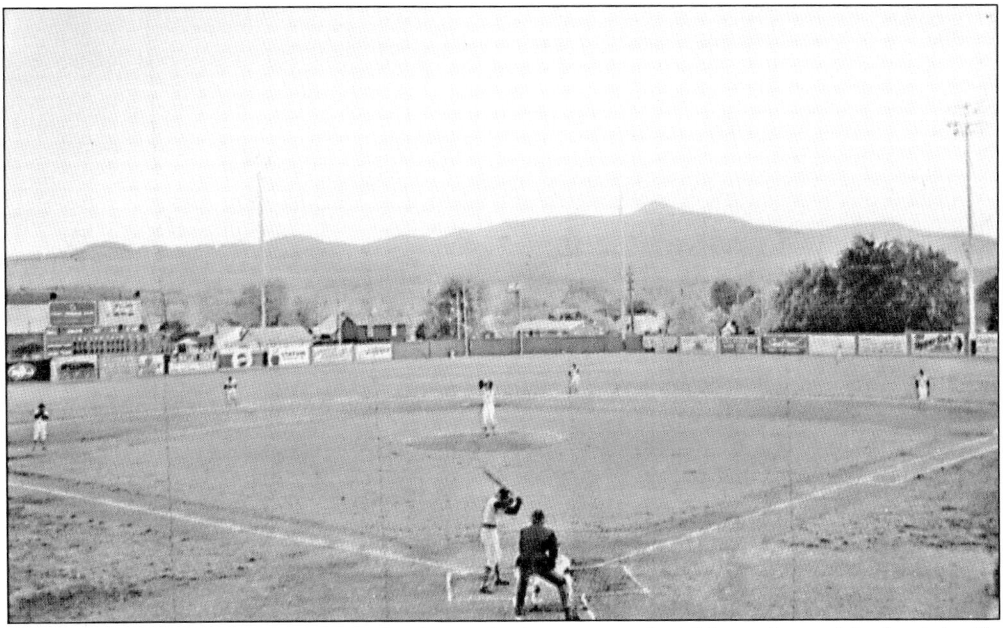

MUNICIPAL FIELD, *C.* 1970. The land on which Municipal Field was located had originally been designated for use as an elementary school site. Further study, however, prompted Salem's leaders to instead appreciate its use for athletics. Thus, in the spring of 1932, Municipal Field was born. Professional baseball debuted there on May 20, 1939, when the Salem Wolves took the field against Lynchburg.

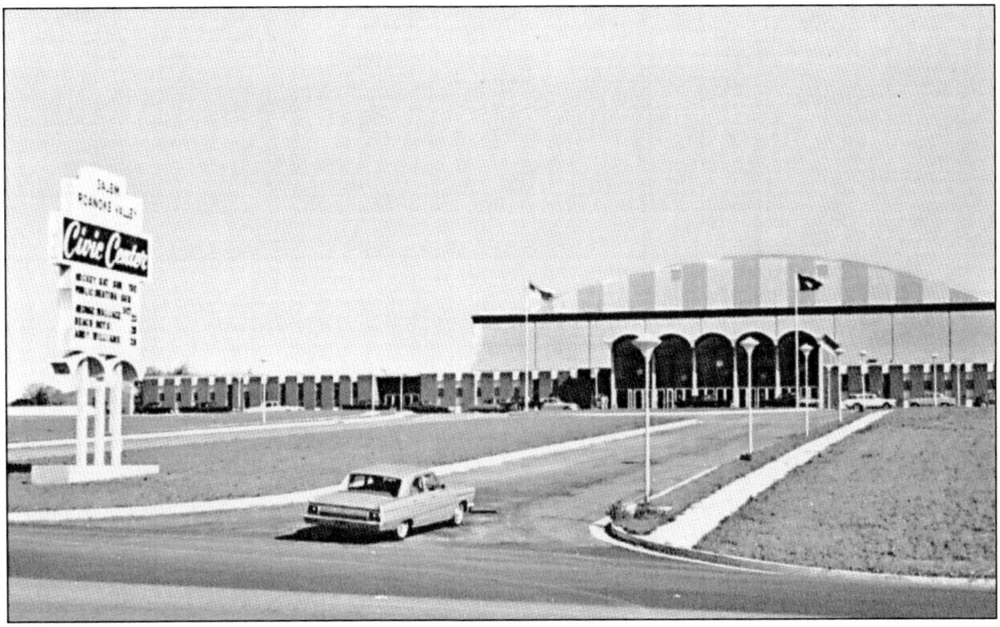

SALEM-ROANOKE CIVIC CENTER, *C.* 1970. Dedicated in 1967 and financed through the sale of bond proceeds, the Salem-Roanoke Valley Civic Center was a recreational and cultural center for Salem. Noted historian Norwood Middleton termed this "the single-most talked-about project in Salem's history." The arena was first used on September 25, 1967, for a meeting of the Virginia Education Association.

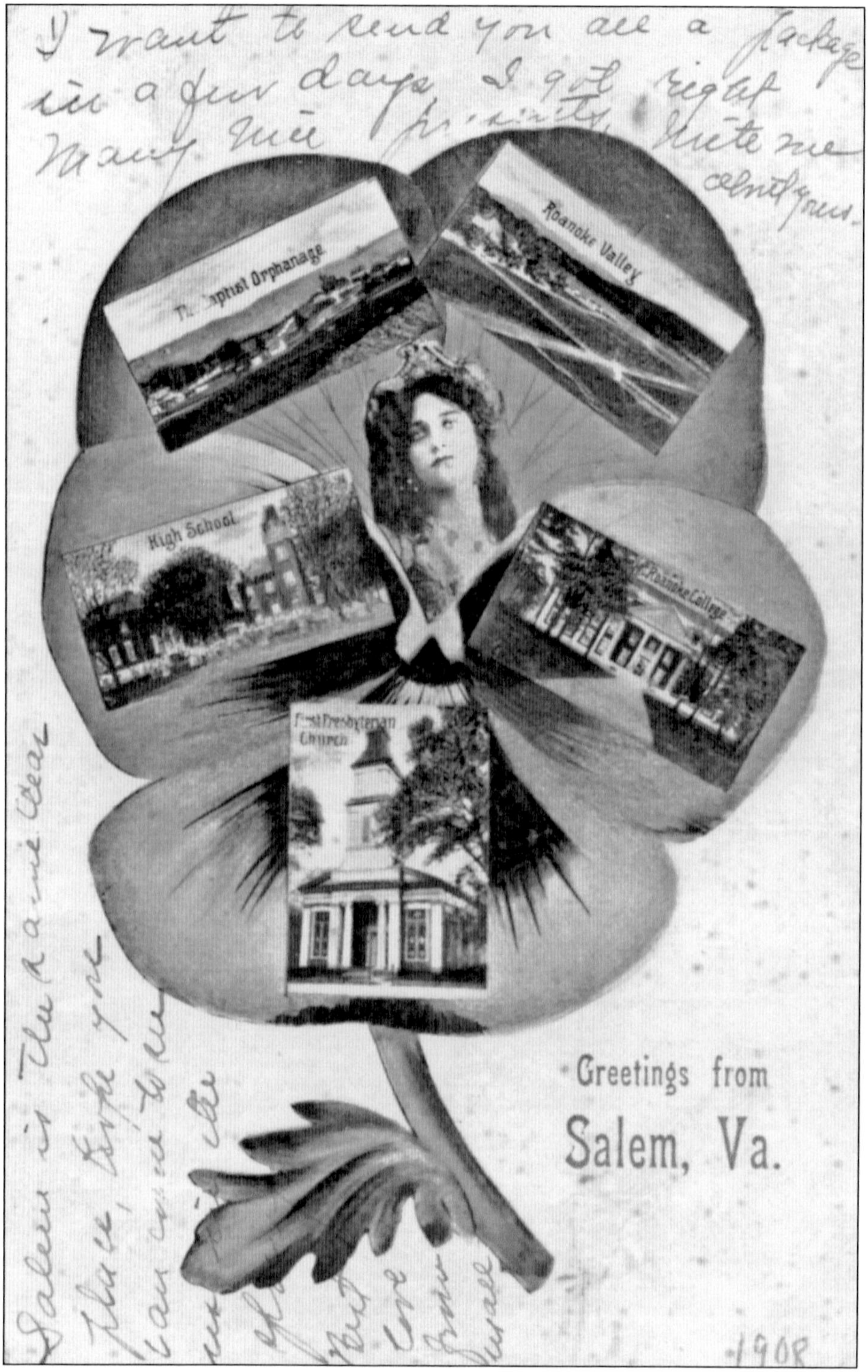

GREETING CARD, 1908. This early greeting card promoted all things Salem. The images are Roanoke Valley (top right), Roanoke College (bottom right), First Presbyterian Church (bottom center), High School (bottom left), and Baptist Orphanage (top left).

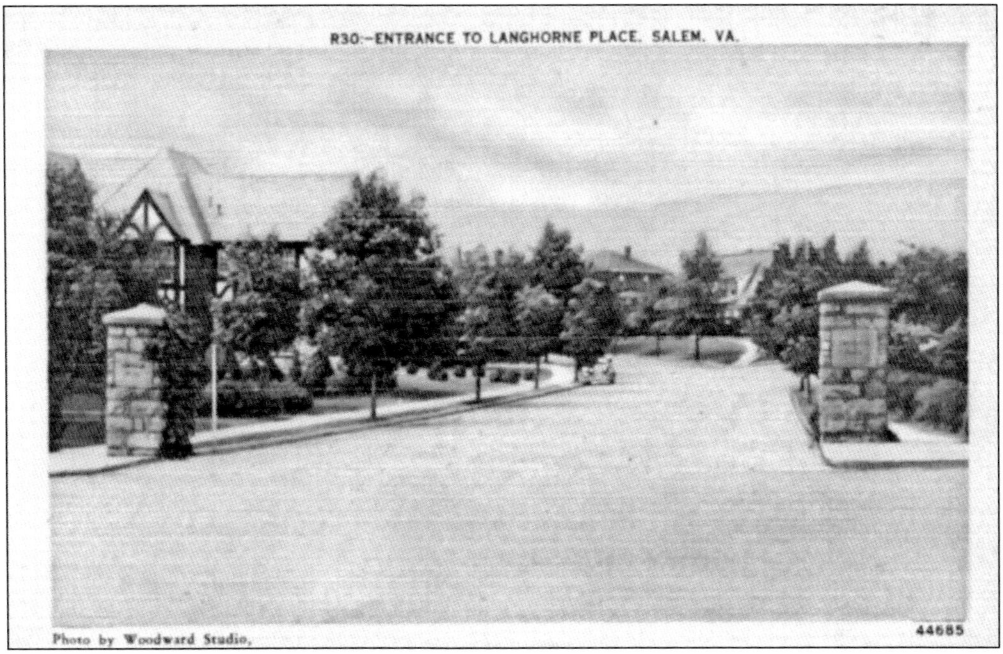

ENTRANCE TO LANGHORNE PLACE, *c.* 1940. Langhorne Place marked the arrival of the first middle-class apartment rental units in Salem not associated with Roanoke College. The Glenmary was built in 1929, and consisted of 10 units (with 8 more added soon thereafter).

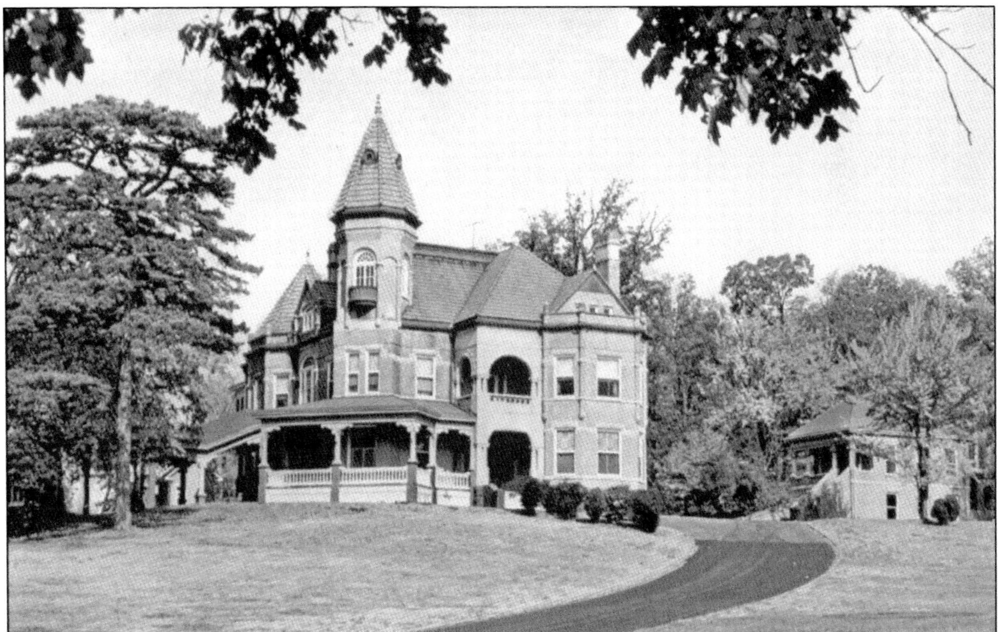

LONGWOOD SALEM COMMUNITY CENTER, *c.* 1960. The Victorian mansion known as Longwood was built by Thomas Henry Cooper *c.* 1904. The majestic structure was destroyed by fire on November 19, 1968.

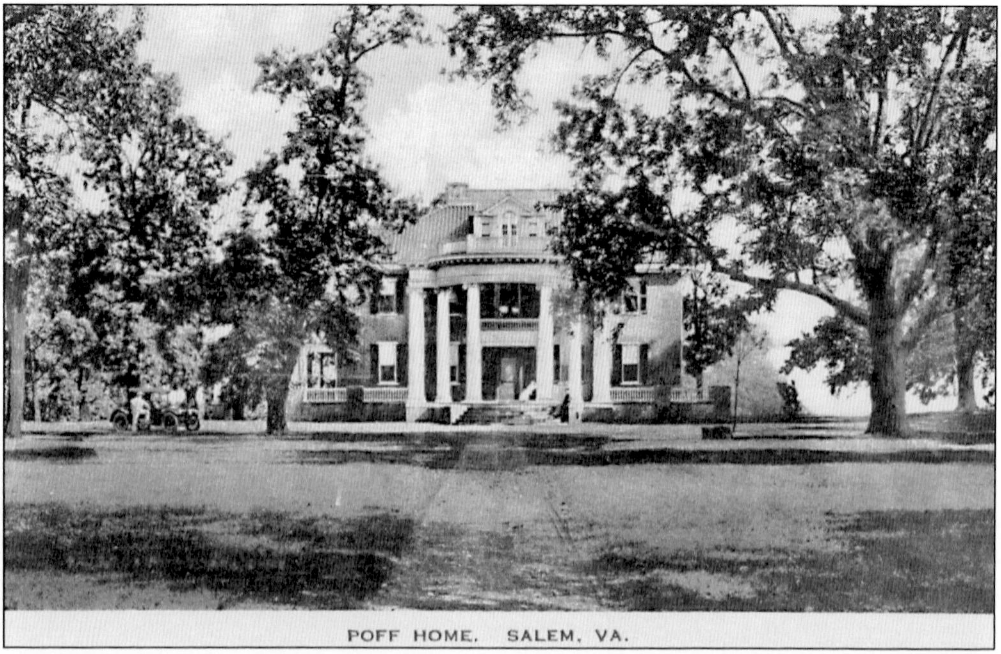

THE POFF HOME, *c.* 1925. Salem boasts many fine residences, including the Poff home (pictured here). Some of Salem's earliest residents were also appointed as town trustees by the state in 1806. Those first official "town fathers" included John Brugh, James Mason, William Lewis, Elijah McClanahan, William Blain, Lewis Cooper, and John King.

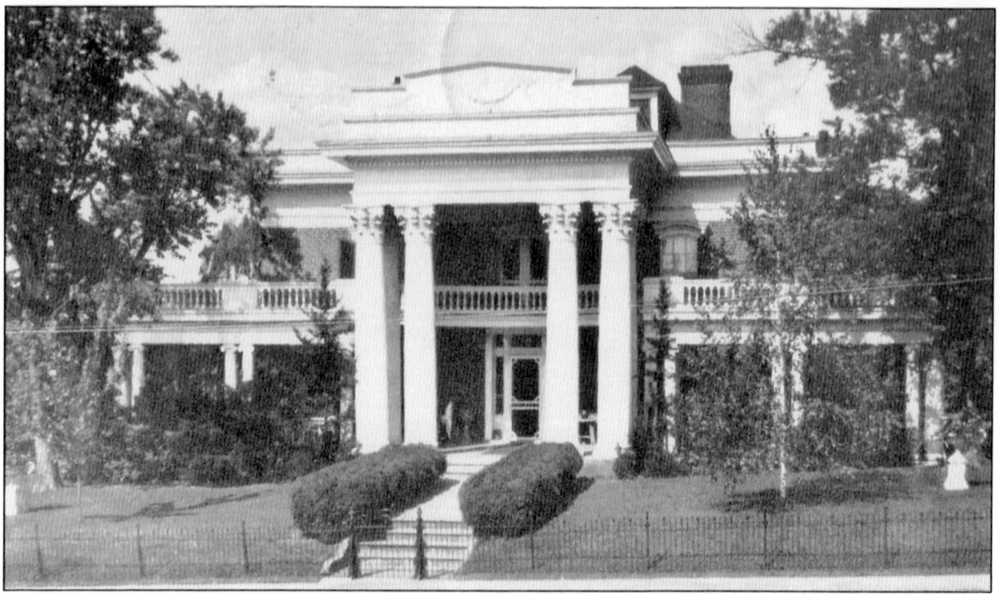

STROUSE HOME, 1947. The impressive home of Salem lawyer Demetrius B. Strouse, on Broad Street, was built around the dawn of the 20th century. Strouse was involved in numerous civic and religious projects in the Roanoke Valley.

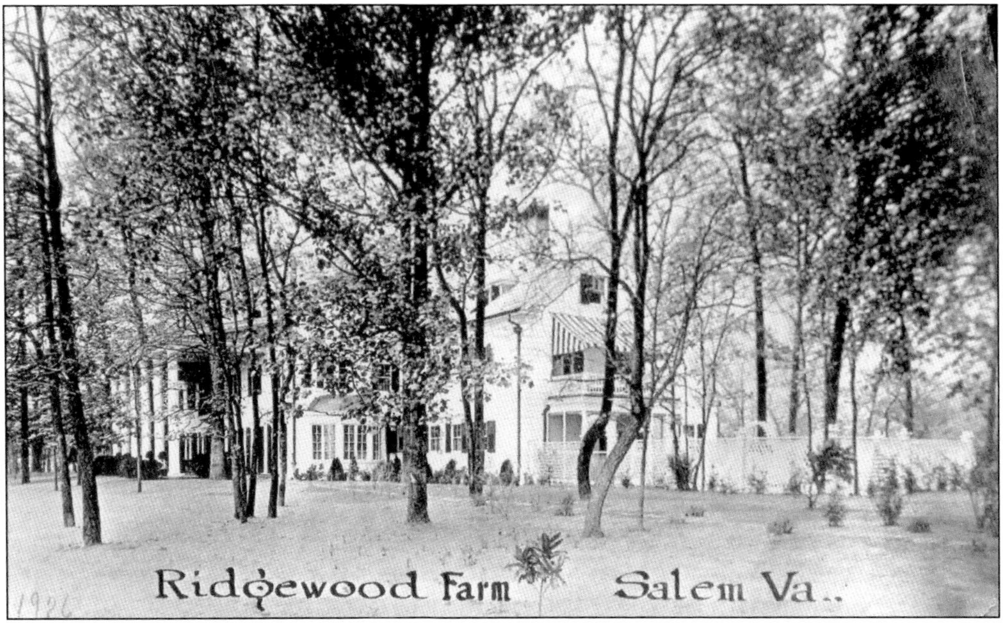

RIDGEWOOD FARM, 1926. Today, the Ridgewood Farm land is a developed retail corridor known as the Ridgewood Village Center. The center opened in 1985 with a variety of stores and restaurants. The home, shown here, remains standing today.

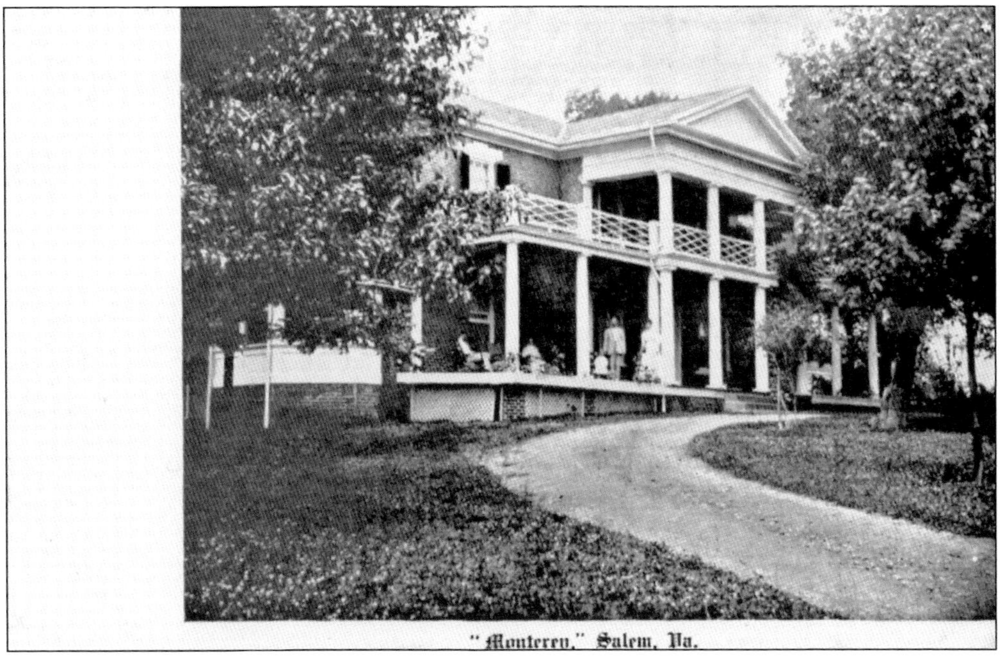

MONTEREY, 1907. Monterey was the pre-Civil War home of the Chapman family. In later years, the home at the corner of High and Clay Streets served as a hotel, hosting visitors by making them feel that they are at a residence.

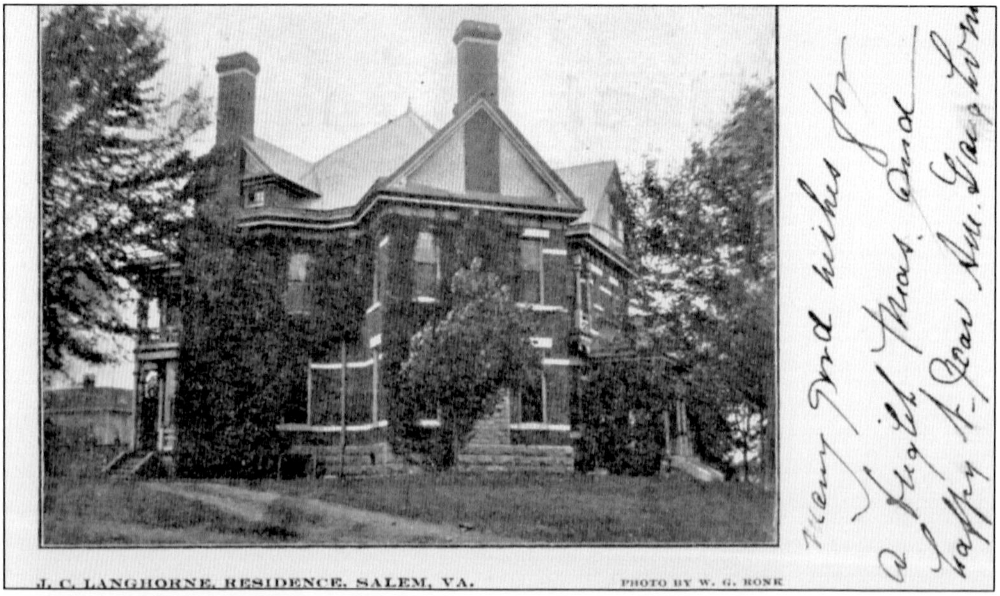

J.C. LANGHORNE RESIDENCE, 1915. James C. Langhorne, who was a prominent figure in the formation of St. Paul's Episcopal Church, also helped to develop Lake Spring Park, served on the Salem Town Council, and operated several business enterprises.

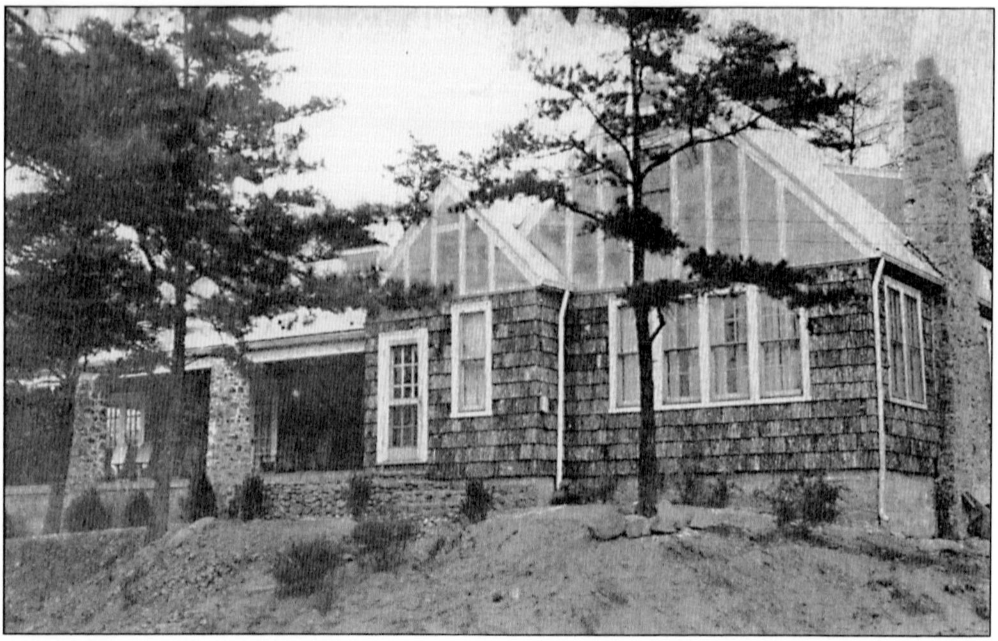

ROANOKE COUNTY WOMEN'S CLUB, *C.* 1940. The Roanoke County Women's Club was formed on June 7, 1923, by 28 women. In May 1929, the club formally dedicated their clubhouse. On year later, the Junior Club added a wing to the main clubhouse and started a library. This effort laid the groundwork for the county's library system.

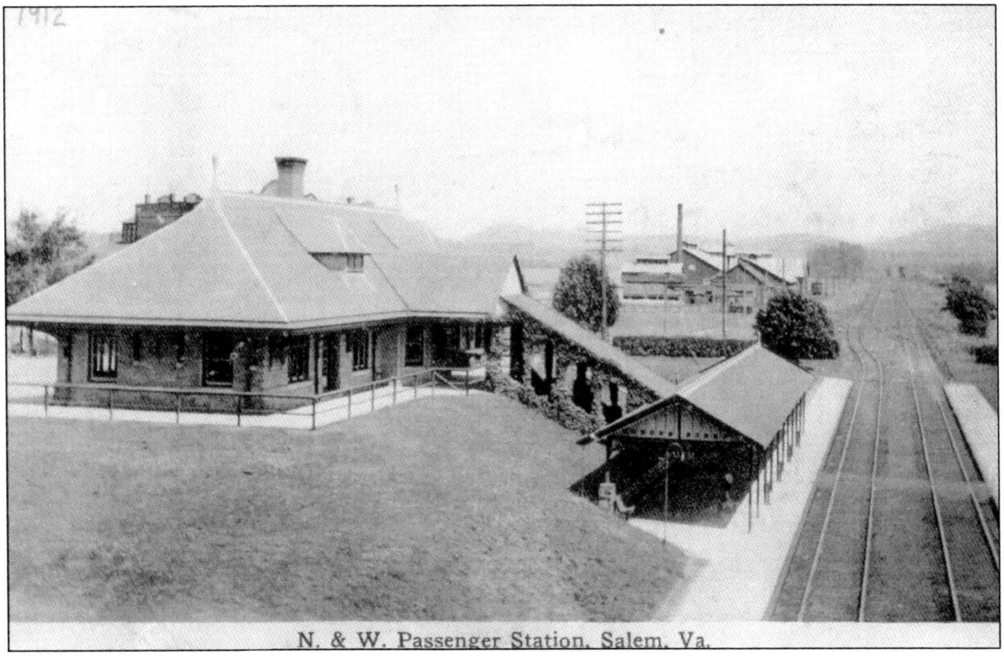

NORFOLK AND WESTERN RAILWAY PASSENGER STATION, 1912. The passenger station hosted a prominent visitor on October 19, 1934, when Pres. Franklin Roosevelt came to dedicate the new veterans' hospital. After the ceremony, the president came to Salem, where he was escorted by Salem's mayor and an assemblage of Boy Scouts to his waiting train.

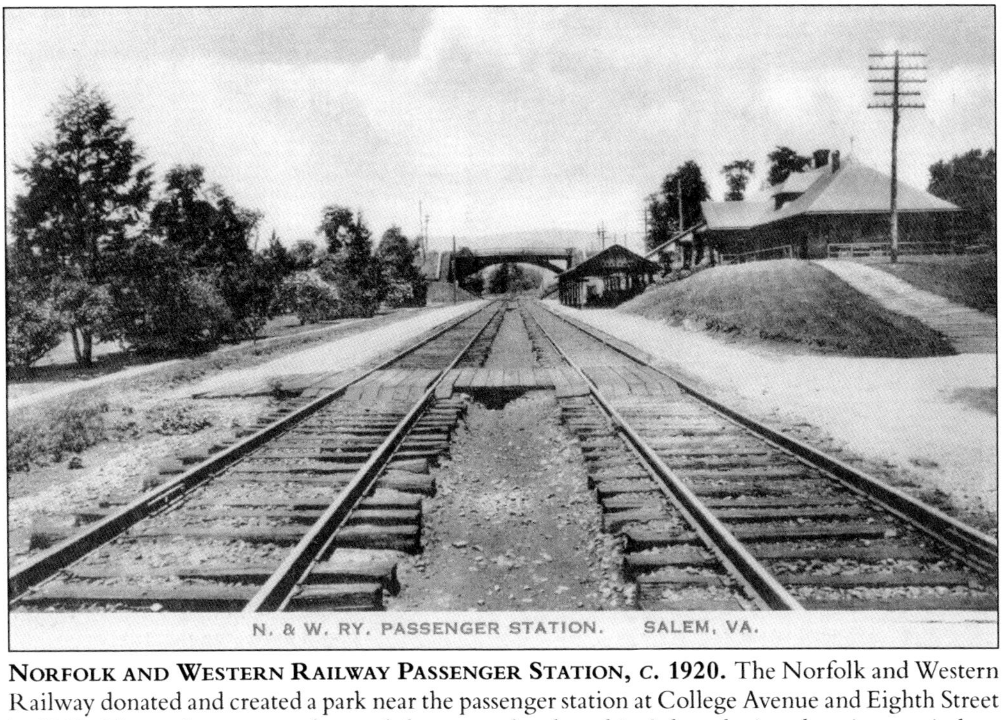

NORFOLK AND WESTERN RAILWAY PASSENGER STATION, *C.* 1920. The Norfolk and Western Railway donated and created a park near the passenger station at College Avenue and Eighth Street in 1933. The park was one of several that were developed in Salem during that time period.

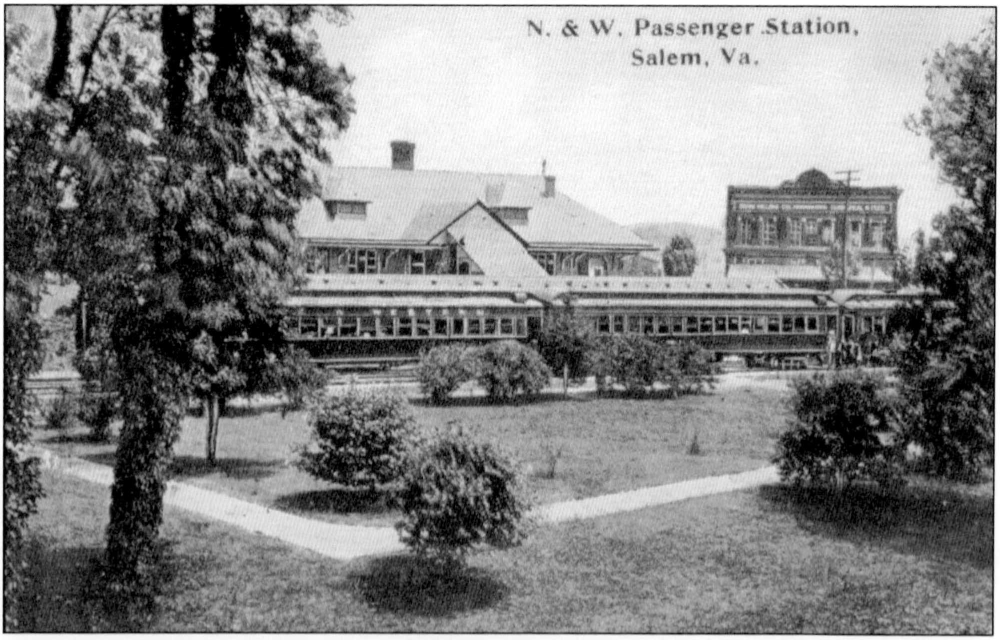

NORFOLK AND WESTERN RAILWAY PASSENGER STATION, 1915. Passenger service at the Salem depot ended on April 30, 1965. On that day, YWCA kindergartners boarded the Powhatan Arrow for a trip to Christiansburg. That same year, the Norfolk and Western donated the station to the town of Salem.

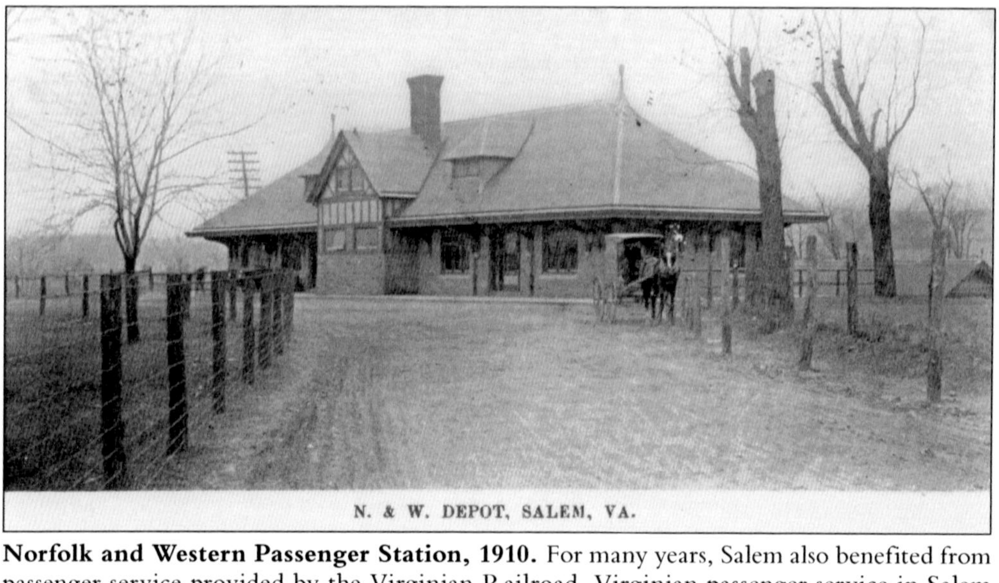

Norfolk and Western Passenger Station, 1910. For many years, Salem also benefited from passenger service provided by the Virginian Railroad. Virginian passenger service in Salem ended in 1954, five years prior to its merger with the Norfolk and Western Railroad.

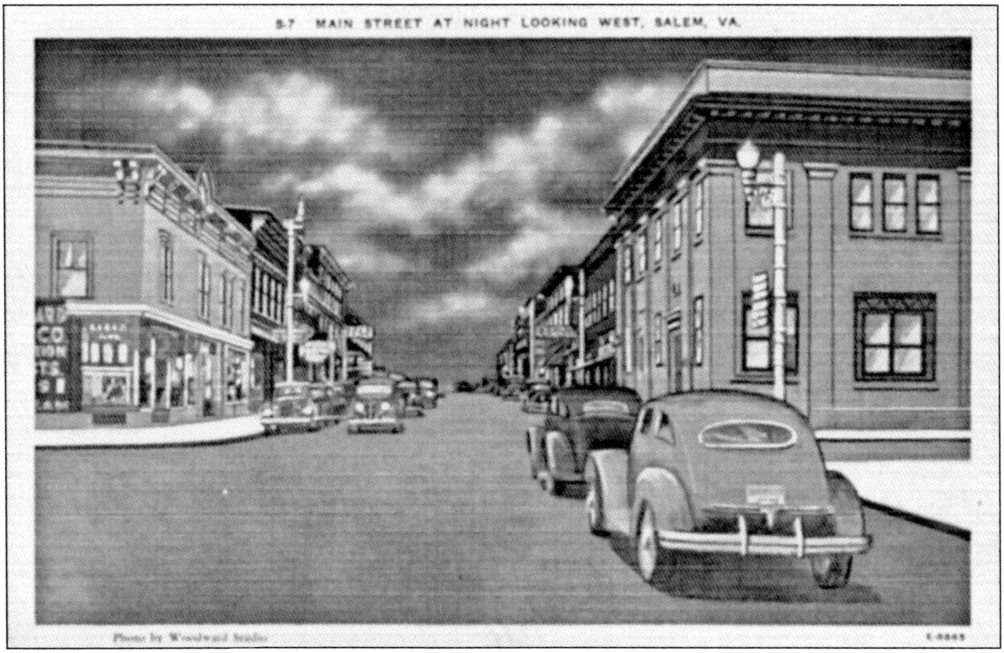

MAIN STREET AT NIGHT, LOOKING WEST, *c.* 1940. Main Street has hosted many parades over the years. The Salem Chamber of Commerce launched the traditional Christmas parade (probably to promote holiday shopping) on November 30, 1956. Within two years, the event was attracting some 15,000 spectators.

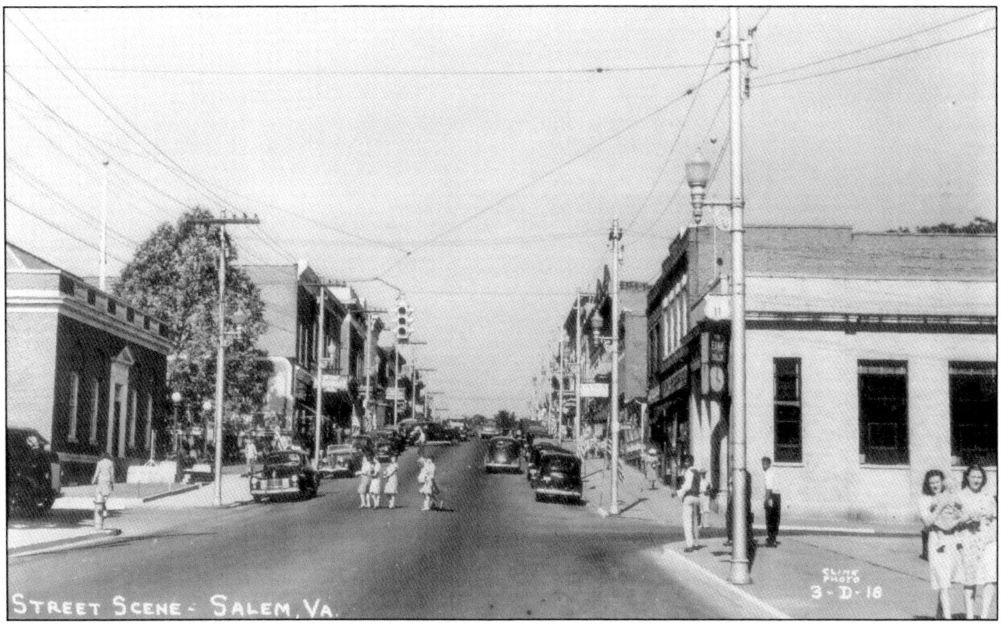

MAIN STREET, *c.* 1950. Main Street has become the setting for one of Salem's most successful civic and commercial events: Olde Salem Days. The event began in 1981 with an estimated 12,000 visitors. By 1985, under the sponsorship of the Jaycees, Olde Salem Days drew some 40,000 people. The event has continued to be a major draw, encompassing a variety of vendors, musicians, crafters, and an antique car show.

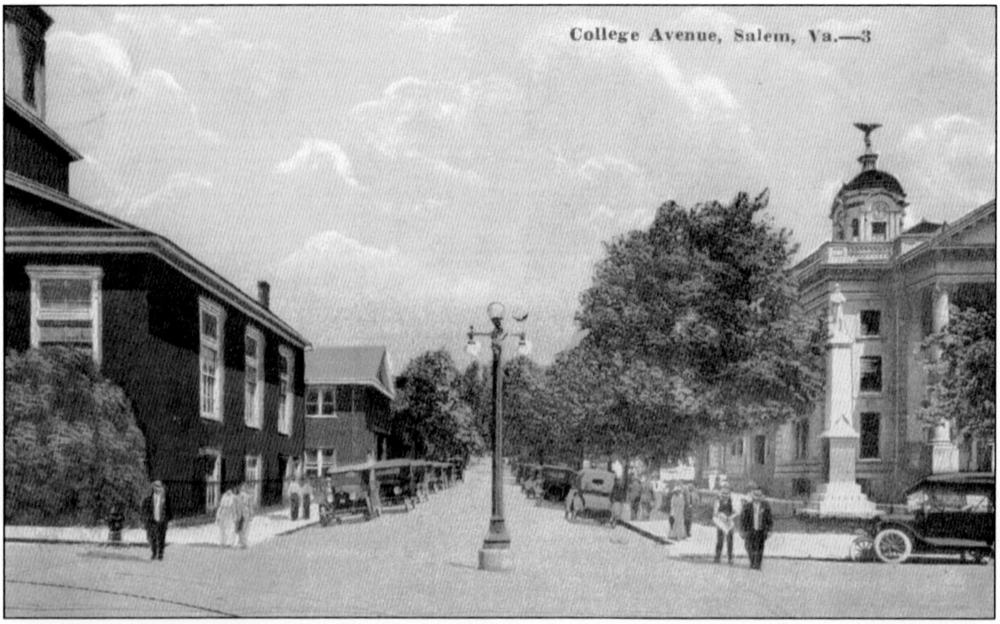

COLLEGE AVENUE, 1925. Good streets have always been one of the basic services provided by any municipality to its citizens. In 1909, a *Salem Times* headline read, "Good Streets Coming." The editor was congratulating Salem leaders for applying crushed limestone to the streets to replace the previous cinder covering. In 1911, the streets were actually "oiled" to suppress dust.

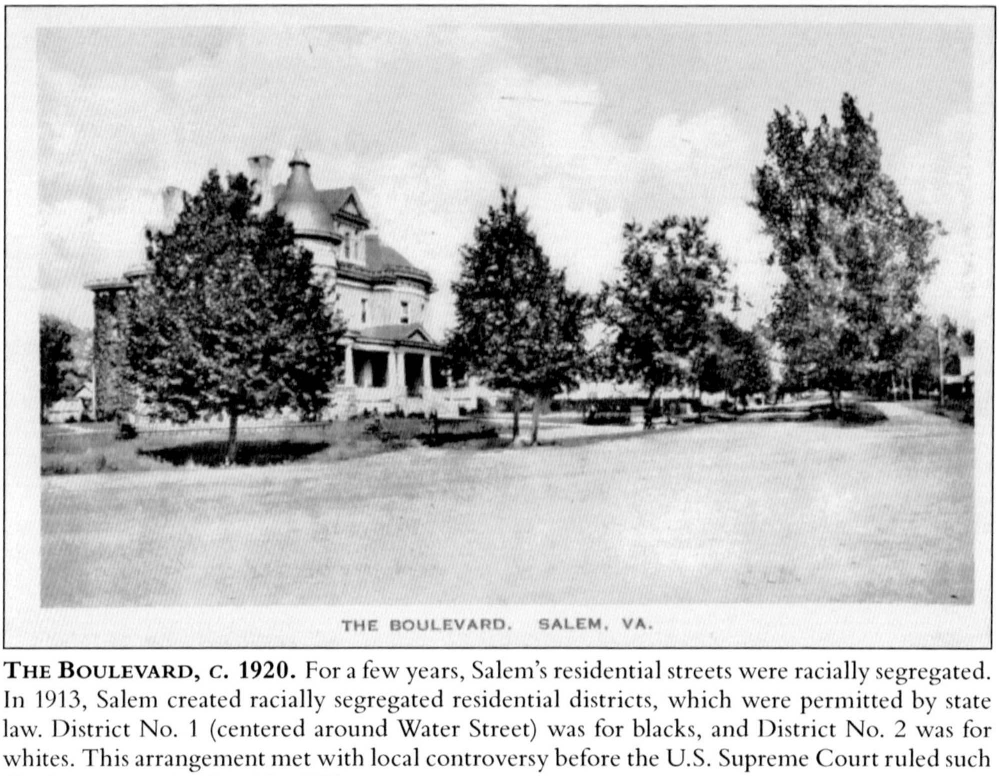

THE BOULEVARD, *c.* 1920. For a few years, Salem's residential streets were racially segregated. In 1913, Salem created racially segregated residential districts, which were permitted by state law. District No. 1 (centered around Water Street) was for blacks, and District No. 2 was for whites. This arrangement met with local controversy before the U.S. Supreme Court ruled such districts unconstitutional in 1919.

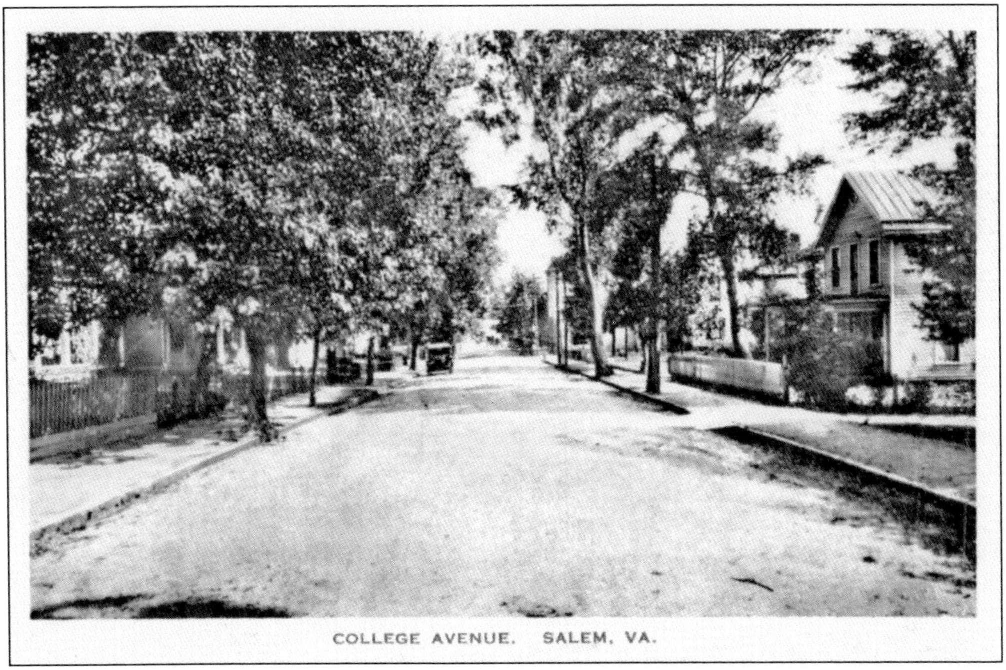

COLLEGE AVENUE, 1920. One early item that continually surfaced regarding Salem's streets was the roaming of cows. In 1907, the *Salem Times* opined, "Our dreams of beautiful streets and unfenced yards have been and will be in vain until the good people of Salem inaugurate an anti-cow movement. . . . Many of the leading streets in our town are veritable barnyards." On February 1, 1913, Salem officially decreed that no cattle, horses, or mules could roam the streets without an attendant.

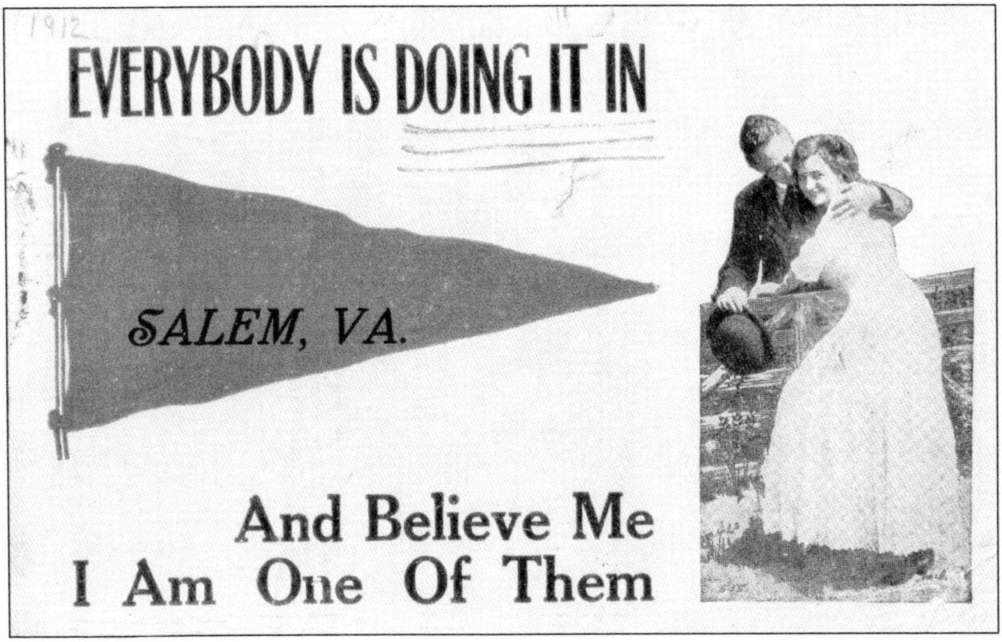

GREETING CARD, 1912. This humorous greeting card proclaimed, "Everybody's doing it in Salem, VA, and believe me I am one of them!"

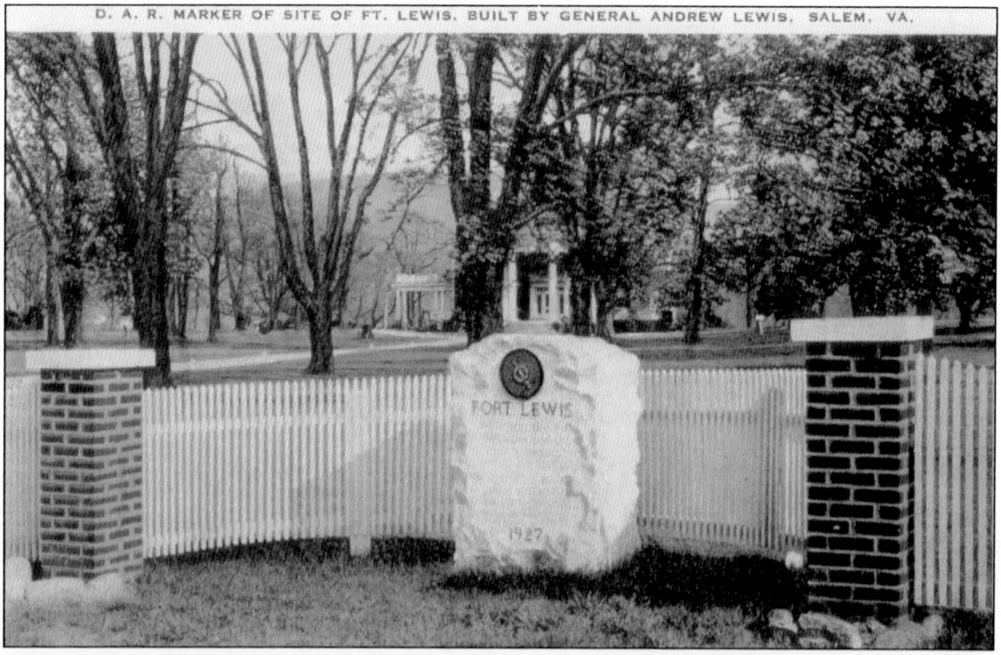

FORT LEWIS MARKER, *C.* 1940. In 1927, the local chapter of the Daughters of the American Revolution erected a monument marking the location of Fort Lewis, which had been built by Gen. Andrew Lewis.

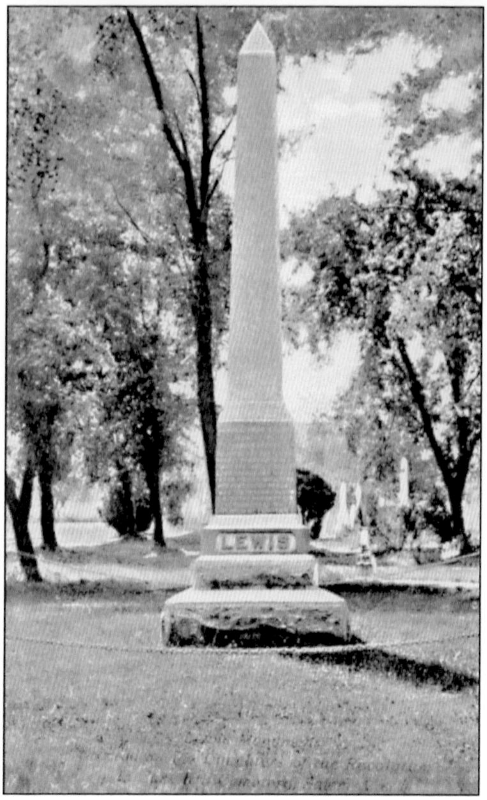

ANDREW LEWIS MONUMENT, 1912. One of the most notable citizens in the region's early history was Gen. Andrew Lewis. Though Lewis died before the town of Salem was officially plotted by James Simpson, his life was spent in its general vicinity. This monument was erected in East Hill Cemetery.

Two

ORPHANAGES

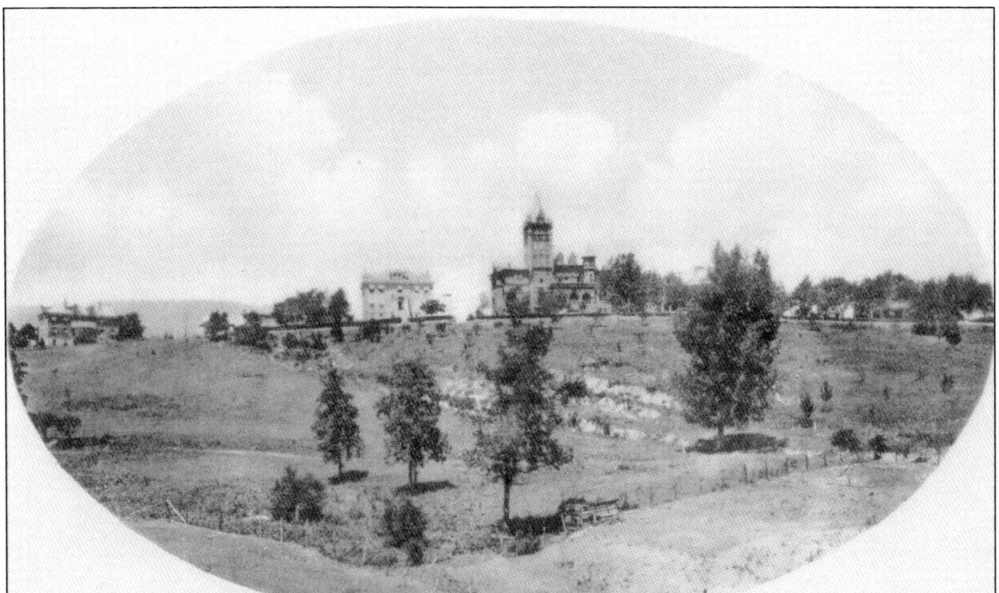

BAPTIST ORPHANAGE, SALEM, 1910. The Baptist Orphanage arrived in Salem in 1892 as a ministry of the Baptist General Association of Virginia. The Baptists had considered other sites in the state, including Fork Union, Glade Spring, Chatham, and Bedford.

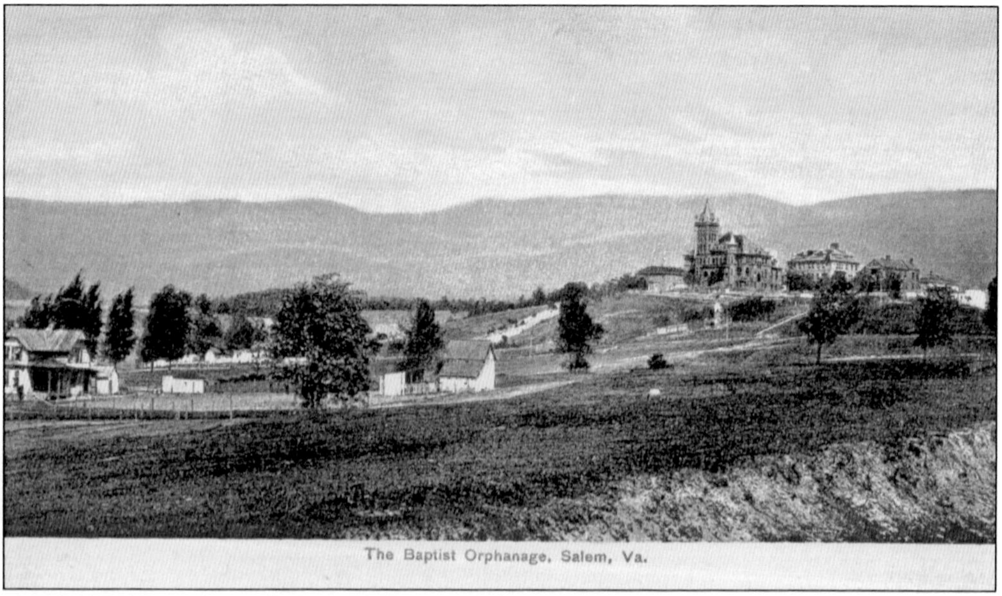

Baptist Orphanage, Salem, 1910. The Baptist Orphanage often brought visiting Baptists from around the state to Salem, who, according to the early Salem newspapers, would bring the local orphans into town for entertainment and recreation.

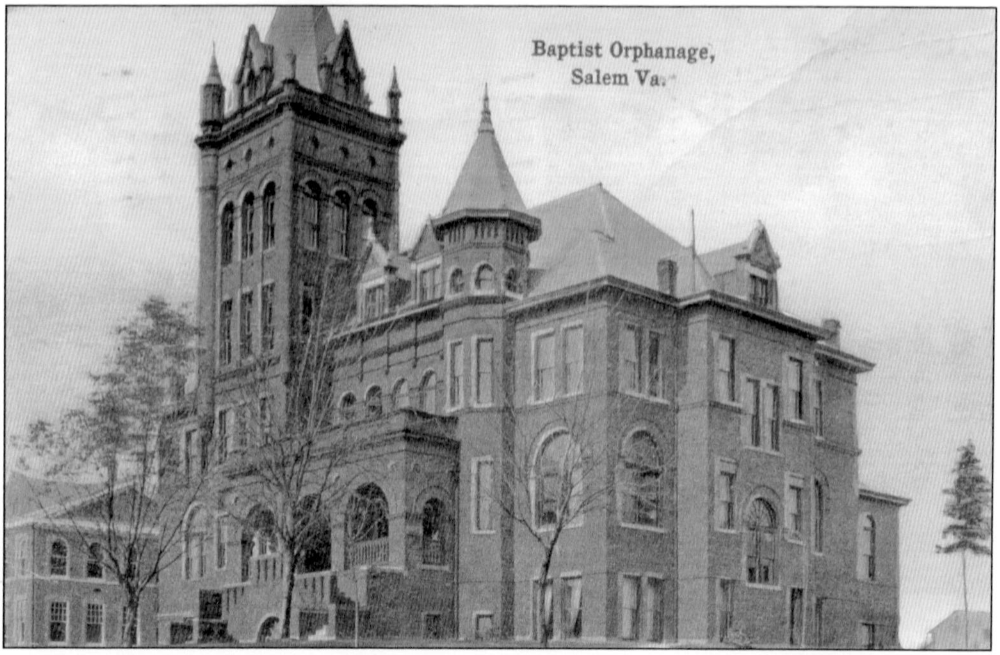

Baptist Orphanage, Salem, 1918. As a measure of Salem's hospitality, many of the local churches, regardless of denomination, became involved with both the Baptist and Lutheran orphanages. In fact, Roanoke College offered free tuition to qualified students from both orphanages.

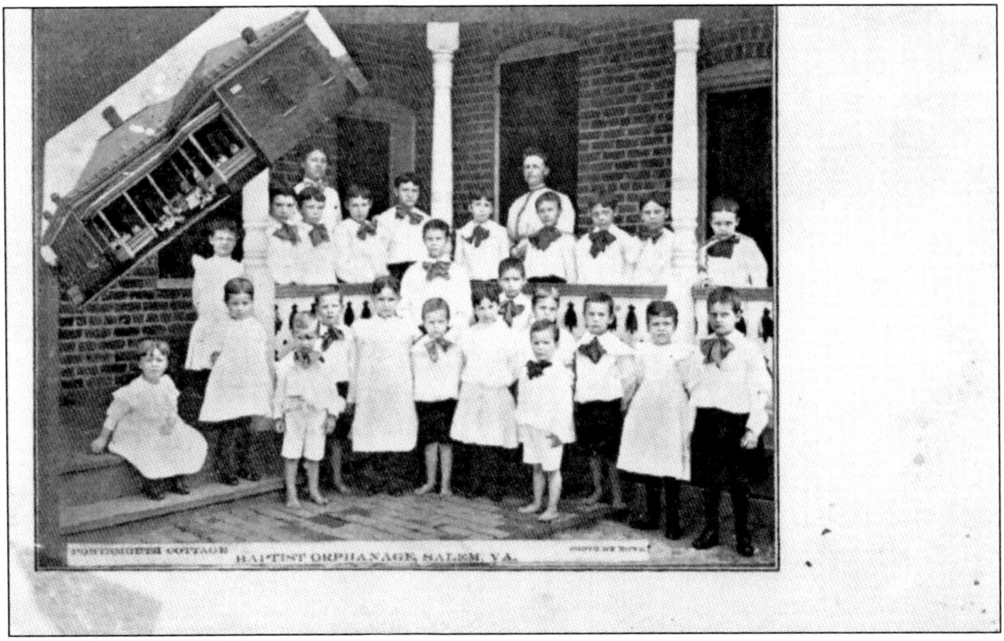

PORTSMOUTH COTTAGE, BAPTIST ORPHANAGE, *C.* 1920. Before the advent of modern medicine, quarantine was often the best strategy to avoid the spread of disease. Salem, like all communities, had to impose its fair share of them. In 1905, the Baptist Orphanage was quarantined for two weeks due to an outbreak of 15 cases of varioloid on its campus.

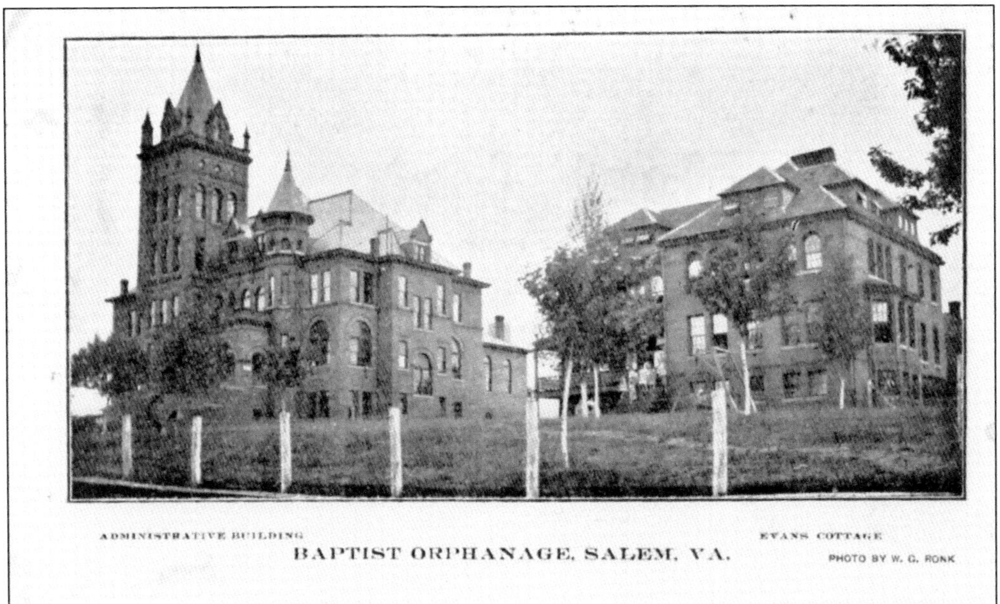

ADMINISTRATION BUILDING AND EVANS COTTAGE, BAPTIST ORPHANAGE, 1910. The cornerstone on the Administration Building was laid on July 4, 1901, and the building was occupied in 1902. Its red-brick castle-like structure was an imposing piece of architecture on the campus. The Administration Building was razed in 1965.

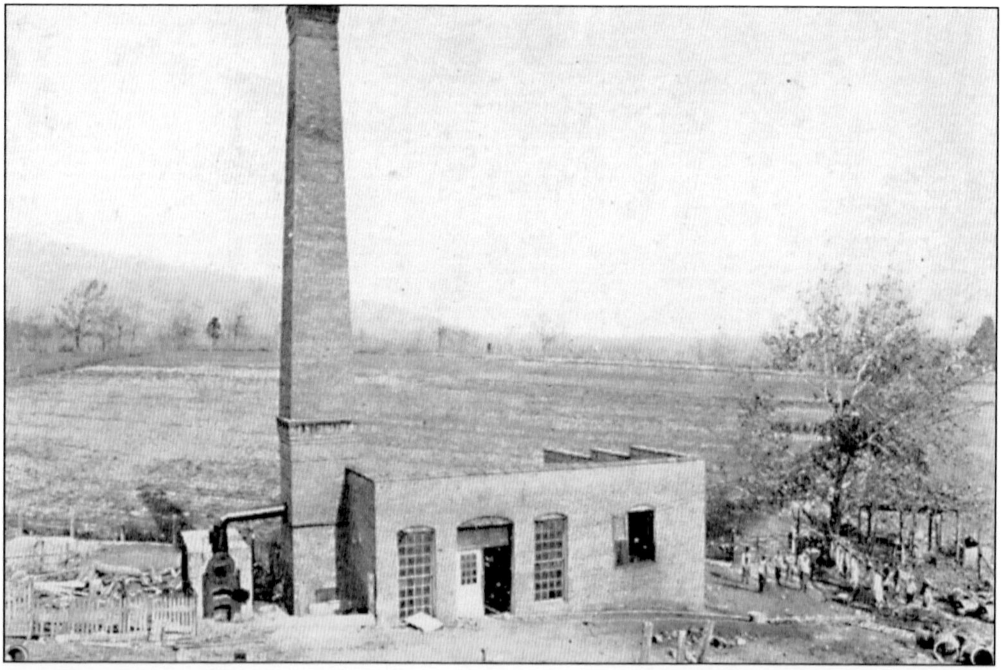

HEATING PLANT, BAPTIST ORPHANAGE, 1915. The hill-top Baptist Orphanage prided itself on being self-sustaining in its early years. A generous donation of an additional 87 acres in 1897 allowed the orphanage to even operate a full-scale farm and dairy herd.

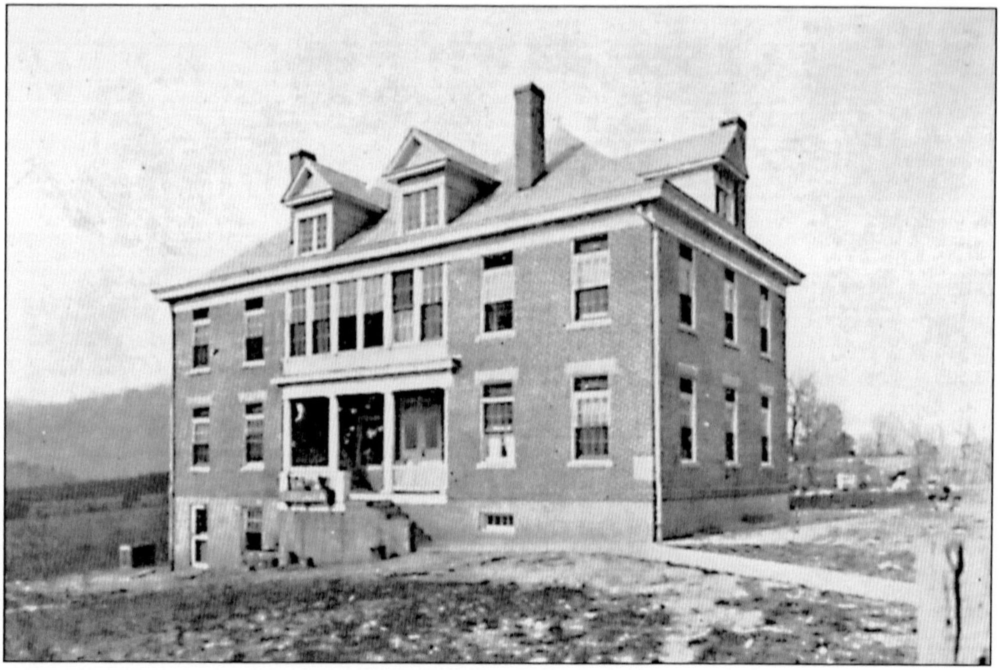

STRALEY INFIRMARY, BAPTIST ORPHANAGE, 1915. By 1905, the Baptist Orphanage, which was just a decade old, was caring for 165 orphans. Some were placed in the institution's care due to loss of parents, while others came to live there because their families were impoverished. All of the needs of the children were met, and they all attended schools in Salem.

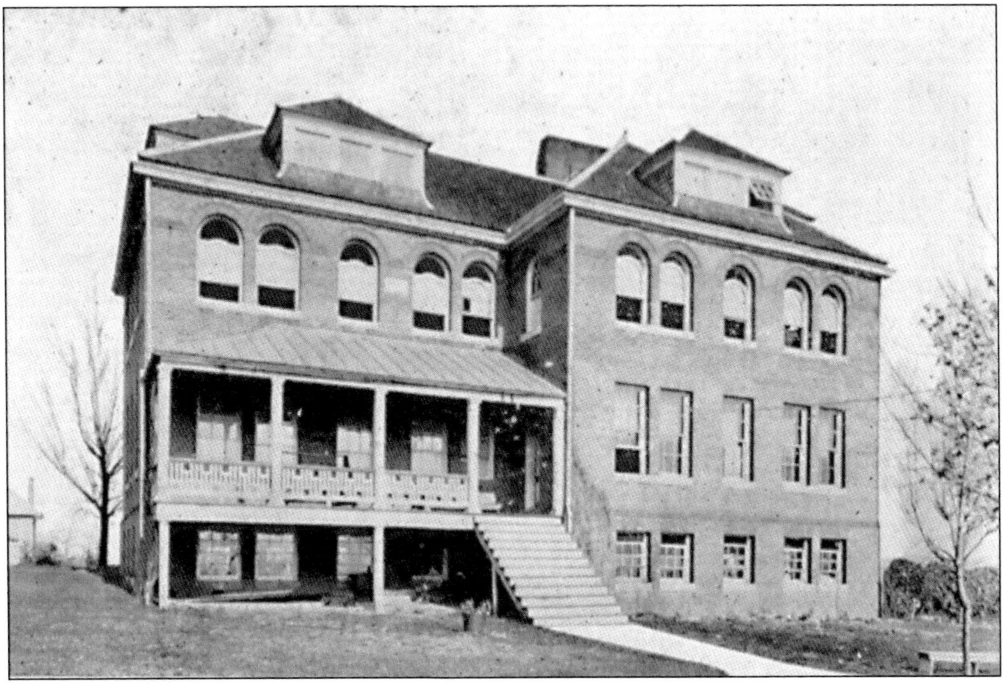

EVANS COTTAGE, BAPTIST ORPHANAGE, 1915. The 16 original acres on which the orphanage sat were donated by businessman John M. Evans. The very first cottage to be built, which was completed on July 1, 1892, was named for Evans.

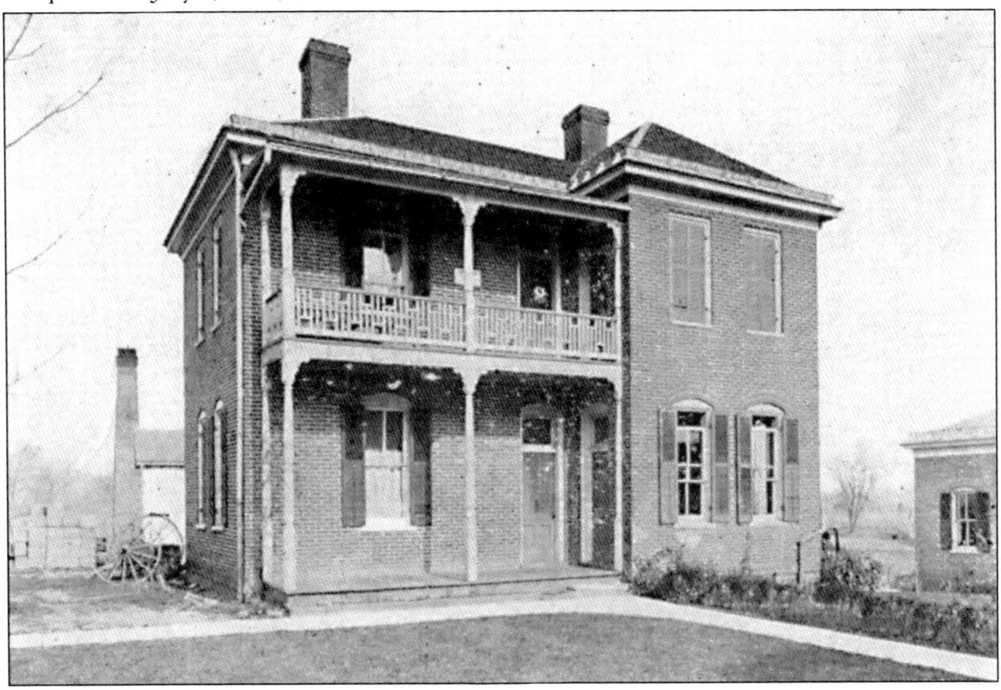

HOBDAY COTTAGE, BAPTIST ORPHANAGE, 1915. This second cottage to be built for the orphanage was named for the institution's first superintendent, the Reverend George J. Hobday, who served the orphanage from 1891 to 1906.

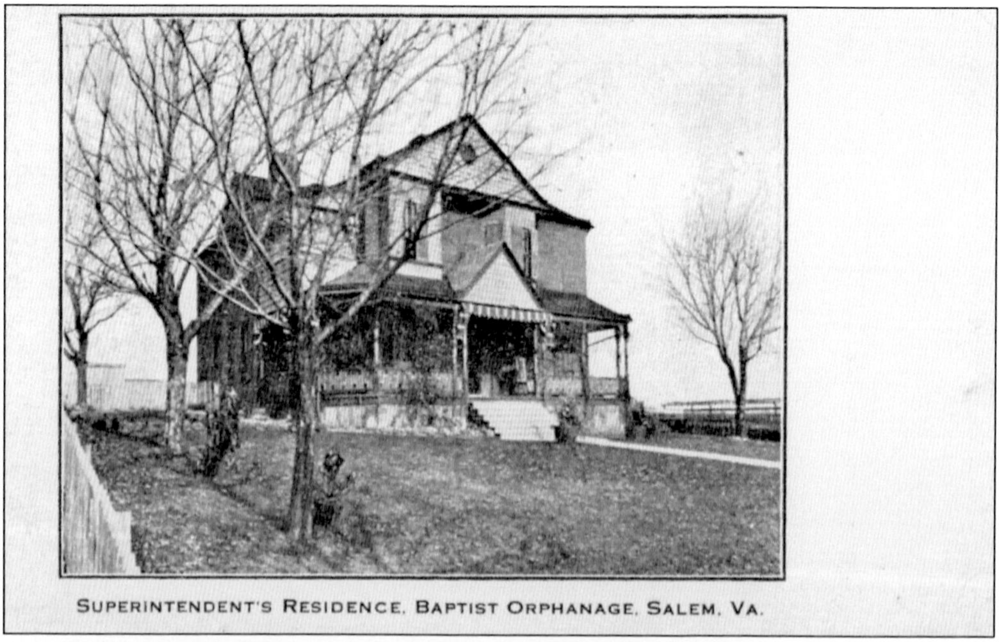

SUPERINTENDENT'S RESIDENCE, BAPTIST ORPHANAGE, 1915. The residence for the superintendent was constructed within the first decade of the orphanage's operation. The residence allowed the superintendent to not only live on the campus but to host visitors and families.

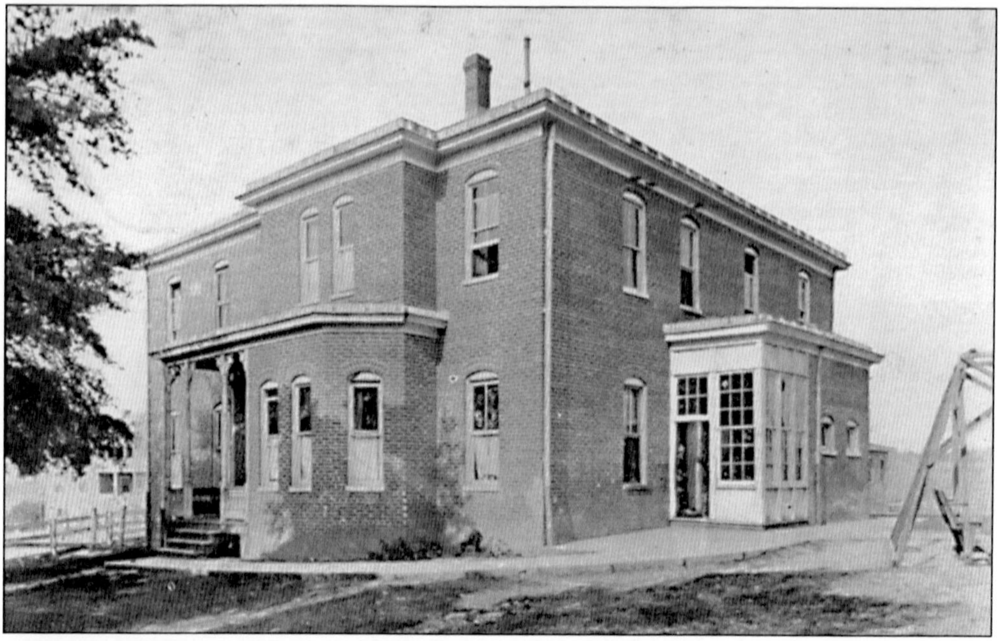

SCHMELZ COTTAGE, BAPTIST ORPHANAGE, 1915. Life at the orphanage often paralleled events in Salem itself, and some of those were not positive. In 1918, a severe outbreak of the Spanish flu closed Salem's schools, churches, and businesses for over a month. Sixty people at the Baptist orphanage contracted the illness, including its nurse, Mary Dunton. Dunton died as a result, having served as the orphans' nurse for 12 years. The epidemic also took the lives of 13 others living in Salem.

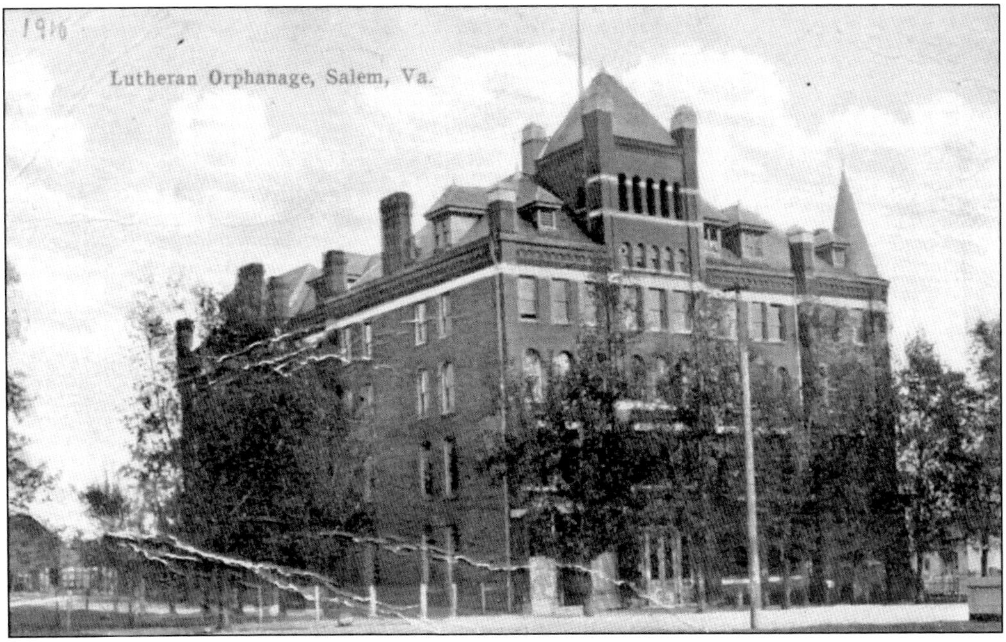

LUTHERAN ORPHANAGE, SALEM, 1910. The Lutheran Orphanage arrived in Salem in May 1896, occupying a brick home on five acres at the corner of present-day Florida Avenue and Boulevard. The orphanage bought the former Hotel Salem on College Avenue (shown here), which it occupied from 1900 until 1927.

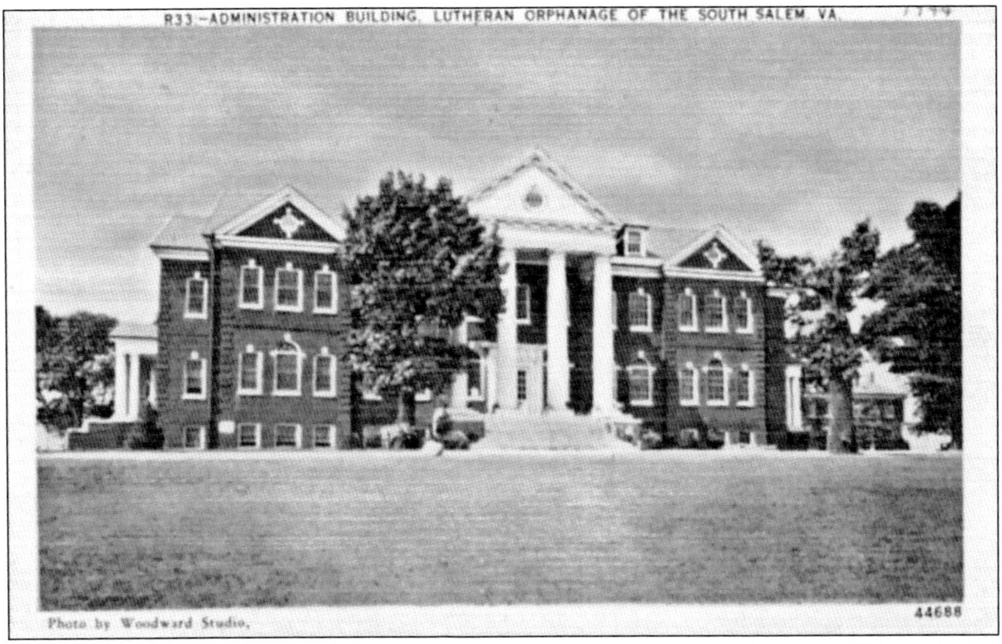

ADMINISTRATION BUILDING, LUTHERAN ORPHANAGE OF THE SOUTH, 1944. Having outgrown its environs, the Lutheran Children's Home built an administration building and two cottages just off Lynchburg Turnpike, on land previously occupied by the plantation home Sherwood. The building, shown above, was occupied and dedicated in November 1926.

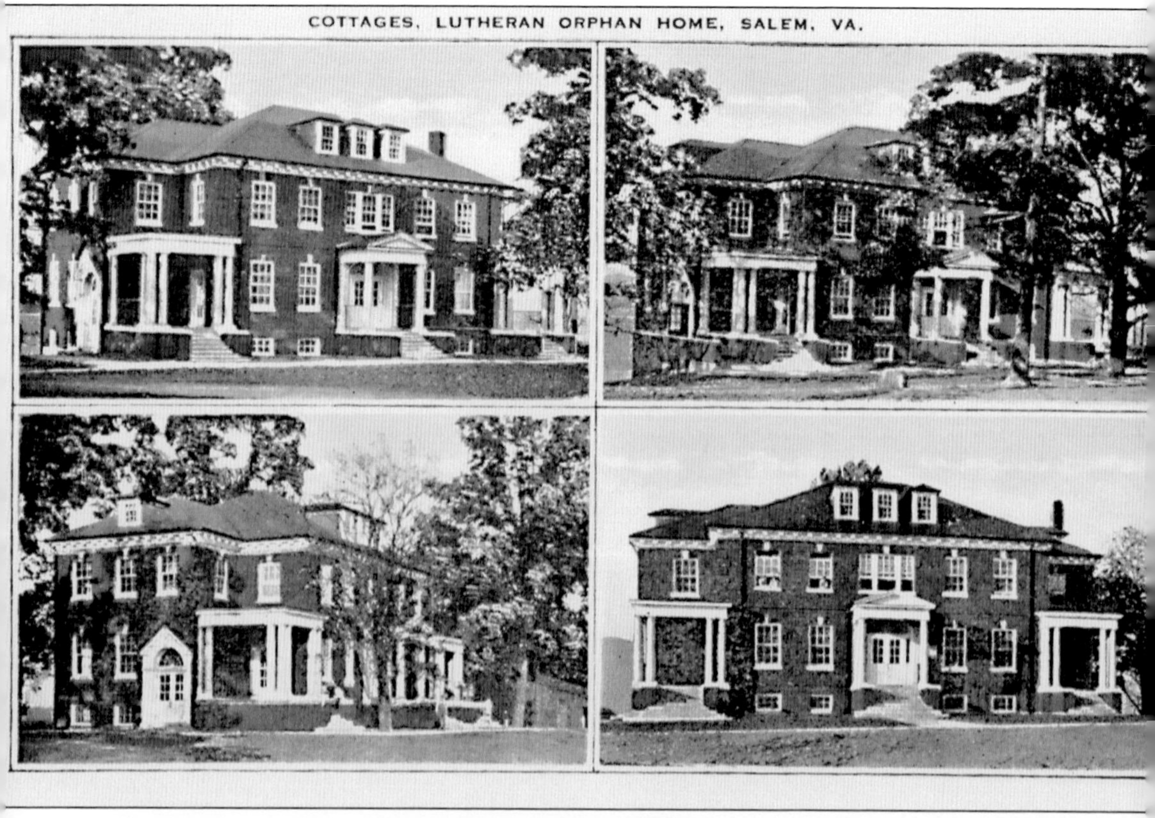

COTTAGES OF THE LUTHERAN ORPHANAGE, C. 1940. In the 1960s, The Lutheran Orphanage sold much of its land to Salem for the purpose of erecting what is now the Salem Civic Center. The buildings were sold to Roanoke College in 1985.

Three

Roanoke College

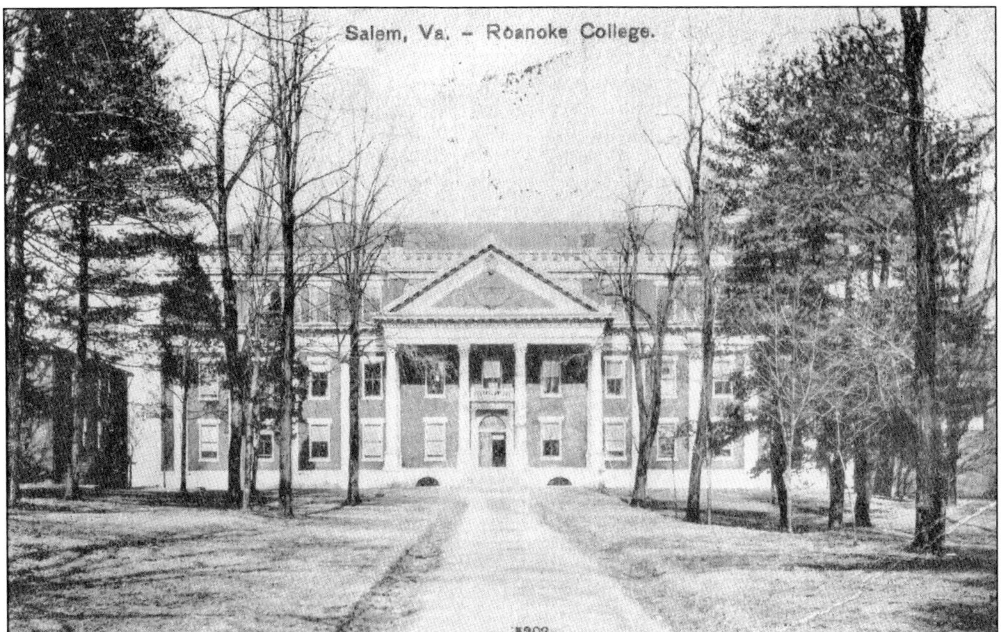

Administration Building, 1908. Roanoke College arrived in Salem in 1847, bringing all of its belongings as an institution in one wagon. The college, originally known as Virginia Collegiate Institute, moved from Augusta County.

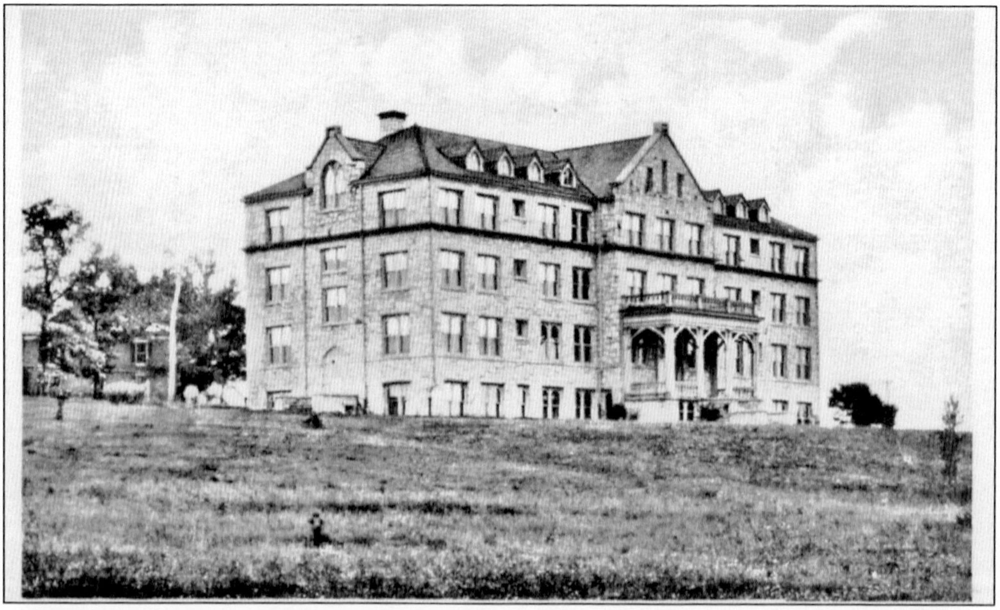

ELIZABETH COLLEGE, 1915. Elizabeth College was the result of the merger of the Elizabeth College and Conservatory of Music in Charlotte, North Carolina, and the Roanoke Women's College. The merged institution was located in Salem because its president had graduated from Roanoke College and thought highly of the Salem community. Elizabeth College officially opened in September 1915 with 88 students. The main building, shown here, was destroyed by fire on December 22, 1921. At that time, the college dissolved, and the campus land was acquired by the Lutherans for their new orphanage. It is known today as Elizabeth Campus, an annex of Roanoke College.

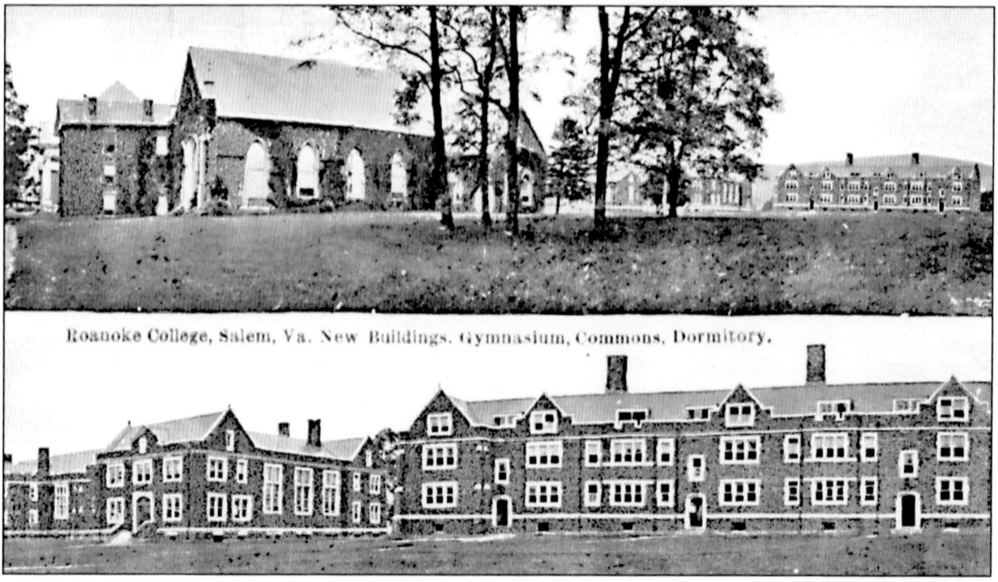

NEW BUILDINGS, GYMNASIUM, COMMONS, AND DORMITORY, 1915. Roanoke College's presence in Salem came as a result of a 9–5 vote by its trustees. The original four-acre campus was acquired through the purchase of land from William C. Williams for $400 in 1847. Until the campus was built, students were boarded in the private homes of many Salem residents.

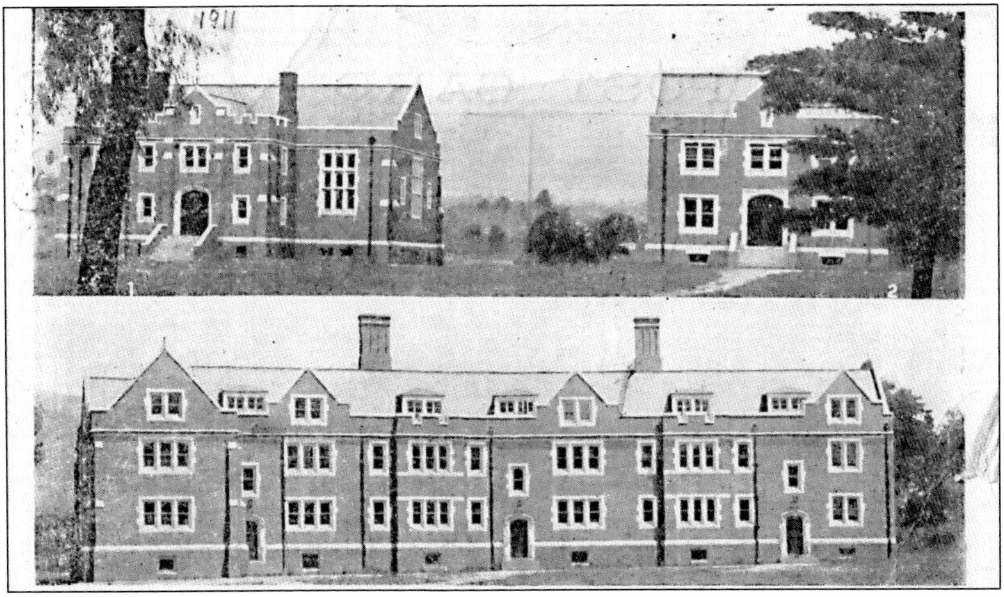

ROANOKE COLLEGE, MULTI-VIEW, 1911. This card shows the early gymnasium (top left), Commons (top right), and Dormitory. A 19th-century writer for the *Lutheran Observer* penned the following about Salem: "I had almost forgotten to state that the society of Salem is generally, and we might also say, universally moral and mostly religious. We recollect but one grog shop in the place."

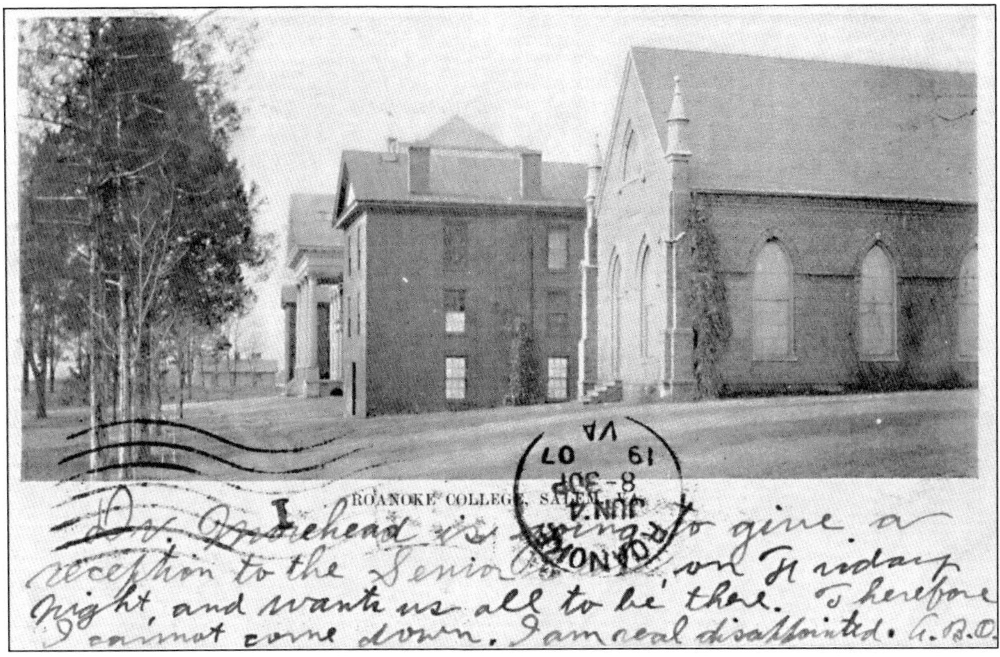

ROANOKE COLLEGE, 1907. The *Fincastle Democrat*, perhaps jealous of Salem's development and the college deciding to locate within its environs, wrote the following soon after its move to Salem: "They have procured a very handsome sight, not far from the courthouse, and intend putting up one or more buildings this summer. We certainly differ with them as to the character of such edifices. We would never put up a four story building where land is so cheap as it is in Salem."

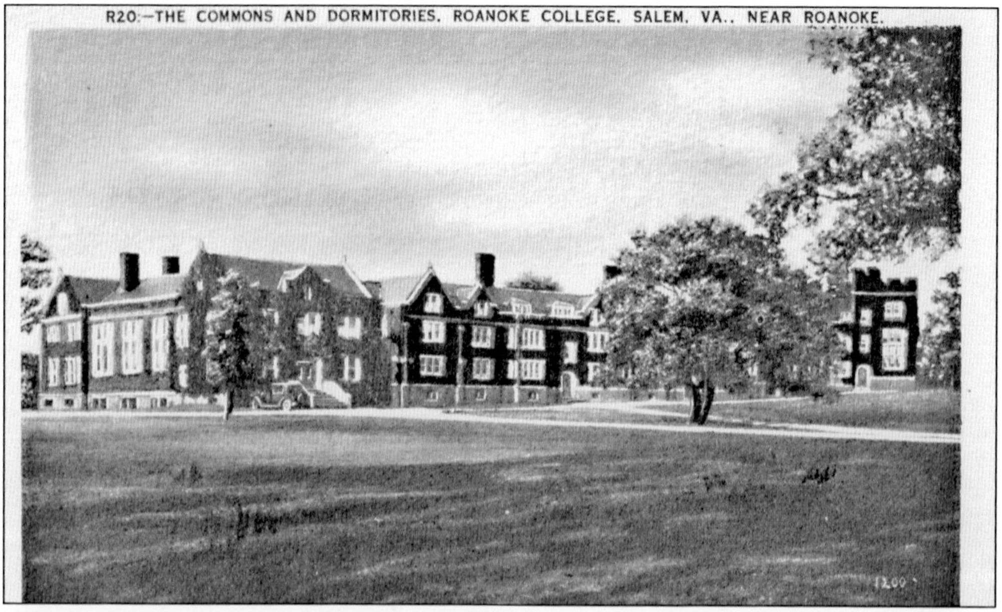

THE COMMONS AND DORMITORY, *c.* 1940. A semi-centennial celebration for Roanoke College occurred in Salem during the week of June 7, 1903. To create a festive atmosphere, Salem businesses decorated with the college colors of blue and yellow. Salem residents joined with the college in a parade, band concert, speeches, and an appearance by Virginia governor Andrew Montague during the week.

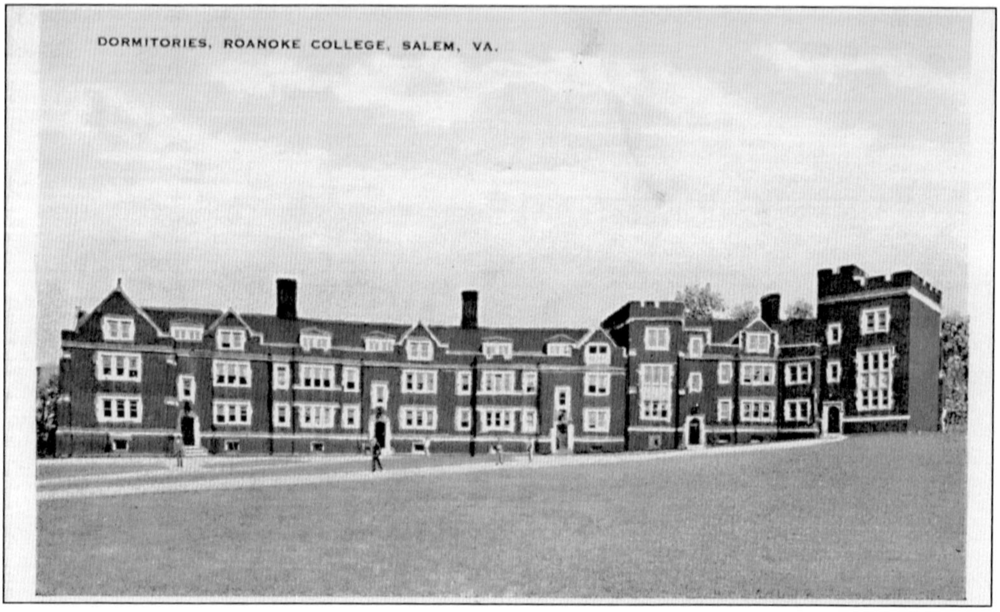

DORMITORIES, *c.* 1940. One of Roanoke College's most esteemed presidents was Dr. Julius H. Dreher. Dreher served the college from 1878 until 1903, when he moved to South Carolina to care for his aging mother. Pres. Theodore Roosevelt appointed Dreher as U.S. consul to Tahiti in 1906. Dreher served in other diplomatic posts including Jamaica (1910), Toronto (1913), and Panama (1915). After his death in 1937, his ashes were brought back to Salem and scattered in East Hill Cemetery. Dreher laid the groundwork whereby enrollment grew and the dormitories were built.

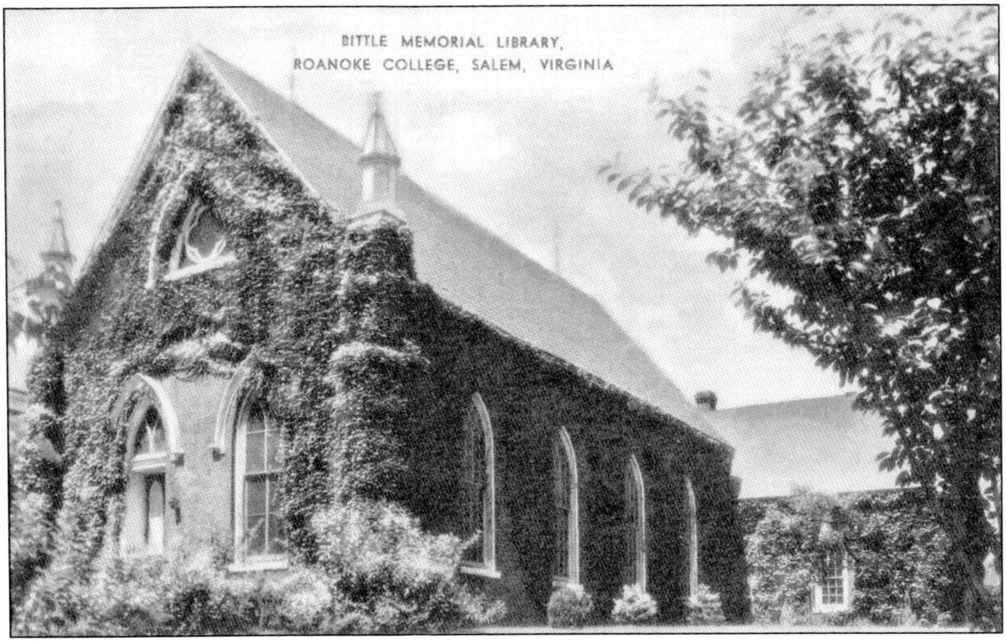

BITTLE MEMORIAL LIBRARY, 1939. Bittle Memorial Library was named for Dr. David Bittle, Roanoke College's early president. Bittle led the college through its move to Salem and during the Civil War. Bittle was one of three Salem leaders who officially surrendered Salem to the Union forces under Gen. William Averell during his invasion of the Roanoke Valley in 1863.

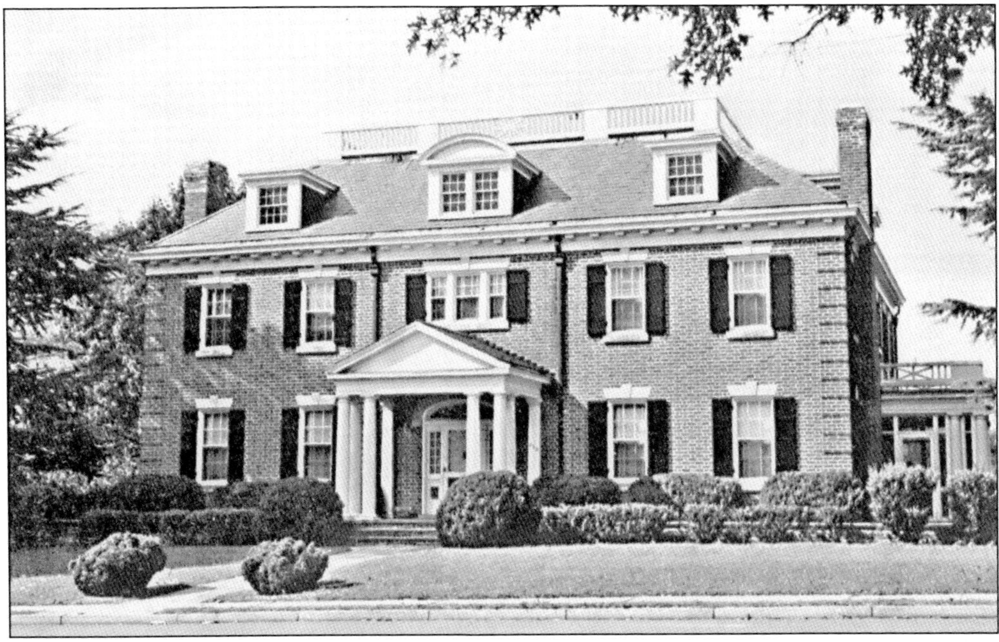

THE PRESIDENT'S HOME, *c.* 1960. The many presidents of Roanoke College have often provided leadership in Salem's civic affairs. They have promoted infrastructure development, settled disputes (and caused a few), offered faculty expertise for fiscal and cultural matters, and one even helped revive Salem's Boy Scout troop in 1923. The president's home, shown here, was built in 1916.

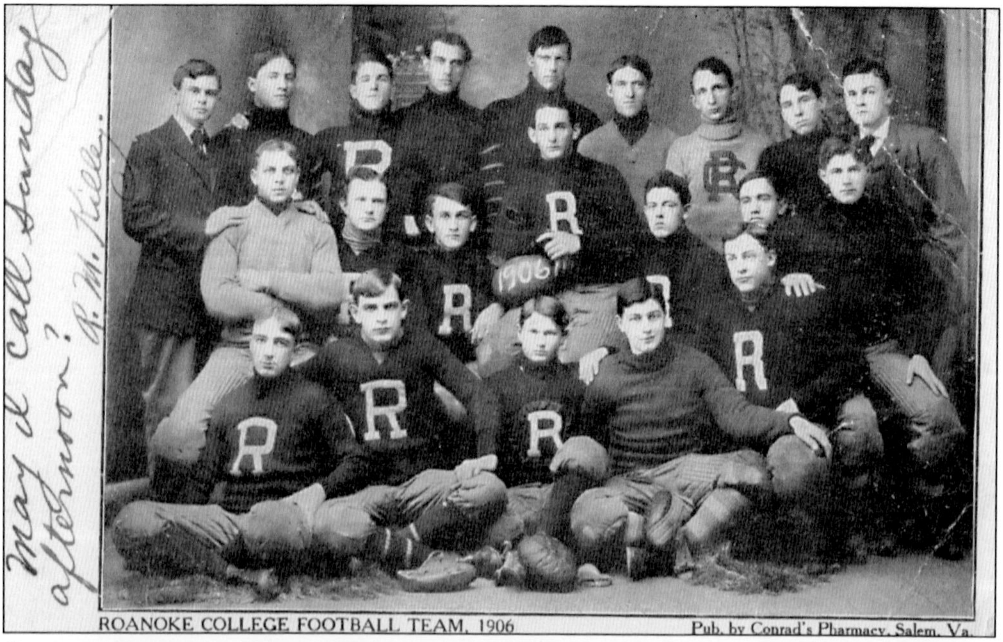

COLLEGE FOOTBALL TEAM, 1906. Raymond Killey sent this postcard to Margaret Rucker, a student at Hollins Institute. The message read as follows: "May I call Sunday afternoon?" Roanoke College's first regular football team was officially organized in 1892, though the game had been played on the campus for several years prior to this time.

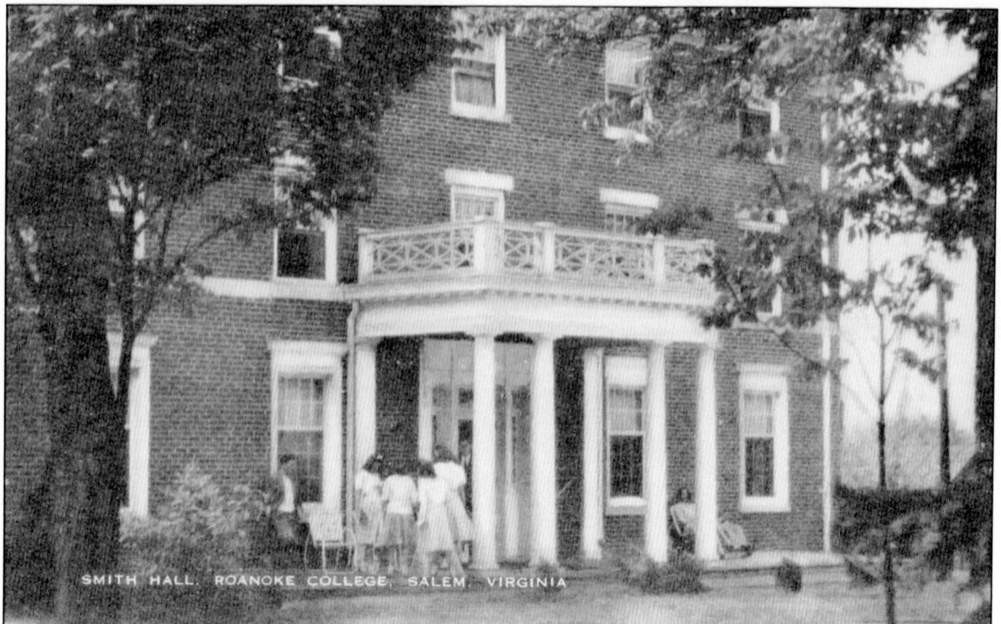

SMITH HALL, *C.* 1950. Smith Hall, named for a past president of the college, was erected in 1941. Designed by the firm of Eubank and Caldwell in Roanoke, the structure (originally a residence hall for 40 women) was built and equipped for a total cost of $50,174.

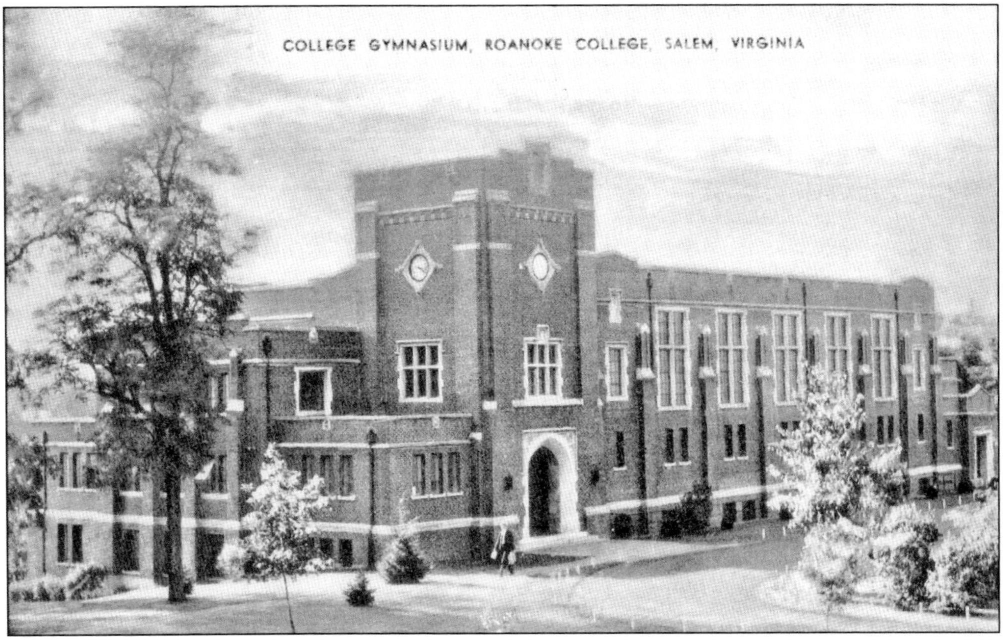

GYMNASIUM, 1939. The gymnasium shown here was built in 1930 for a total cost of $138,354. The gym was but one component of a large master plan to expand the college's facilities. Only the gymnasium was completed on time, as the Depression stopped work at the college for a number of years.

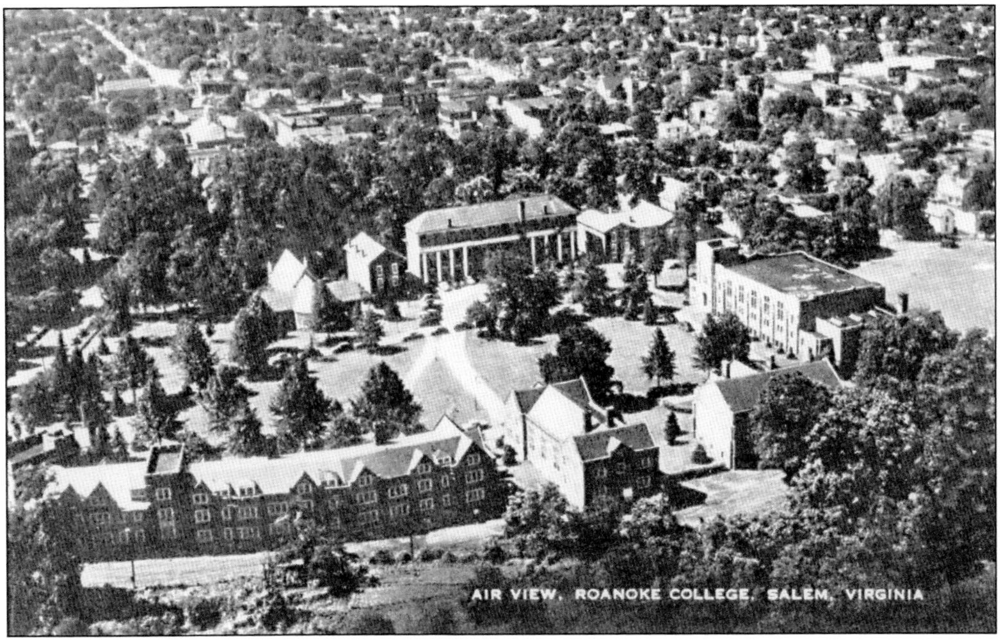

AERIAL VIEW, C. 1930. The campus as it looked when this postcard was printed was largely the result of the leadership of its president at that time, Dr. C. J. Smith. Smith had led the college through the Depression, developed an aggressive master plan for expansion, and admitted women to college courses. Upon his retirement, the trustees stated, "For what Roanoke College is today, and for where it stands in the field of education, Dr. Smith is very largely responsible."

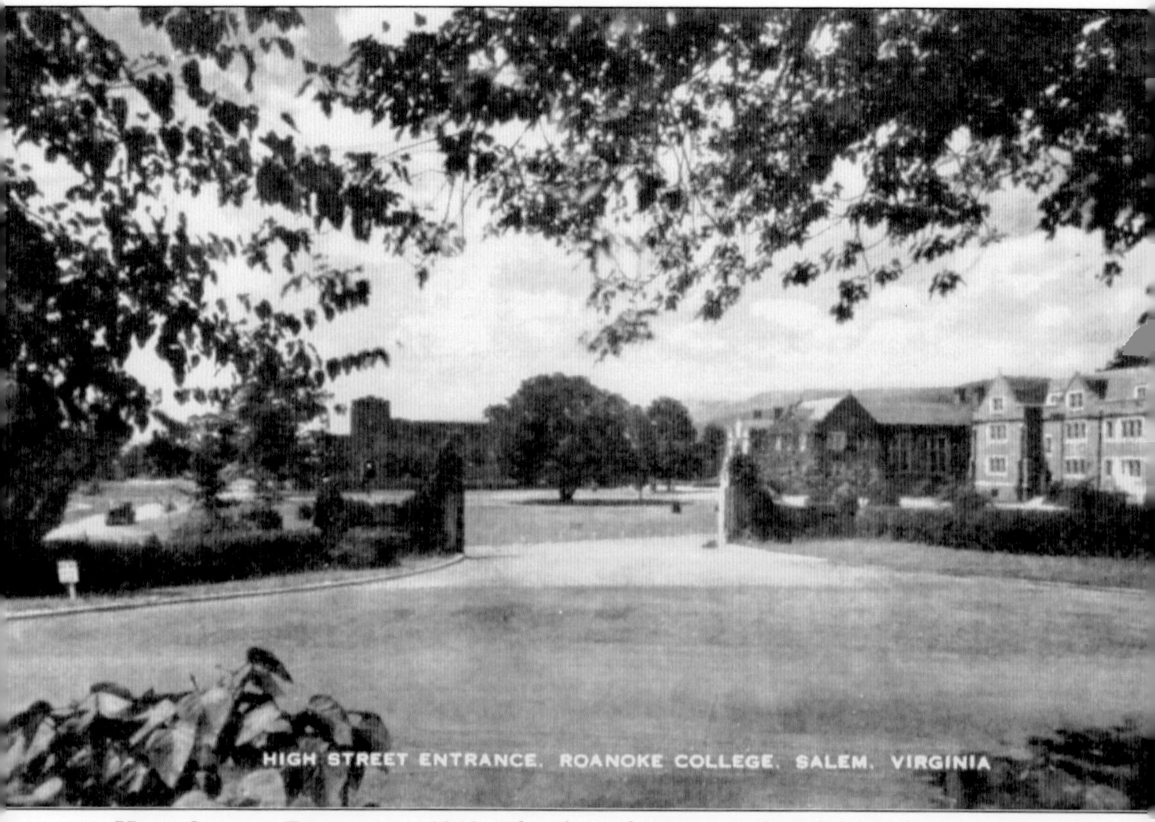

HIGH STREET ENTRANCE, 1948. The class of 1933 contributed funds for the landscaping and drive that made the High Street Gateway. The entrance and subsequent drive were made necessary at the time by the large number of students possessing automobiles, as well as increasing enrollment.

Four

Hollins University

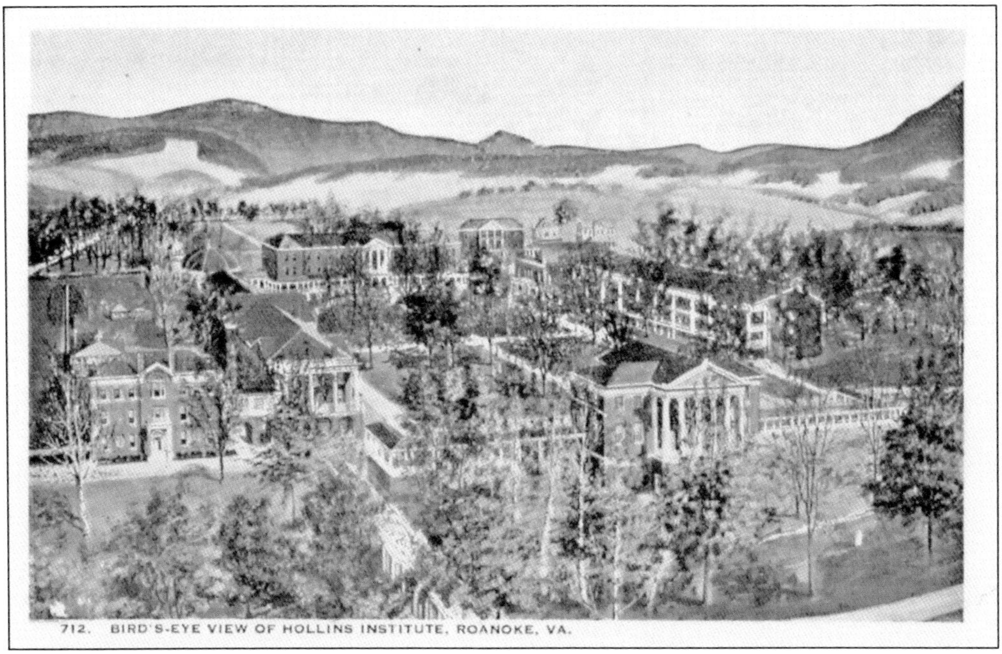

Bird's-Eye View of Hollins Institute, *c.* 1940. The history of Hollins University actually begins in New York with Joshua Bradley, a Baptist minister. Bradley purchased the property of the defunct Roanoke Female Seminary in 1842 for the purpose of forming an education union to "conduct an institution for all denominations." This postcard shows how Hollins looked a century after Bradley's purchase.

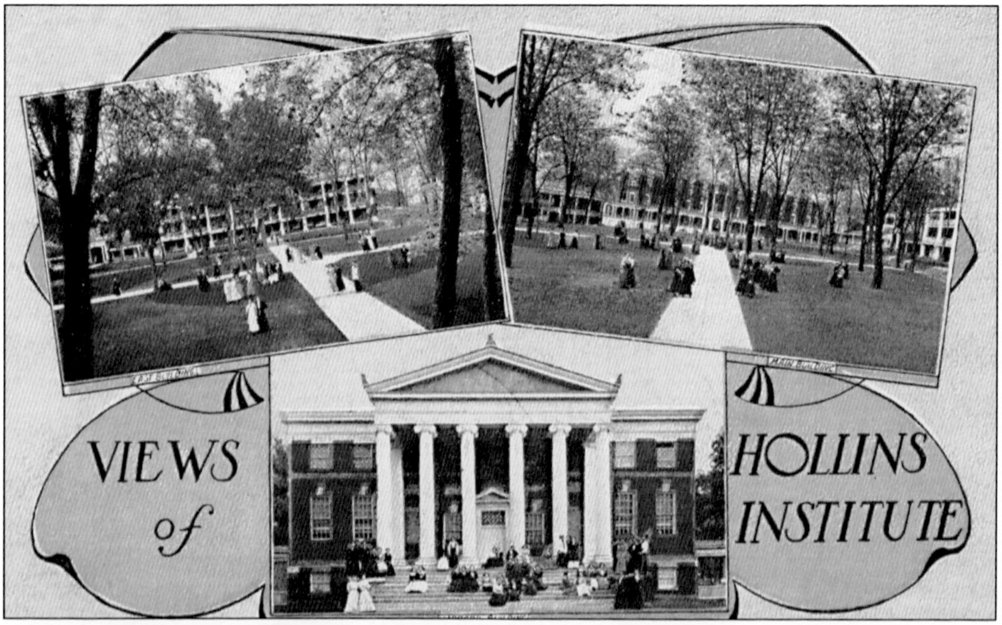

VIEW OF HOLLINS INSTITUTE, *C.* 1930. This collage postcard shows a number of structures on the campus, including the East Building (top left), Main Building (top right) and the library (bottom).

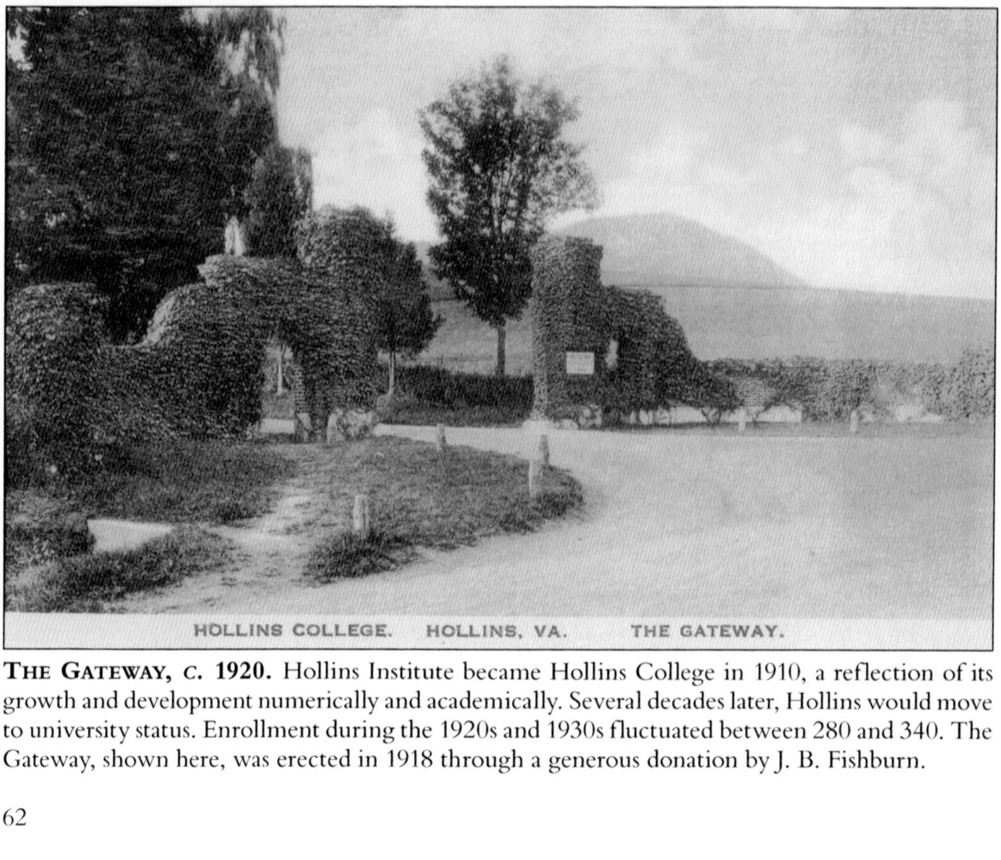

THE GATEWAY, *C.* 1920. Hollins Institute became Hollins College in 1910, a reflection of its growth and development numerically and academically. Several decades later, Hollins would move to university status. Enrollment during the 1920s and 1930s fluctuated between 280 and 340. The Gateway, shown here, was erected in 1918 through a generous donation by J. B. Fishburn.

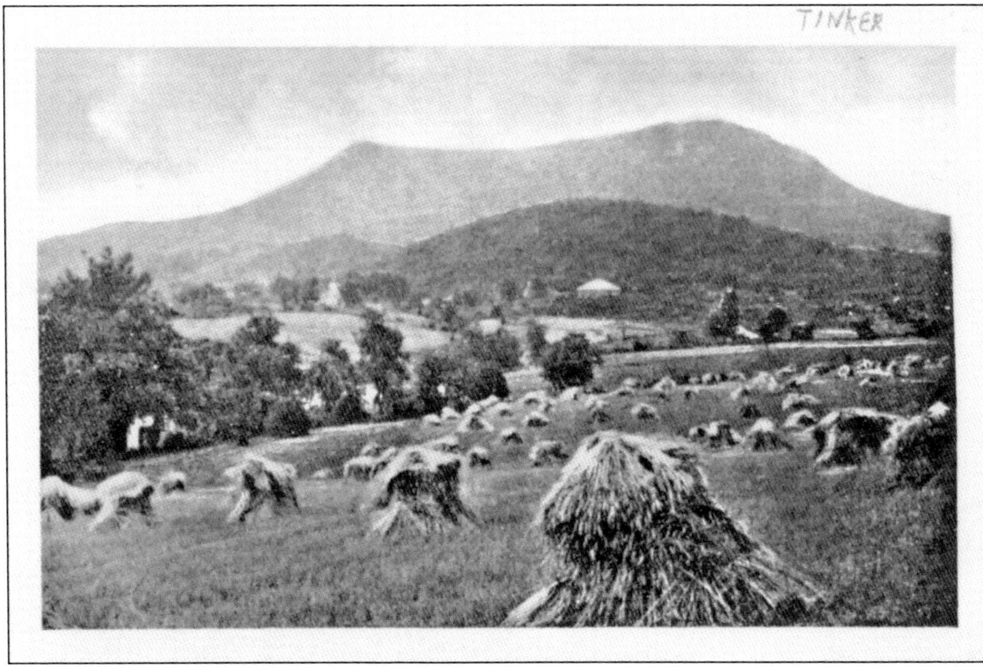

TINKER MOUNTAIN AS SEEN FROM HOLLINS COLLEGE CAMPUS, c. 1920. Tinker Mountain became the focal point for a standard Hollins holiday, Tinker Day. "Off to the mountains!" read a Hollins periodical in 1897, denoting a day off from school. Tinker Day became an official school holiday in 1895, being set in October.

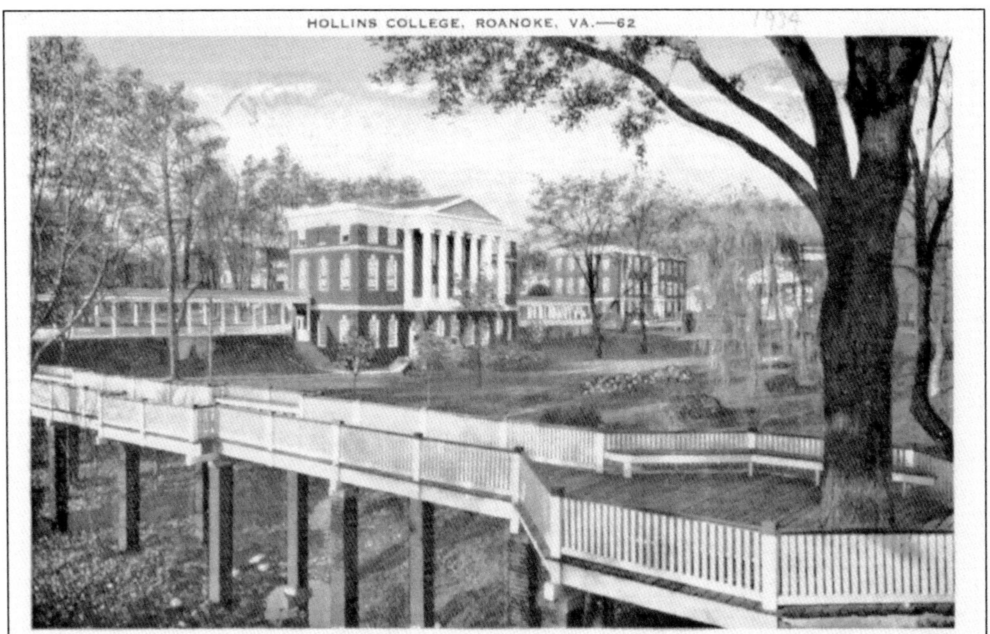

THE OLD BRIDGE, 1935. The bridge shown here was built in 1908, replacing an older one. The bridge was part of an extensive landscape plan developed for the campus at the time that consisted of gardens, boardwalks, bridges, and recreational areas.

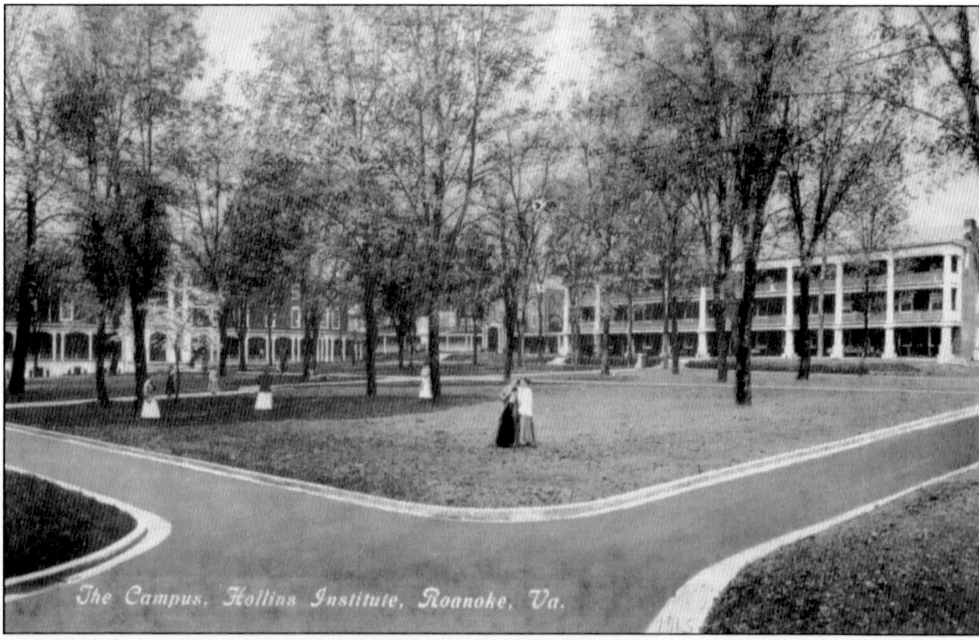

THE CAMPUS, 1911. Early in Hollins's history, social life for the students was very structured and limited. For example, in 1925, female students could receive gentlemen callers only on weekend nights and Sunday afternoons. Off-campus dates required a chaperone and parental permission, although seniors could accompany first-year students on the buses to Roanoke.

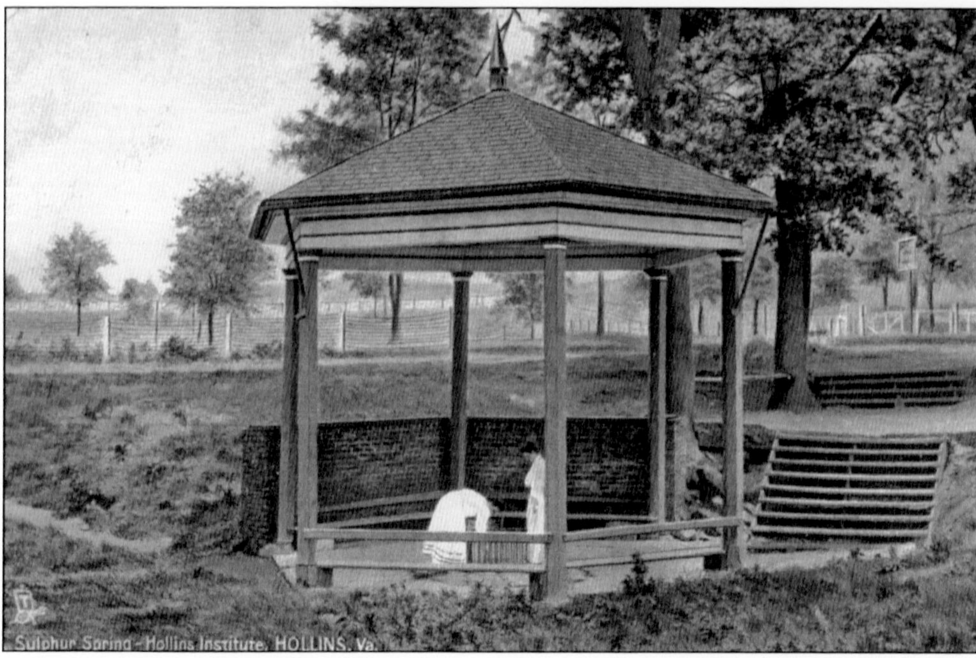

SULPHUR SPRING, 1909. The sulphur spring on the Hollins campus was discovered in the early 19th century in the bed of Carvins Creek. The message on this postcard boasted, "Its water has wonderful curative powers, and many prominent men, among them Pres. Andrew Jackson and General Lafayette, have enjoyed it."

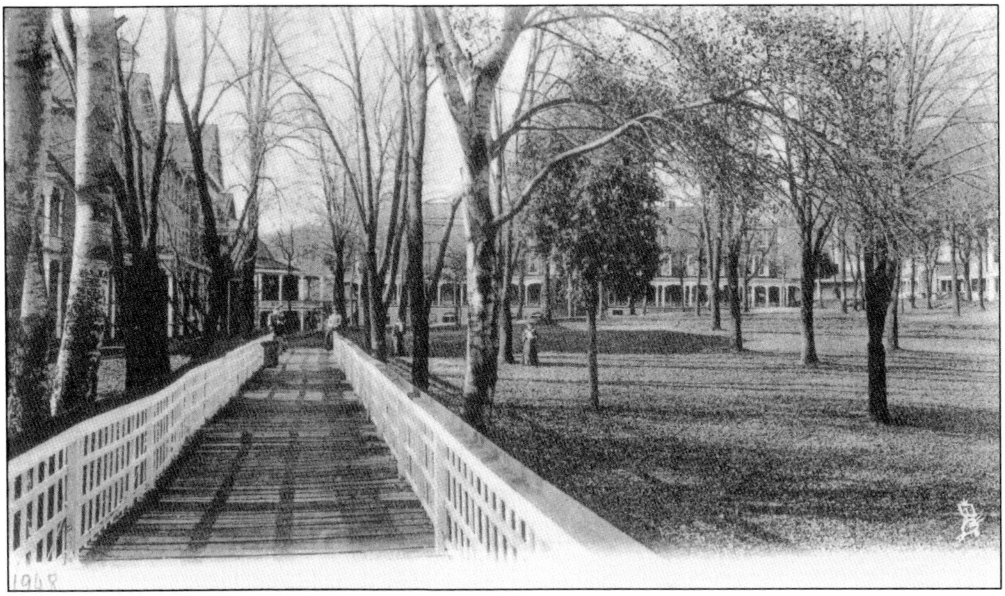

THE BRIDGE, 1908. When this postcard was sent, Hollins students were on a reinvigorated academic schedule that covered six days per week. Students could no longer attend for two years and get an academic certificate; they had to complete all four years and received a bachelor's degree. These academic changes were the result of the school's visionary president, Matty Cocke, who served from 1901 until 1933. "Hollins with its comfortable special courses is no more; we have become a more exact college," noted a student reporter in 1909.

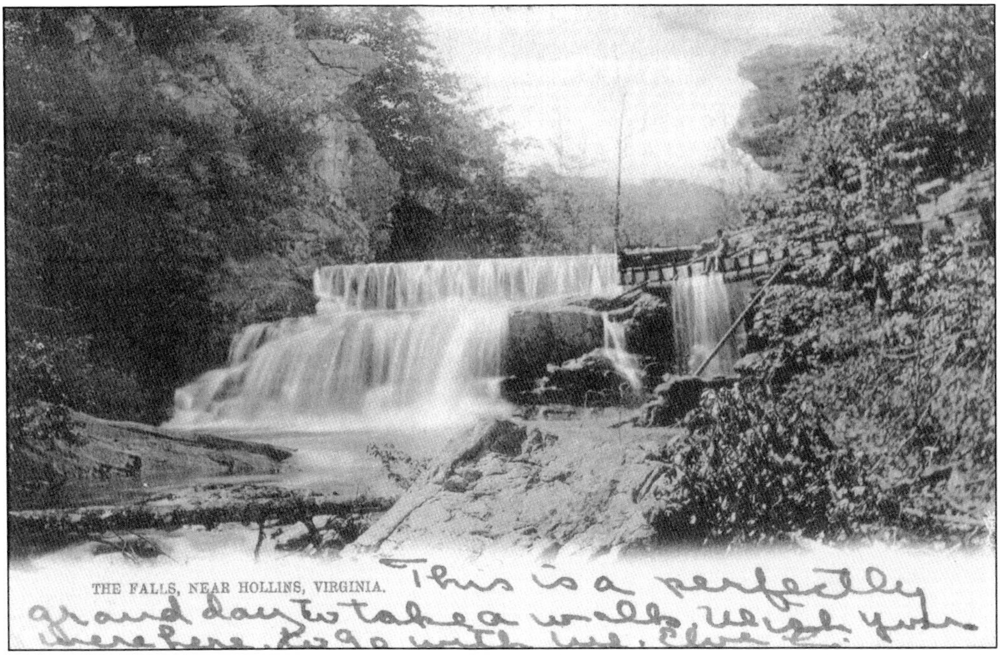

THE FALLS NEAR HOLLINS, 1909. Elva wrote to Albert Reinhold on the back of this card the following: "Received your postal from Washington, thank you so very much. Tell your dear mother that I will write to her tomorrow. This is a perfectly grand day to take a walk. Wish you were here to go with me." The falls shown here were along Carvins Creek.

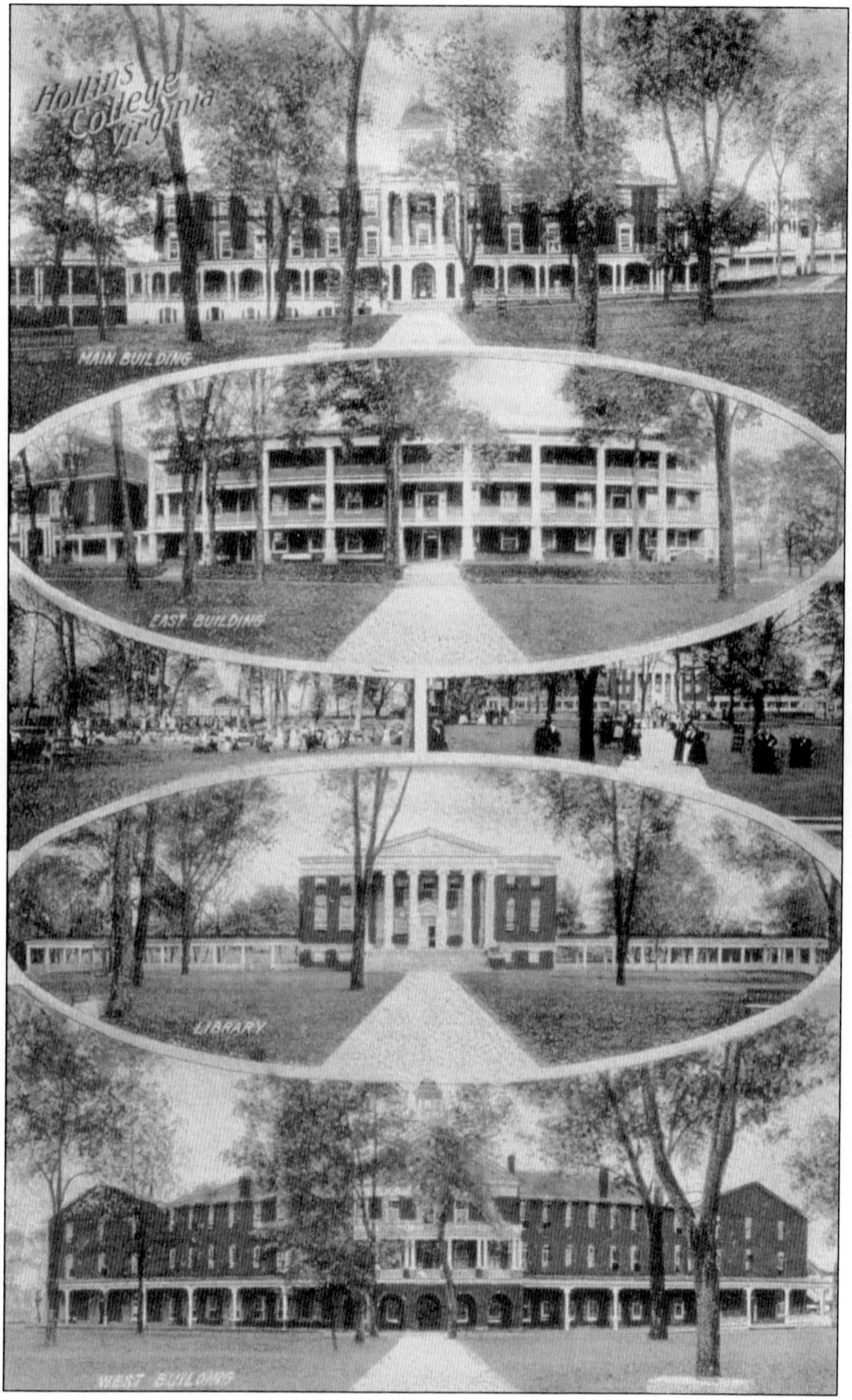

HOLLINS COLLEGE, *c.* 1920. This four-image card shows the Main Building (top), East Building (top center), Library (bottom center), and West Building (bottom). Interestingly, the campus underwent few physical changes between 1920 and 1950.

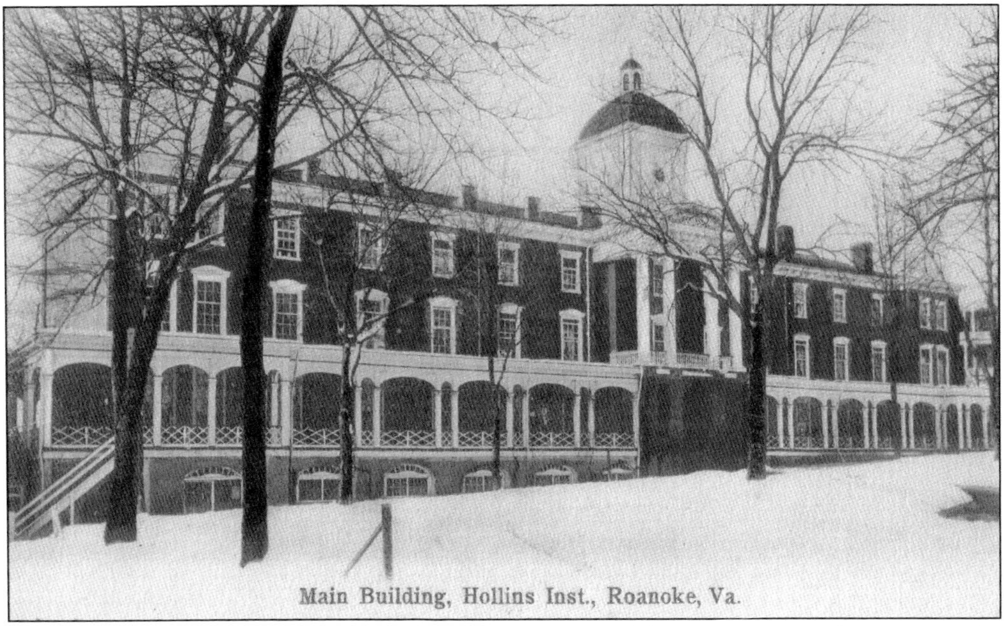

MAIN BUILDING, 1908. The Main Building is one of the oldest structures on the campus. The building was erected in between 1861 and 1863. The day the building was started was the same day Virginia seceded from the Union. With the onslaught of the Civil War, construction was often delayed, and the builder, David Deyerle, was not fully paid until 1882 due to the economic collapse of the South. The total cost for Main was $20,000.

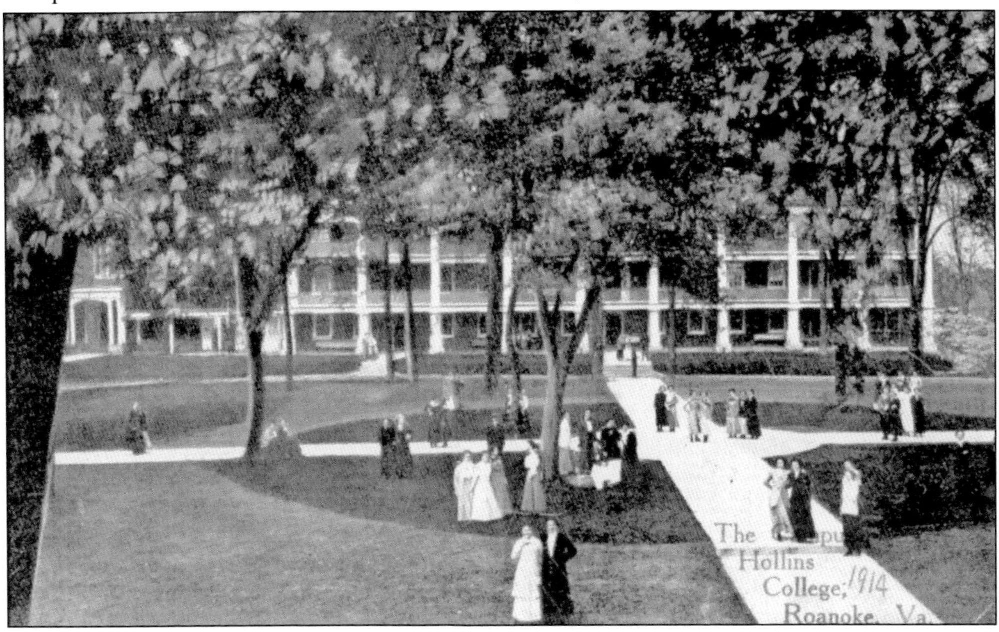

THE CAMPUS, 1914. The quadrangle that has long dominated the campus, as seen on this postcard, was included in the campus's early design in deference to Thomas Jefferson's style for a campus. Hollins's early leaders thought it best to have the quadrangle face the main highway (as opposed to Tinker Mountain). As buildings were erected, Jeffersonian colonnades were added to their facades.

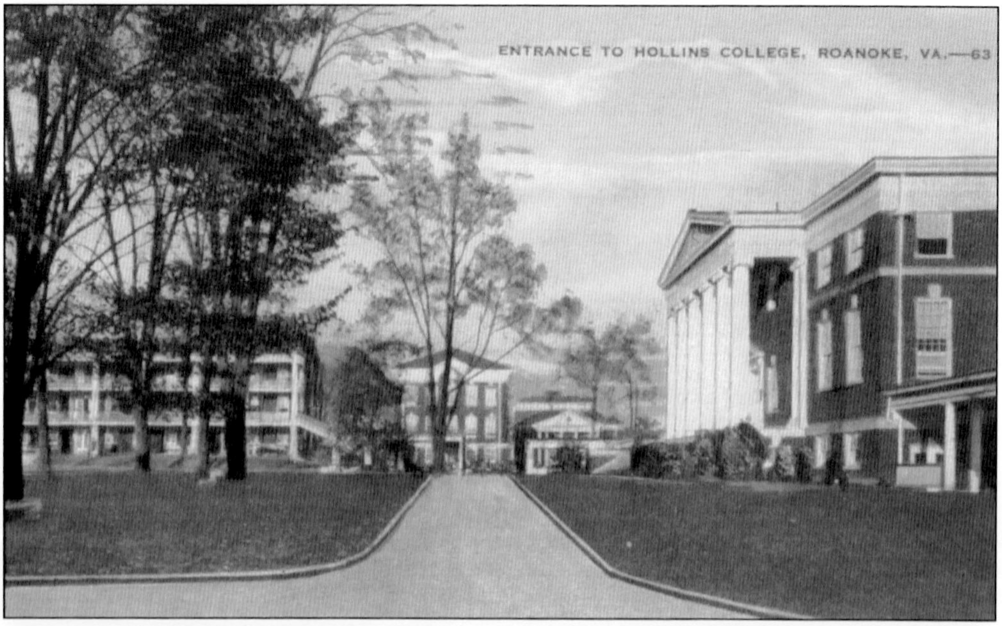

ENTRANCE TO HOLLINS COLLEGE, 1929. The 1920s saw the emergence of student leadership in the affairs of the college. In 1920, a student forum was organized for the purpose of providing input on a variety of issues. One reoccurring issue was dress. Could female students wear short skirts, rolled hose, and French heels in lab classes? Students' judicial and executive councils merged into a legislative committee in 1928.

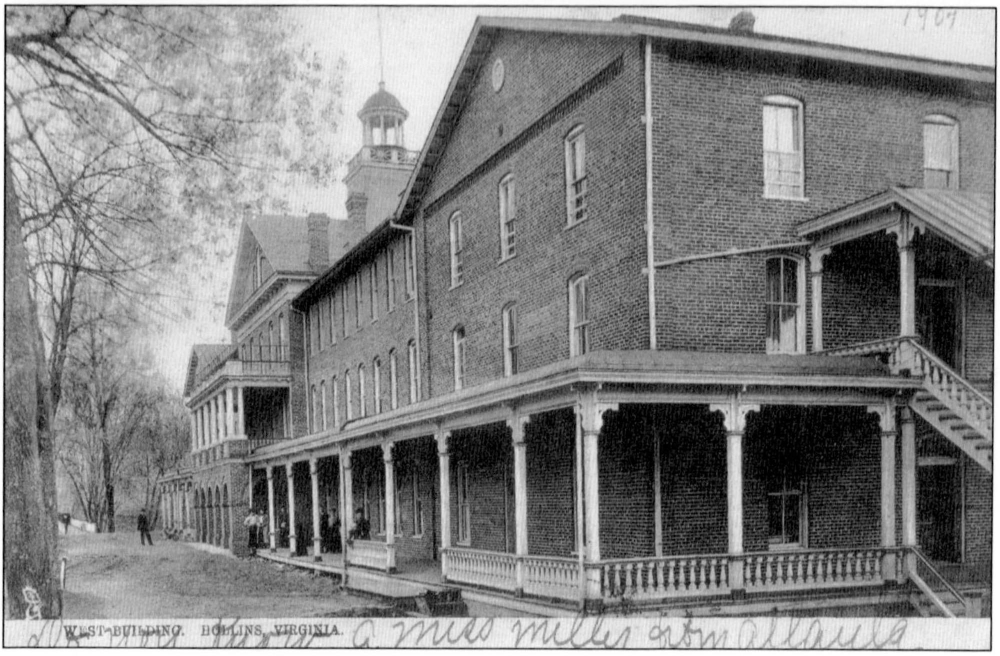

WEST BUILDING, 1907. The West Building was totally rebuilt in 1890. The left wing contained the infirmary, doctor's office, and faculty living quarters, and the right wing contained two large halls for Hollins's two early literary societies. The portico, completed in 1900, was done to echo that of the Main Building.

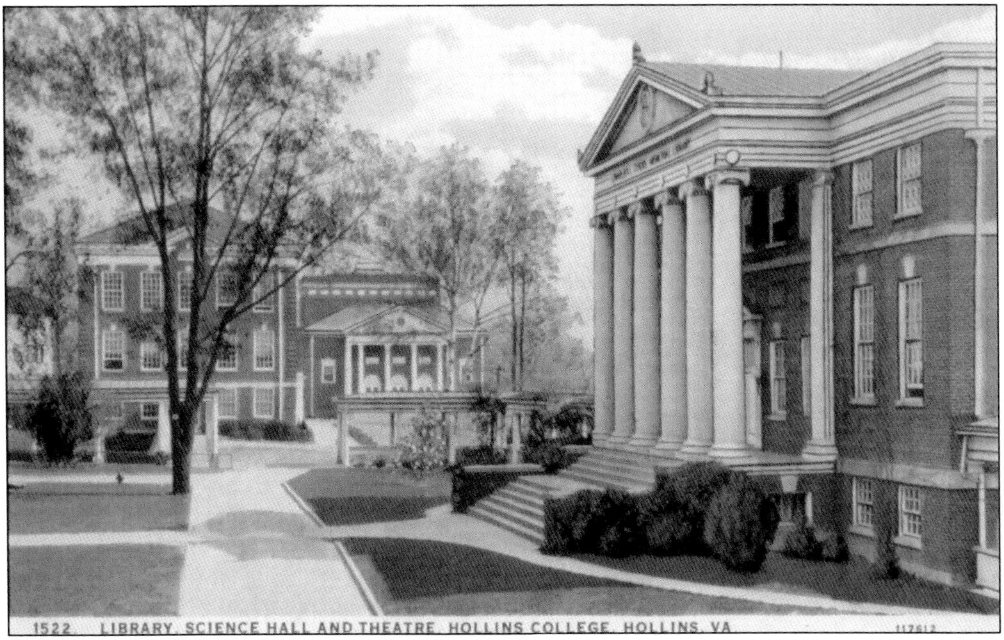

LIBRARY, SCIENCE HALL, AND THEATER, C. 1920. The Science Hall, shown here, was constructed in 1914. This building contained the first elevator to appear in any Hollins campus facility. When originally constructed, the roof contained an observatory for uranography, and the second floor contained a museum dedicated to Southwest Virginia's bird, plant, and animal life. The building was damaged by fire in 1925, but the affected areas were rebuilt shortly thereafter.

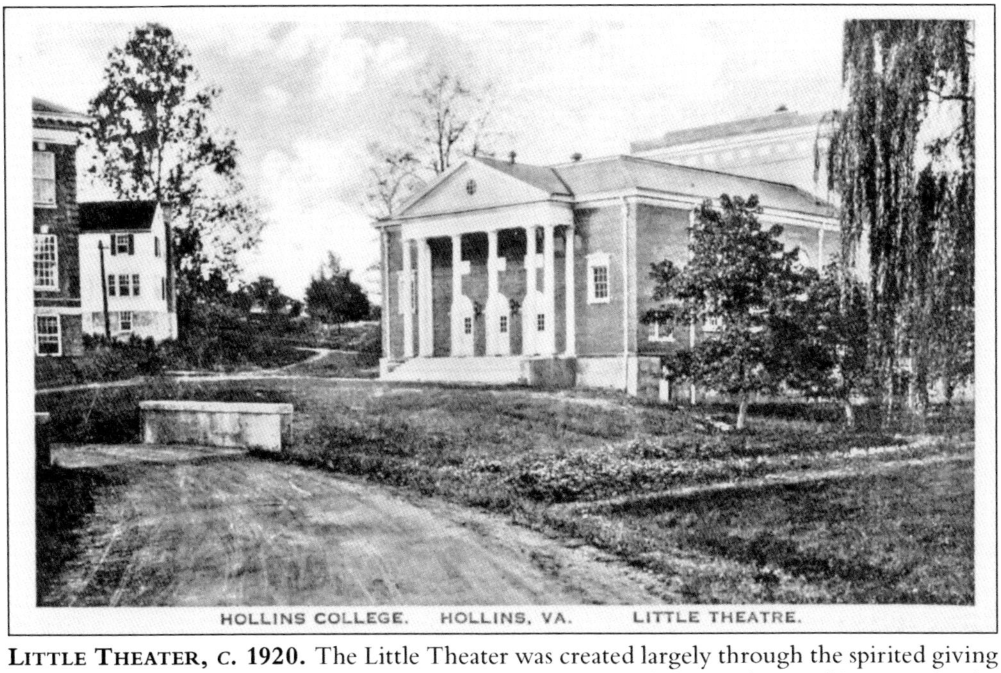

LITTLE THEATER, C. 1920. The Little Theater was created largely through the spirited giving of Hollins students, who, in the 1920s, raised $45,000 toward the total cost of $65,000 for the structure. The theater was built in 1924, replacing an old auditorium that was in the basement of the school's library. The theater contained 540 orchestra and 240 balcony seats.

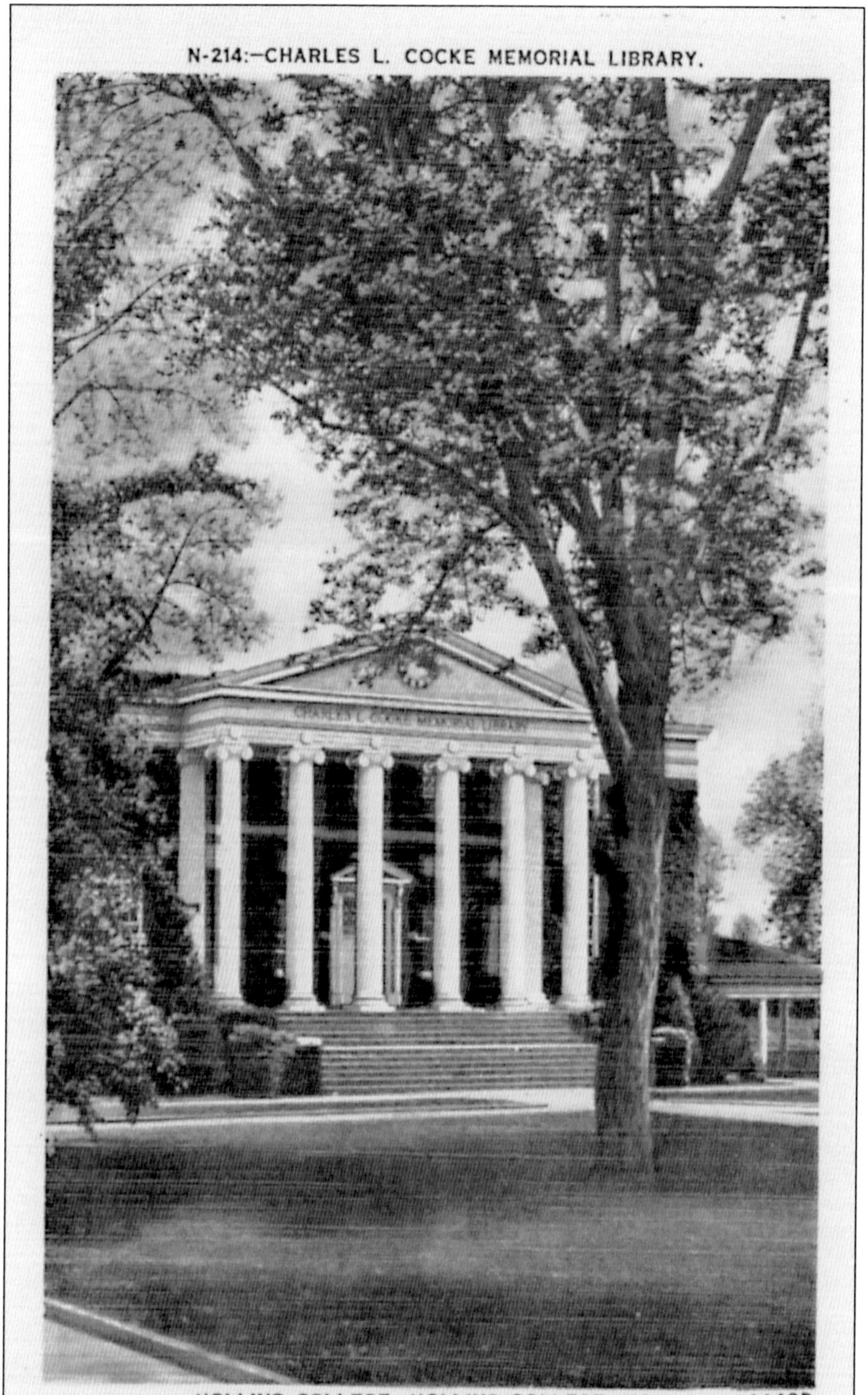

CHARLES COCKE MEMORIAL LIBRARY, *c.* 1940. The Cocke Memorial Library was dedicated in 1908 as a memorial to Cocke. The library was designed with an Ionic portico that faced Main Building. In addition to housing a library, the facility also was home to literary societies. The central hall was adorned with portraits of members of the Cocke family and their relations.

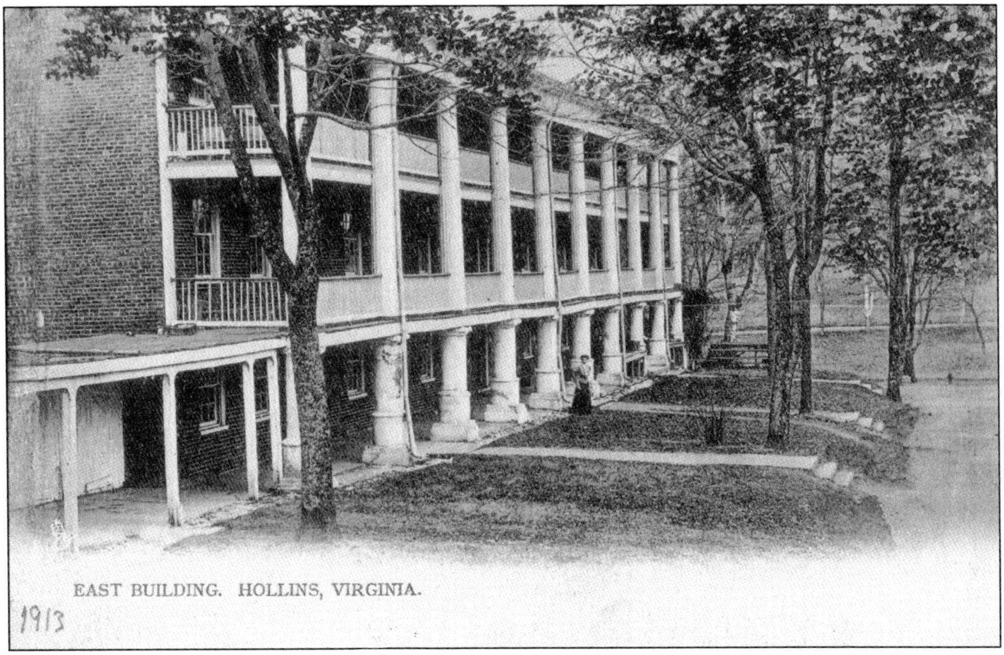

EAST BUILDING, 1913. Construction on East Building began in 1856 and was completed two years later. The East Building, complimenting Main and West, completed the quadrangle courtyard. According to early Hollins historians, East was designed to imitate in appearance the resort hotels popular during that era at many of Virginia's sulphur springs.

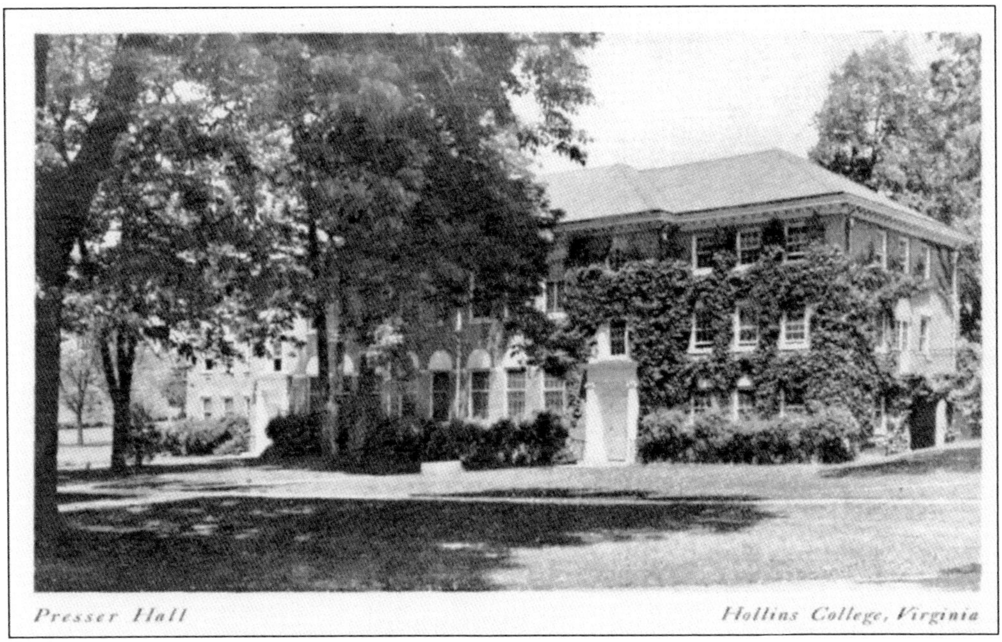

PRESSER HALL, 1930S. Presser Hall was erected in 1925, a gift of Theodore Presser (a music publisher). Presser was a music professor at Hollins from 1880 to 1883. Presser died before the building was completed. At the time of its dedication, the structure's final cost was $56,000.

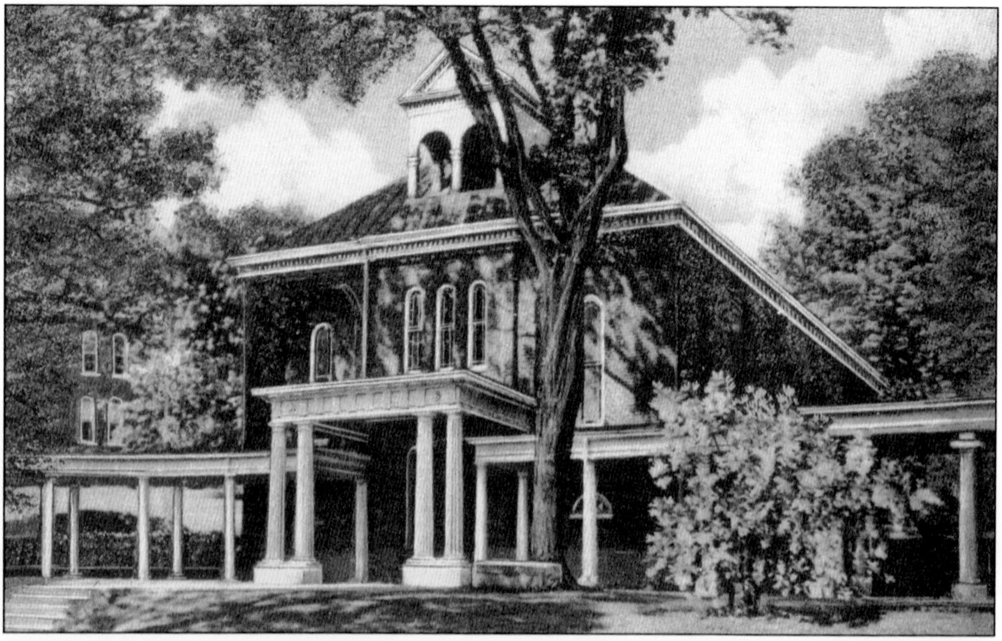

Bradley Chapel, c. 1930. The Bradley Chapel was built in 1883, but not named for Joshua Bradley until the 1930s. The chapel served as the center for campus religious activities. During the early years, Hollins students were expected to attend chapel services daily after supper.

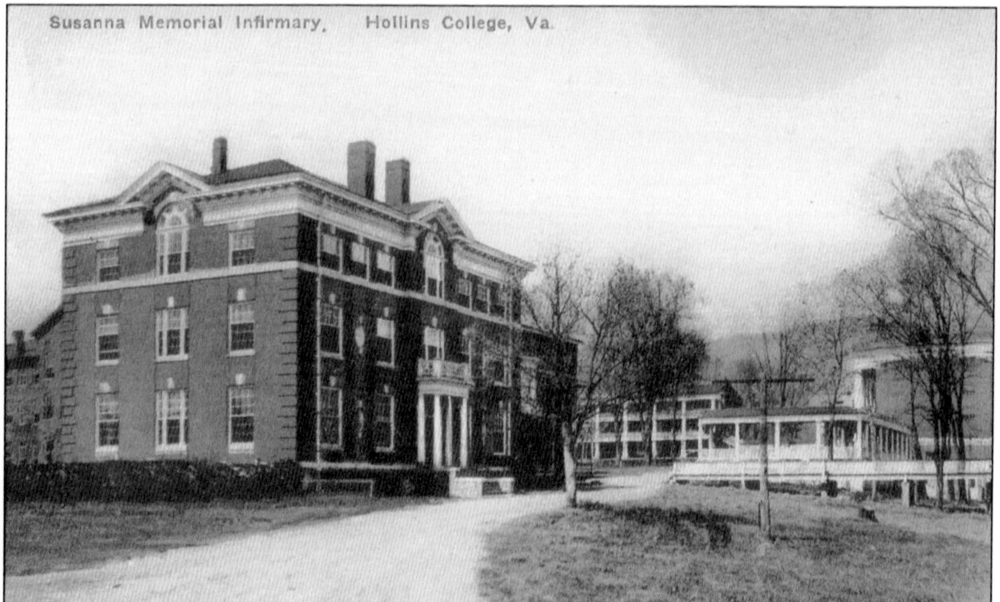

Susanna Memorial Infirmary, c. 1920. The infirmary, constructed in 1910, was named for Susanna Cocke. Utilizing Georgian and Federal architecture, the infirmary was actually the first building included in part of the new quadrangle on the southeast section of the campus.

Five

Vinton

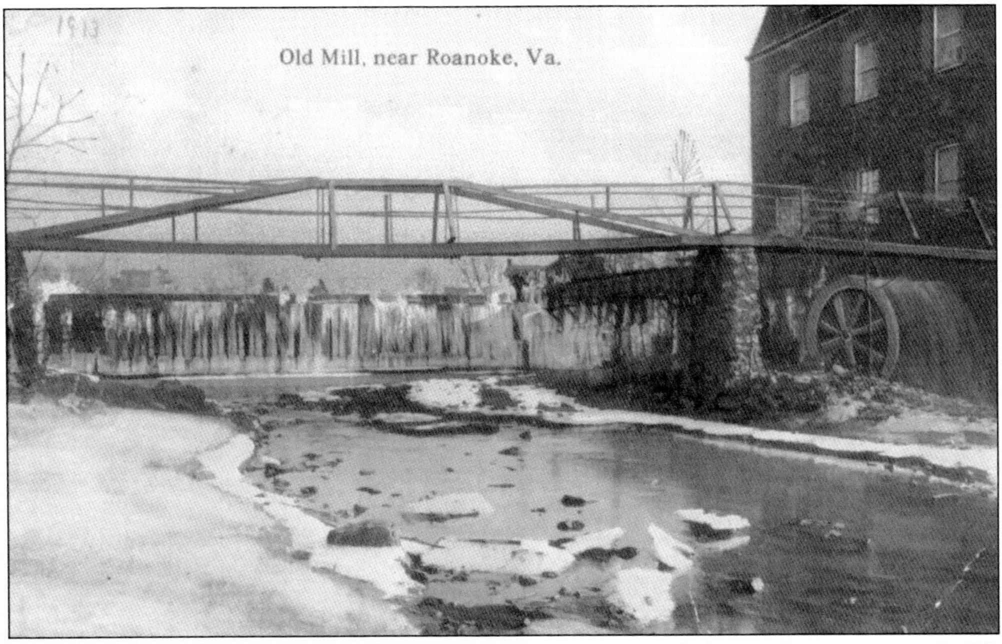

Vinton Roller Mill, 1913. Vinton Roller Mills, along Glade Creek, grew out of mills originally built by David Gish that predated the Civil War. By the 20th century, the remaining mill was owned and operated by James Bowie and produced three kinds of flour. By 1924, the operation was known as Vinton Milling Company.

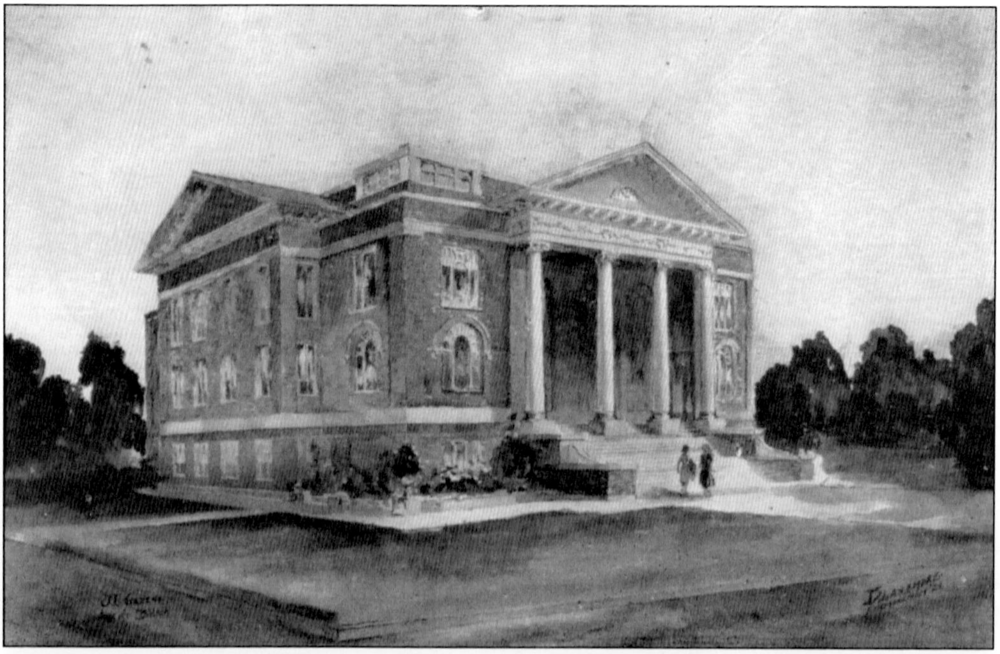

ARCHITECTURAL RENDERING OF VINTON BAPTIST CHURCH, *c.* 1920. Vinton Baptist Church began in 1892. The building shown in this postcard rendering was constructed in 1924, replacing the original sanctuary of 1894.

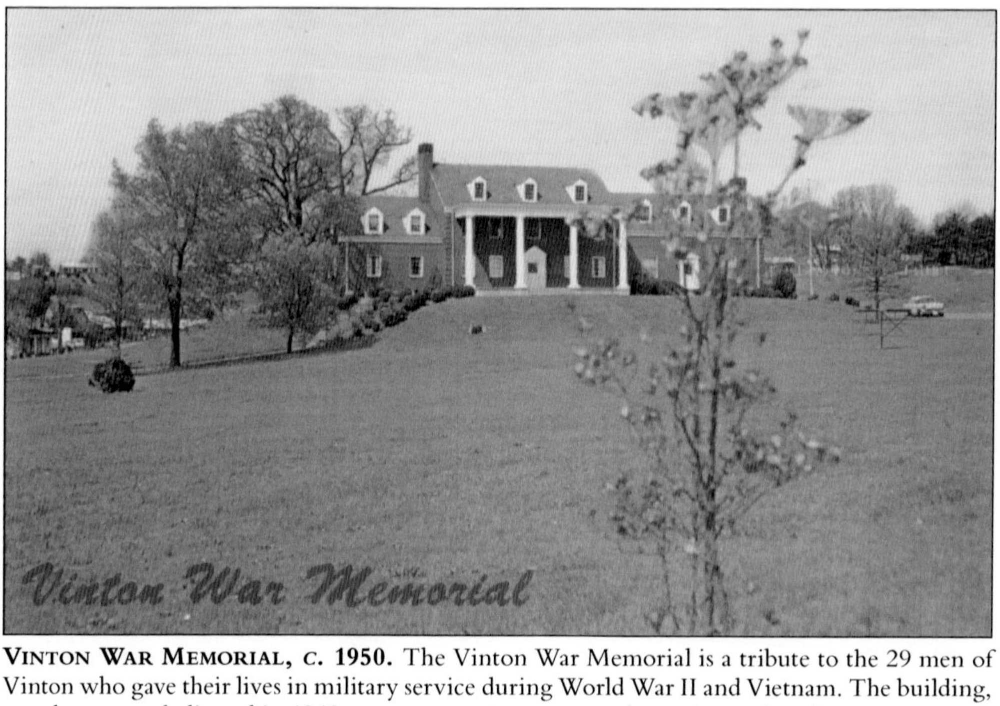

VINTON WAR MEMORIAL, *c.* 1950. The Vinton War Memorial is a tribute to the 29 men of Vinton who gave their lives in military service during World War II and Vietnam. The building, seen here, was dedicated in 1948 as a community center and remains such today.

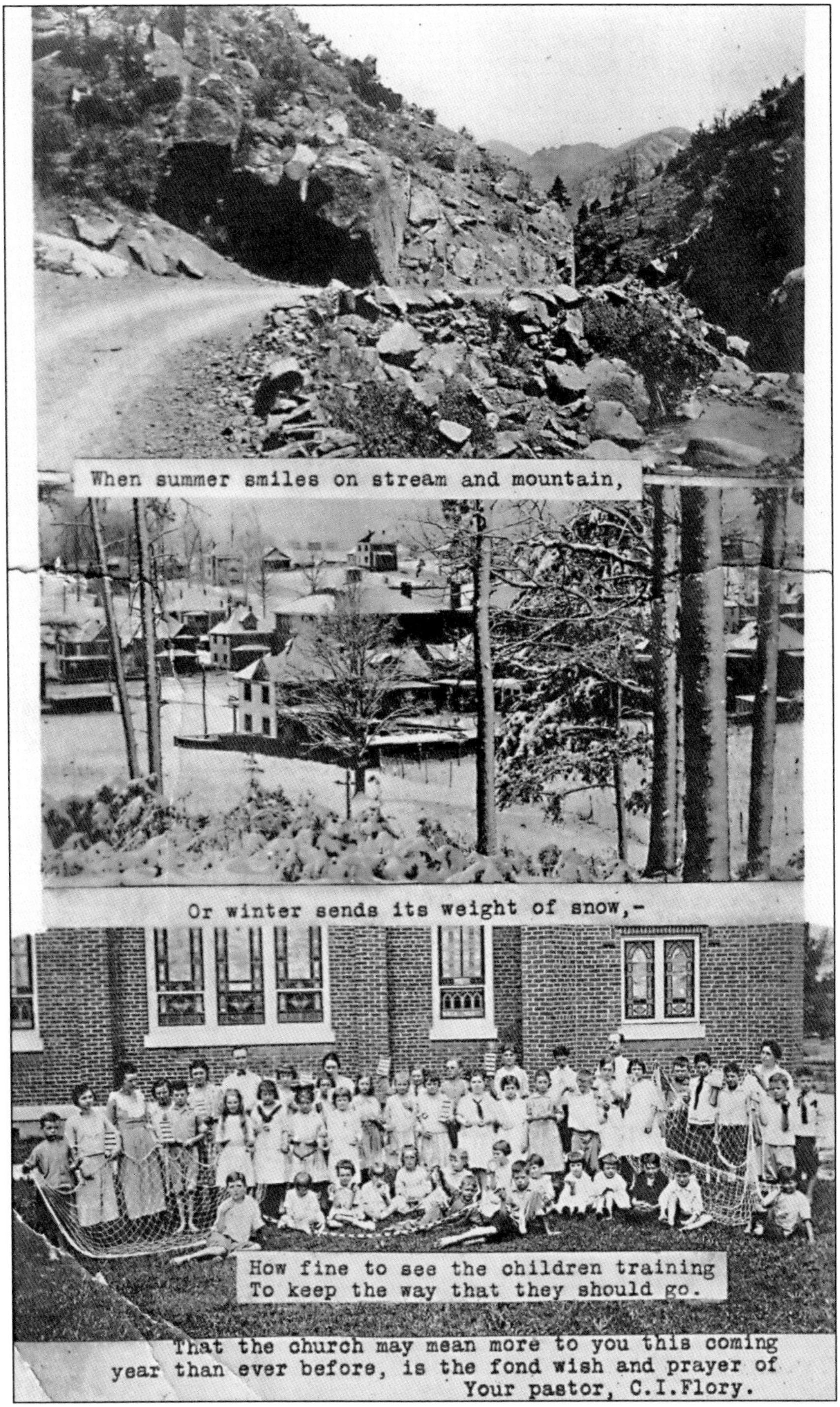

CHURCH CARD, 1911. Pastor C. I. Flory of Vinton sent this card out with the following message: "When summer smiles on streams and mountains, Or winter sends its weight of snow, How fine to see the children training to keep the way that they should go." Flory's personal message was his hope "that the church may mean more to you this coming year than ever before."

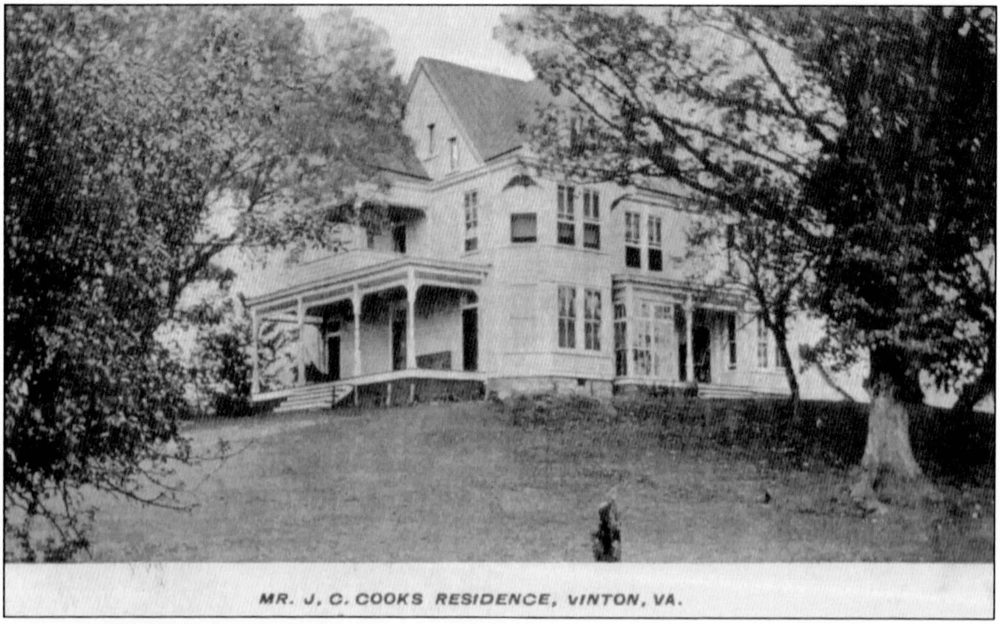

J. C. Cook's Residence, 1909. This residence belonged to prominent businessman J. C. Cook, originally of Bonsack. Cook later moved to the Vinton area and owned the land on which the Vinton War Memorial was built.

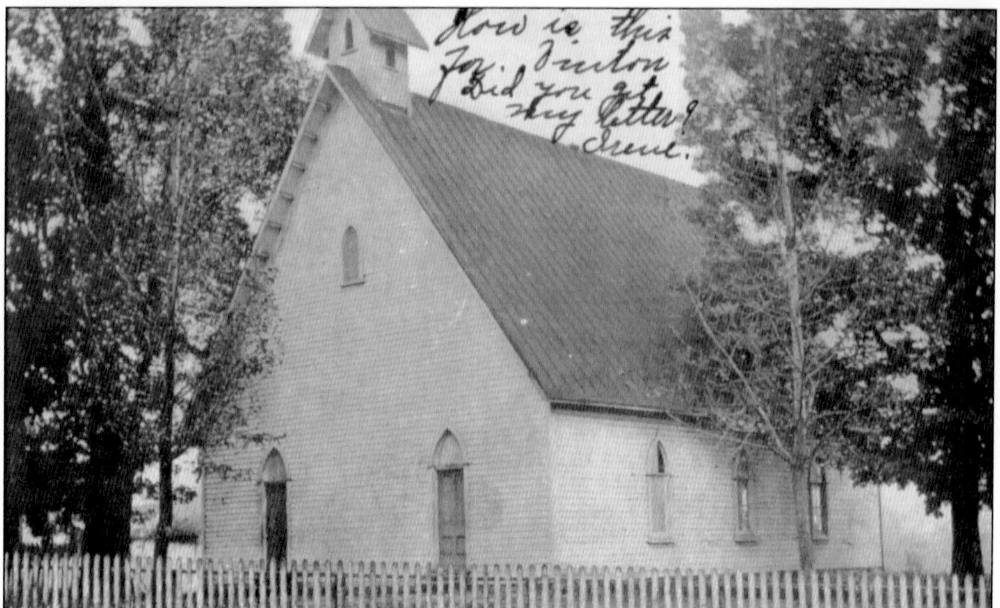

Methodist Church, 1908. This Methodist church was an early sanctuary of the present-day Thrasher Memorial United Methodist Church. The present sanctuary was built in 1963. The church was named for Paul and Sallie Thrasher, pioneer Methodists in the Roanoke Valley. The church traces its origins back to 1815.

Six

Recreation and Leisure

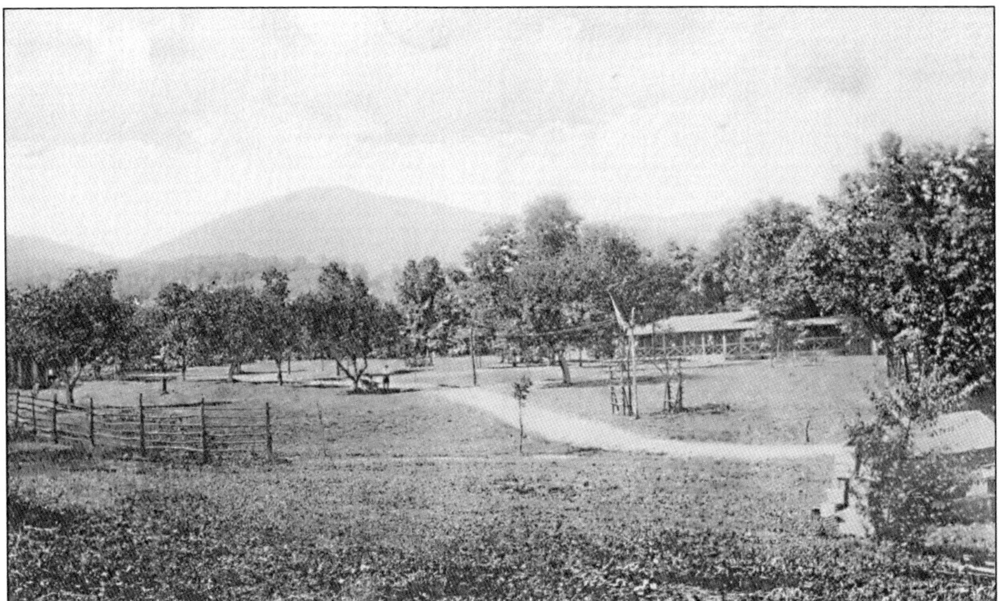

Cavern Hill Lawn, Cavern Hill, Roanoke County, *c.* 1930. Cavern Hill Lawn was part of the Cavern Hill Inn property (later Dixie Cavern Inn), a popular gathering spot in the 1920s and 1930s.

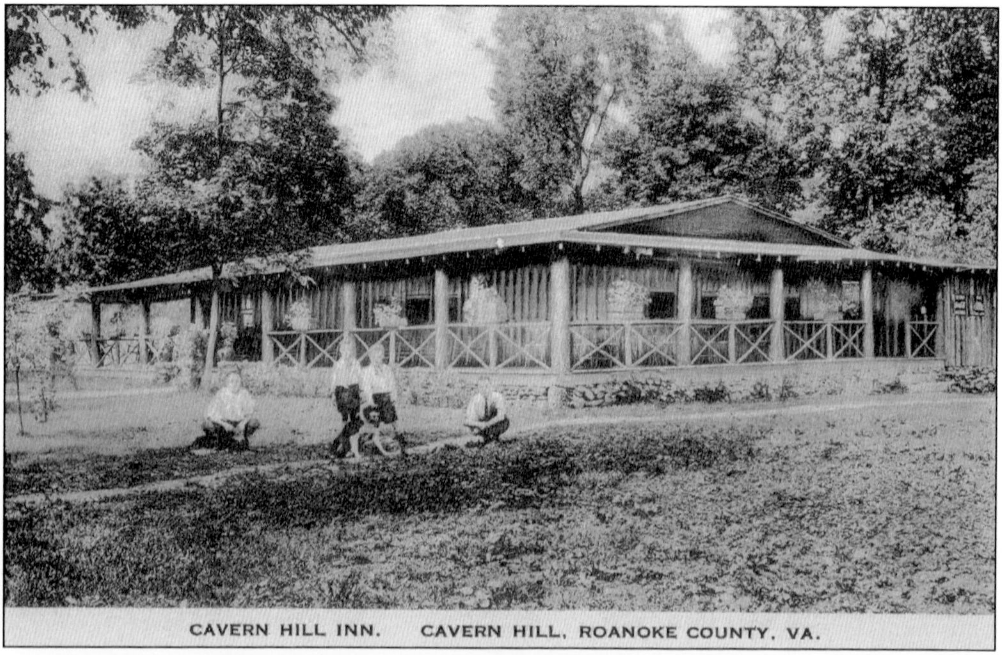

CAVERN HILL INN, ROANOKE COUNTY, *c.* 1930. The Cavern Hill Inn served as the meeting place for numerous civic and charity organizations in the west Salem area. As Dixie Caverns grew in popularity, the inn served tourists in greater numbers than locals.

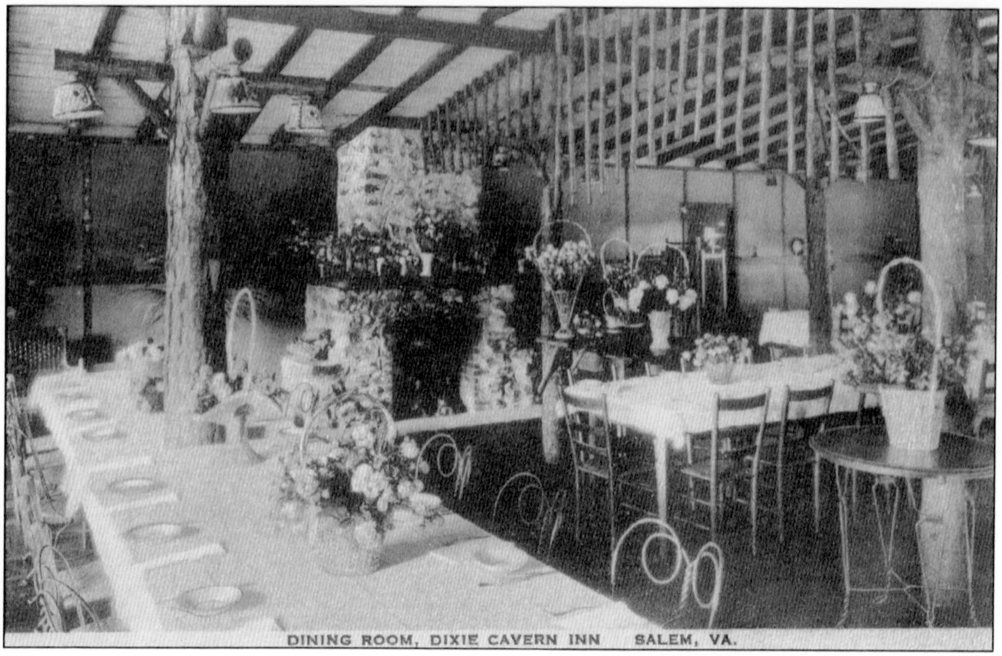

DINING ROOM, DIXIE CAVERN INN, *c.* 1935. The inn provided lodging, campgrounds, and a popular restaurant (shown here). The Inn was located near Dixie Caverns, close to the Roanoke County-Montgomery County line.

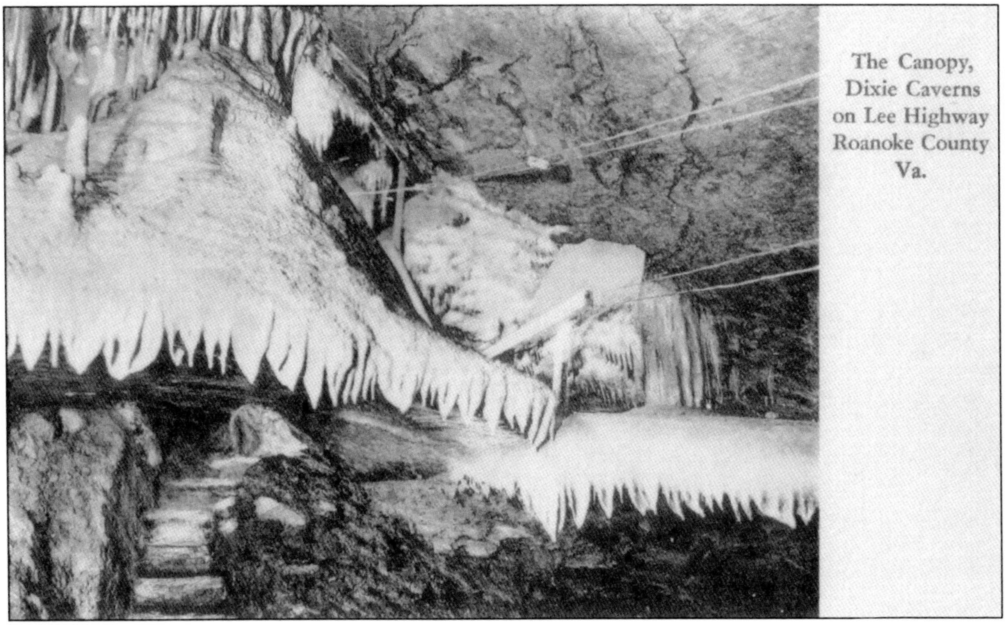

The Canopy, Dixie Caverns, Roanoke County, c. 1930. Dixie Caverns are Roanoke County's only natural wonder. Discovered in the 1920s by Bill McDaniel, they was believed to be known to early Native Americans and considered by them to be sacred. Since McDaniel's boyhood discovery, the caverns have been a popular tourist draw.

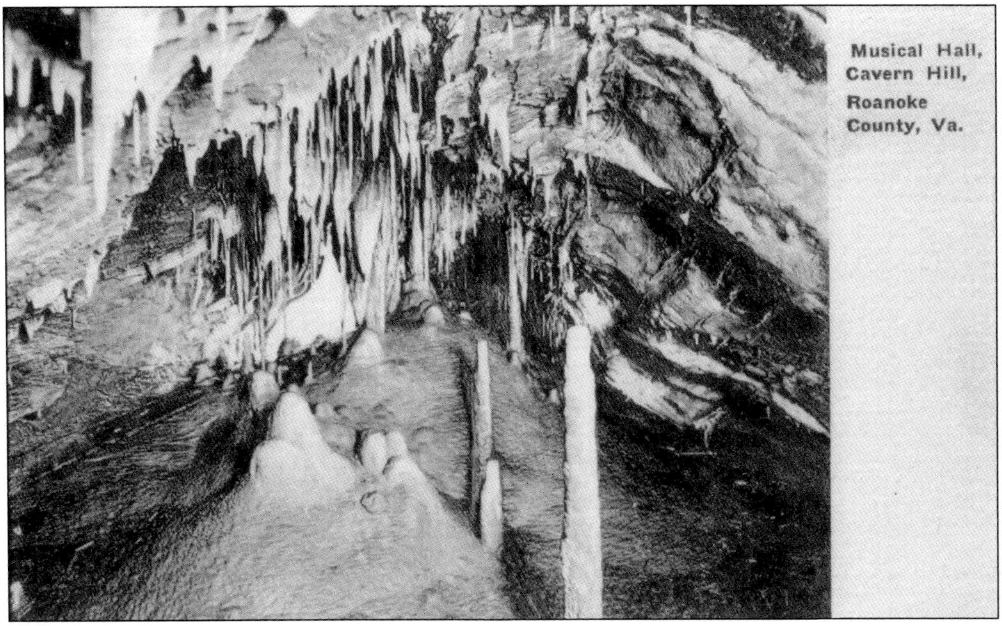

Musical Hall, Dixie Caverns, c. 1930. The caverns contain numerous subterranean features that have been given various descriptive names. Dixie Caverns officially opened in 1923 and were originally called Glenvar Caverns.

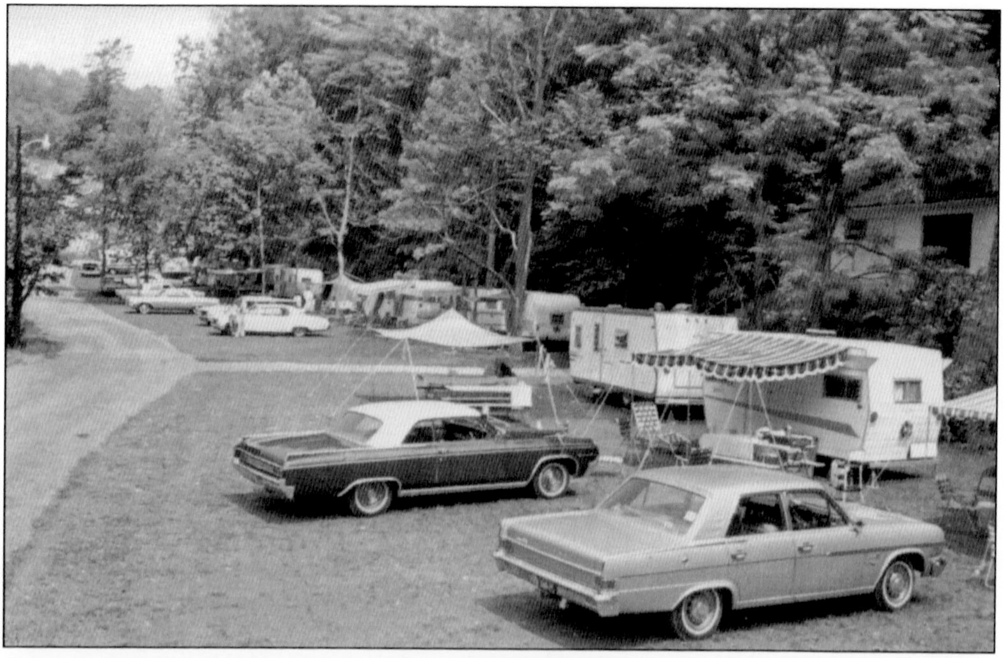

DIXIE CAVERNS CAMPGROUND, C. 1960. As the caverns grew in popularity, so did the amenities surrounding the area. The campground was promoted via this postcard as having an all-tile restroom, flush toilets, showers with hot and cold water, and electrical and water hook-ups.

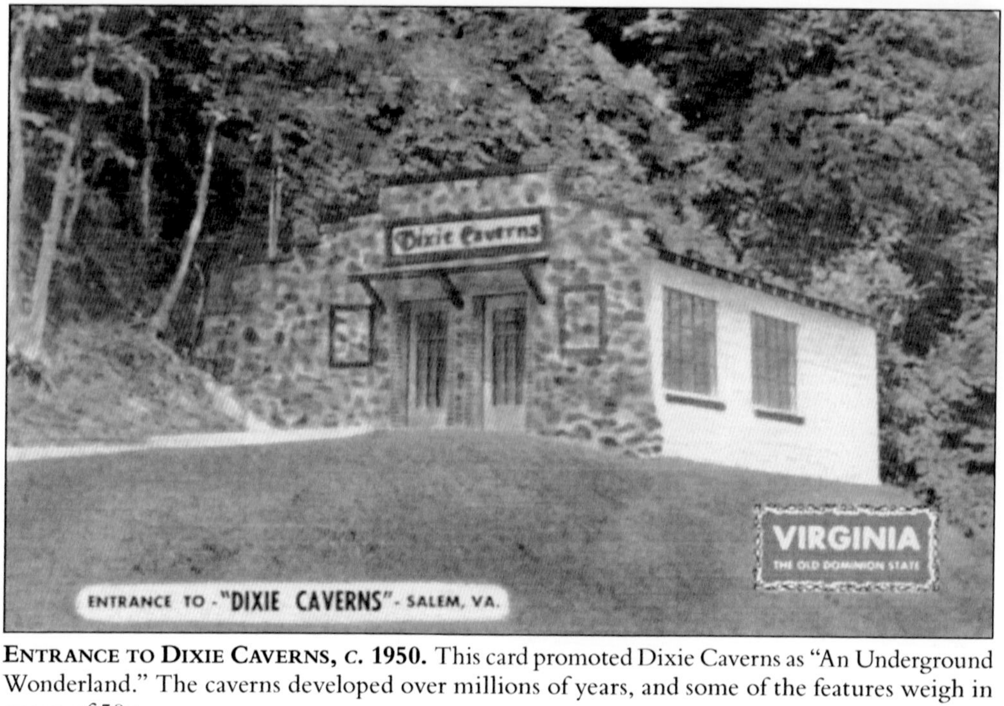

ENTRANCE TO DIXIE CAVERNS, C. 1950. This card promoted Dixie Caverns as "An Underground Wonderland." The caverns developed over millions of years, and some of the features weigh in excess of 50 tons.

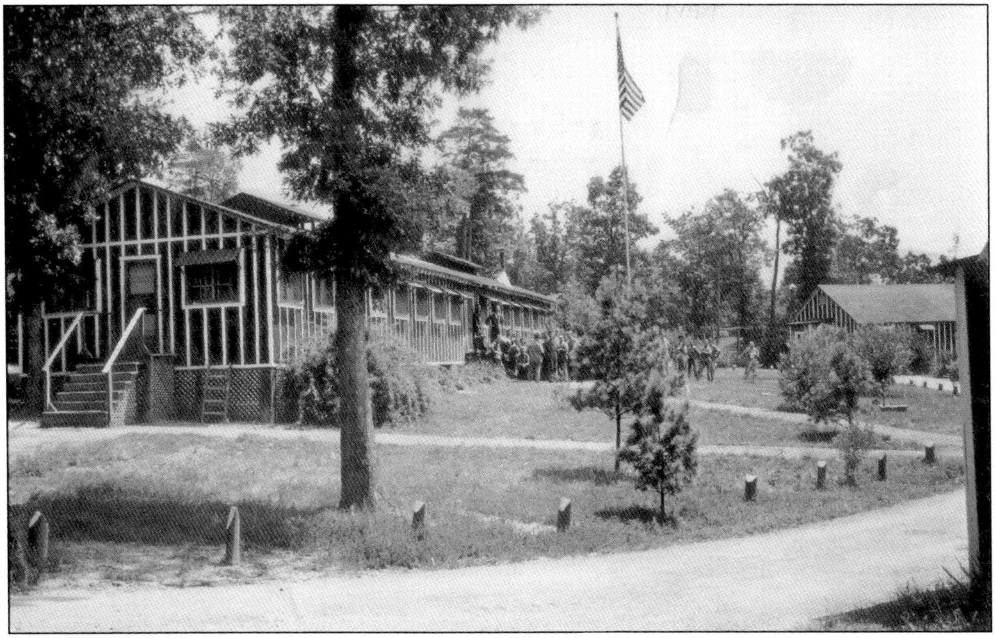

WARD HAVEN CAMP, CATAWBA, 1942. This camp was originally constructed in 1933 by the Civilian Conservation Corps. In 1941, it became an Army mechanical training camp. From 1943 until 1946, the camp housed 150 German prisoners of war who worked in nearby orchards. Today, the camp is owned and operated by the Roanoke Valley Baptist Association as a retreat center.

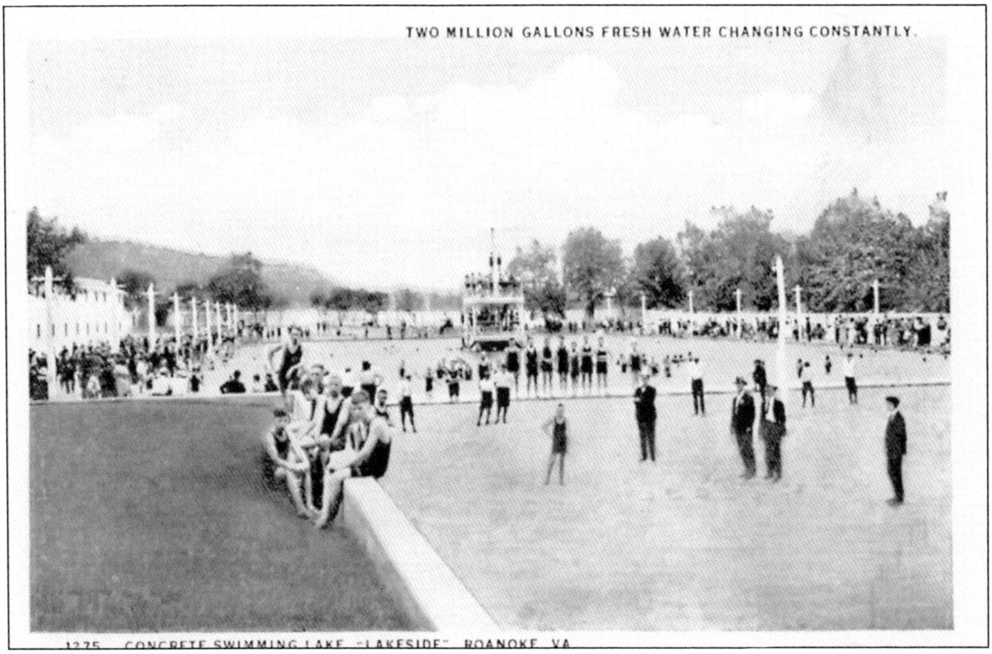

CONCRETE SWIMMING LAKE, LAKESIDE, 1925. Lakeside was opened in 1920 by Robert Lynn Sr. and featured a public swimming pool, roller coaster, and one additional ride. The original 50-acre tract on which Lakeside was built was an orchard owned by John Bower.

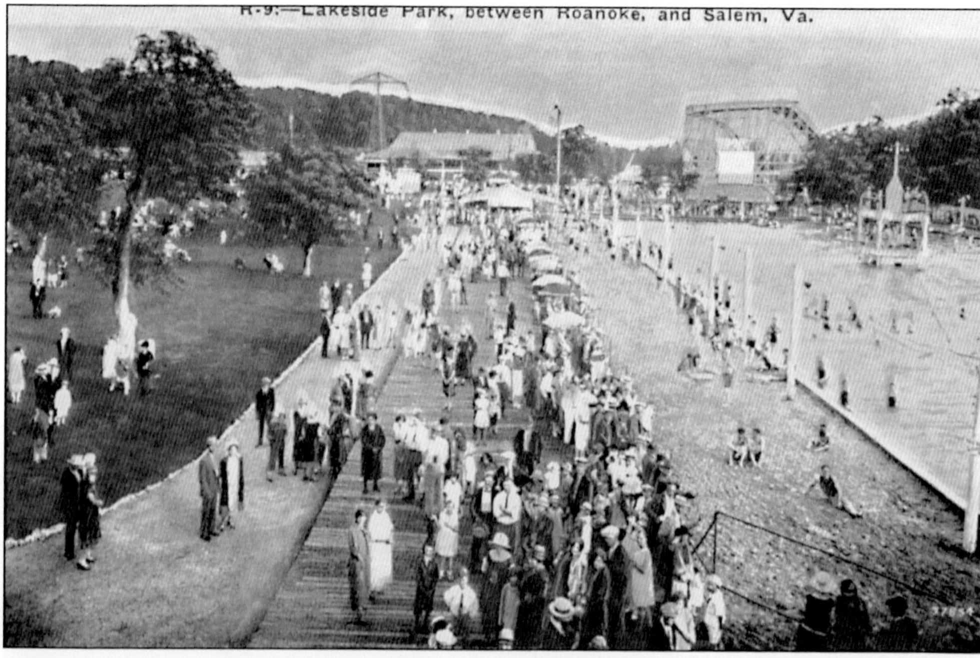

LAKESIDE PARK, 1930. In 1936, Lakeside was purchased by H. L. Roberts, and his family owned and operated Lakeside for the next 50 years. When the amusement park opened, it was described by the *Roanoke Times* as "the largest pool anyone had ever seen," complimented by a beach of imported sand and a boardwalk.

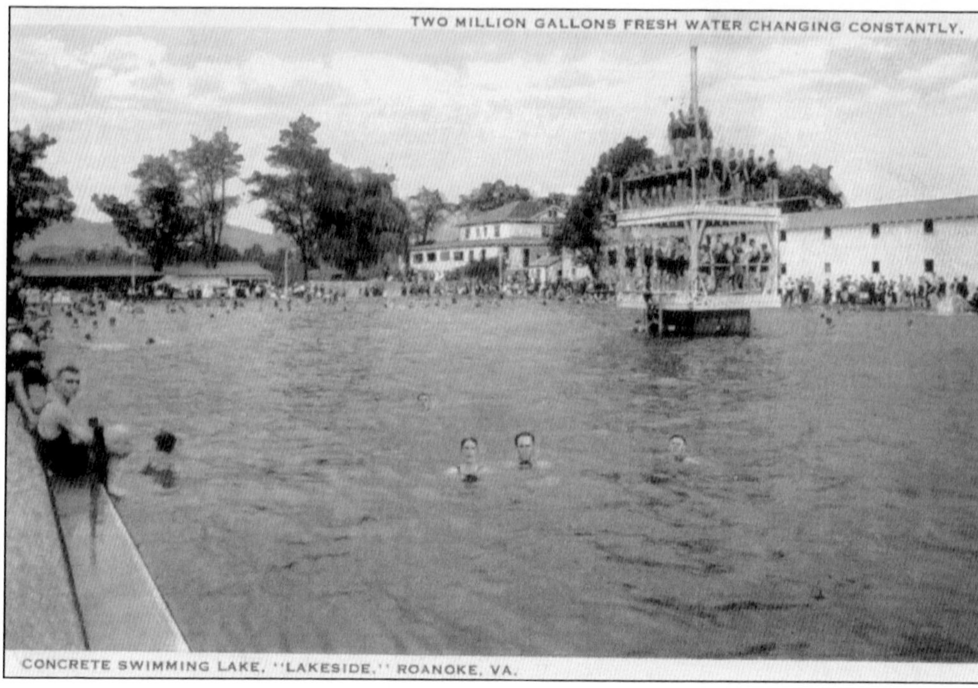

CONCRETE SWIMMING LAKE, LAKESIDE, 1925. The swimming pool contained nearly two million gallons of water. In 1924, an arcade-pavilion was added to the park. By 1926, rides included Lindy Planes (named after Lindbergh), the Whip, Dodgem, Tiltawheel, and a Ferris wheel.

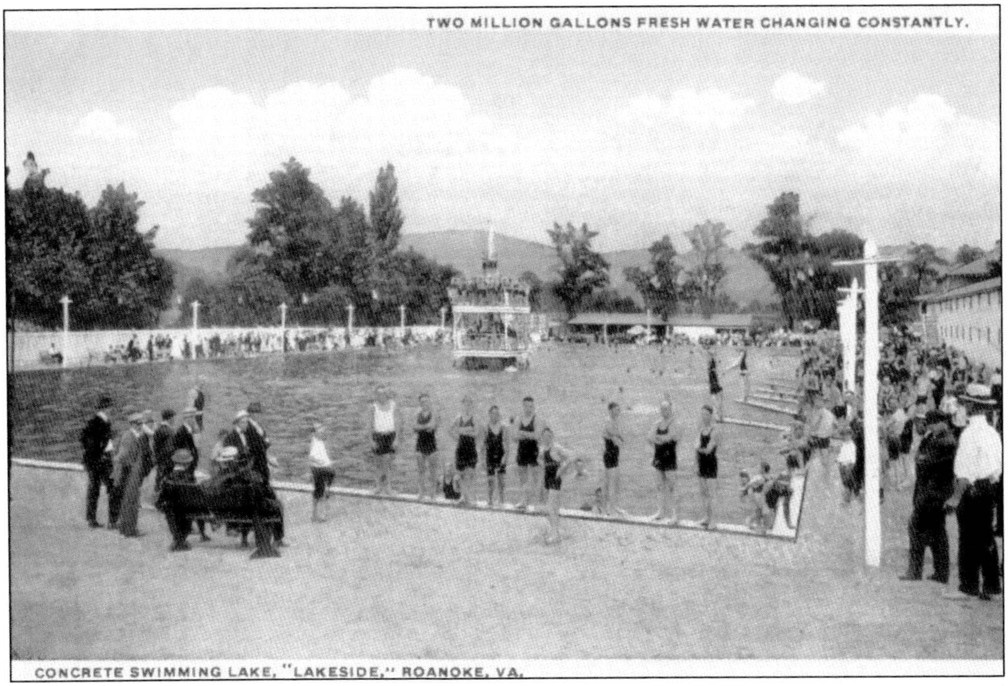

LAKESIDE, 1925. Lakeside survived the Depression by offering low admission prices and cheap entertainment. During World War II, the United Service Organization (USO) provided servicemen complimentary tickets. There was even a movement in 1958 by nearby residents to constitute themselves as the town of Lakeside.

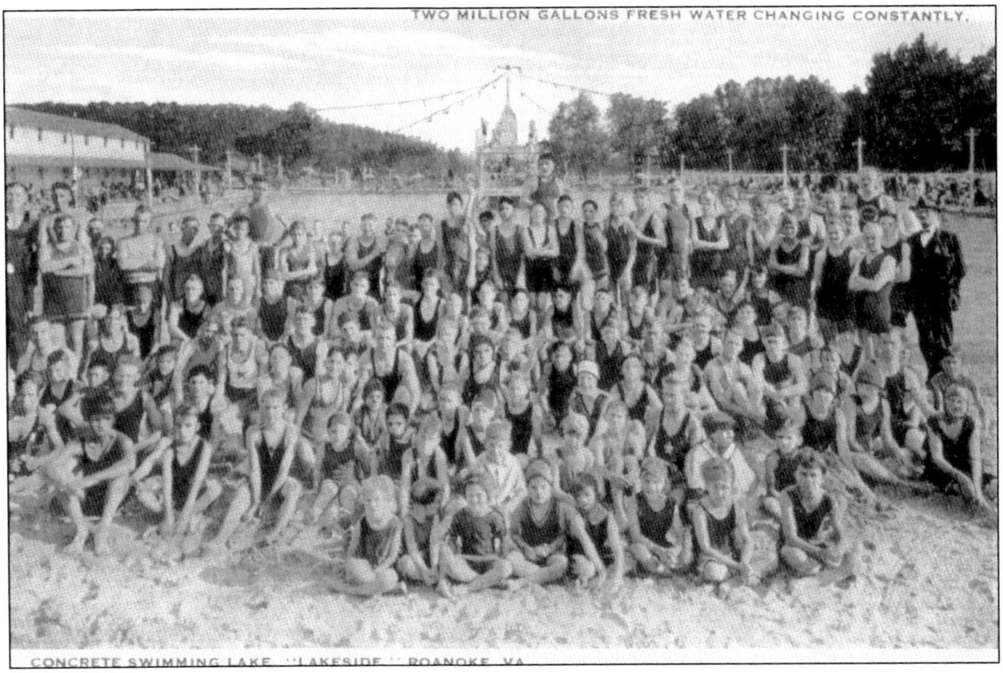

LAKESIDE, 1925. Like most public venues in the South, Lakeside was not racially integrated until 1964. At about this same time, park owners closed the pool, filled it in, and expanded the park.

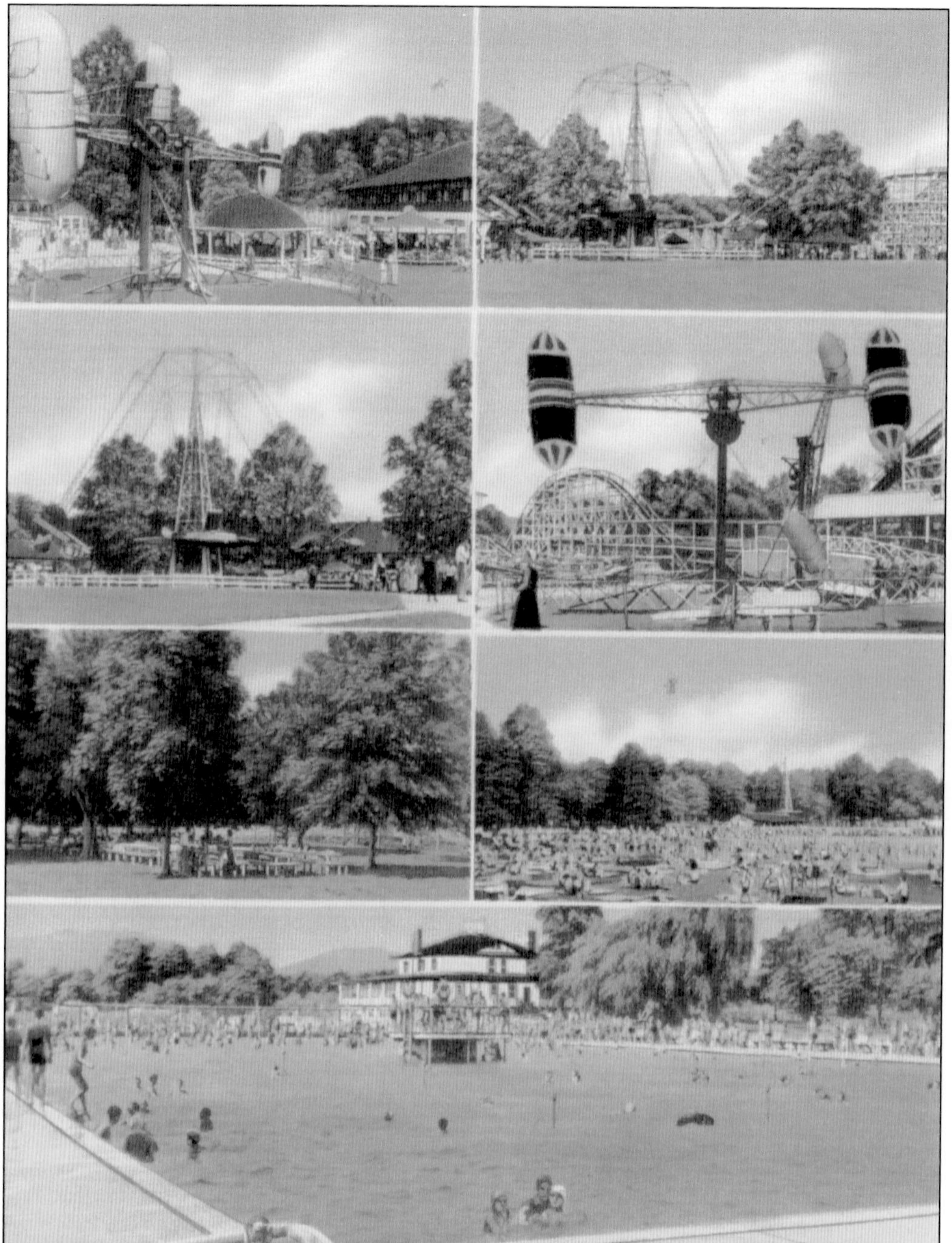

Multi-View of Lakeside, *c.* 1955. This card shows how much the park had developed under the Roberts family, who owned the park from 1936 to 1981. This card advertises, "South's Finest Swimming Pool, Joy Rides for Children and Adults, Beautiful Picnic Grounds."

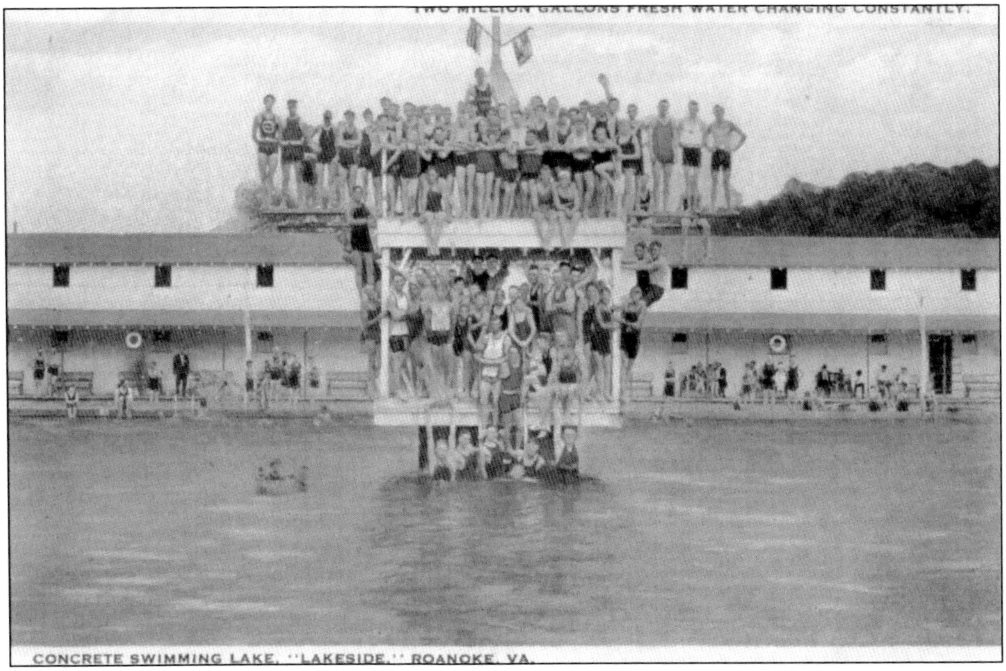

LAKESIDE, 1925. Lakeside was, for many decades, the most popular draw for Valley residents and tourists in the region. Offering rides, amusements, recreation, and concerts, Lakeside was complimented by Dixie Caverns, the Blue Ridge Parkway, and its situation at the intersection of present-day Routes 419 and 460.

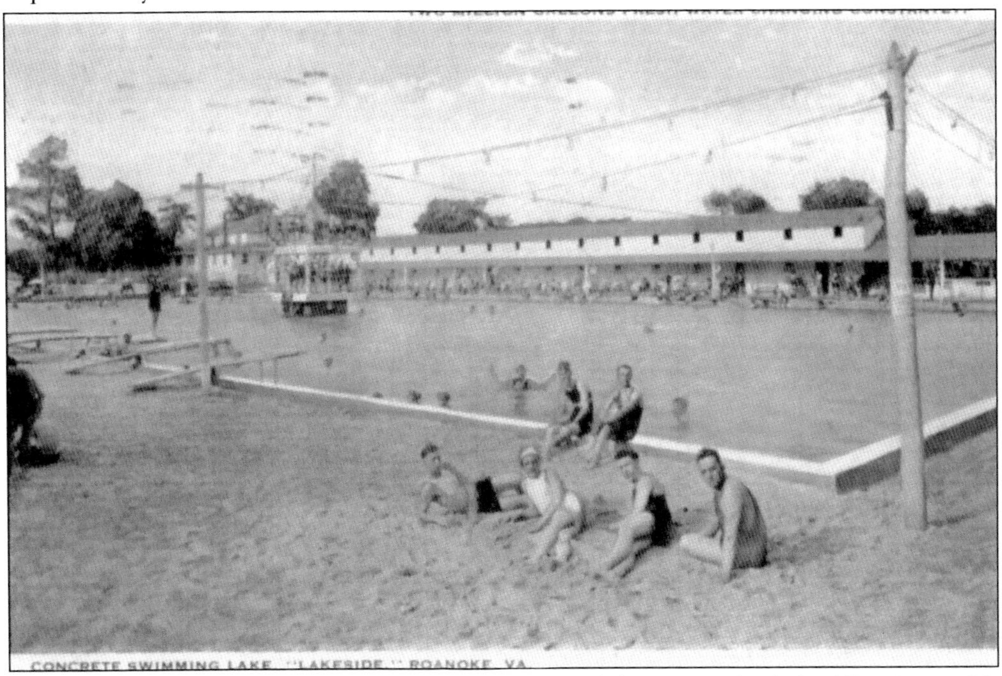

LAKESIDE, 1923. Aunt Katherine wrote her nephew in Salisbury, Maryland, the following on this card: "How would you like to go in bathing here? Uncle Frank and the boys are in now. It is fresh water. They have slides and swings and acting bars and every kind of exercise in the pool."

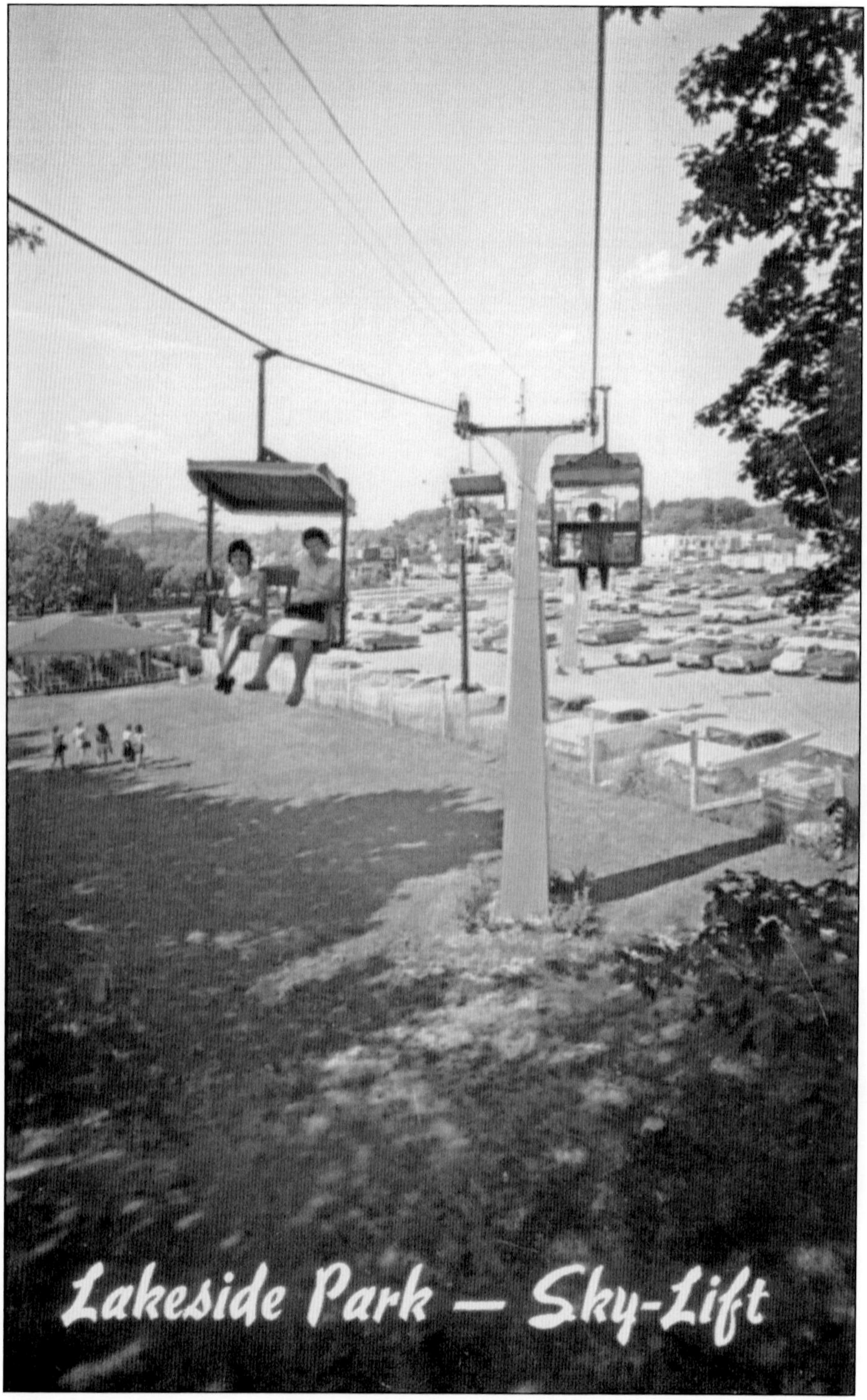

LAKESIDE PARK SKY LIFT, *c.* 1960. The sky lift took patrons on a nine-minute, 1,800-foot panoramic trip above the park. The Roberts family relinquished ownership of the park in 1981, when they sold Lakeside to Frank Selbe.

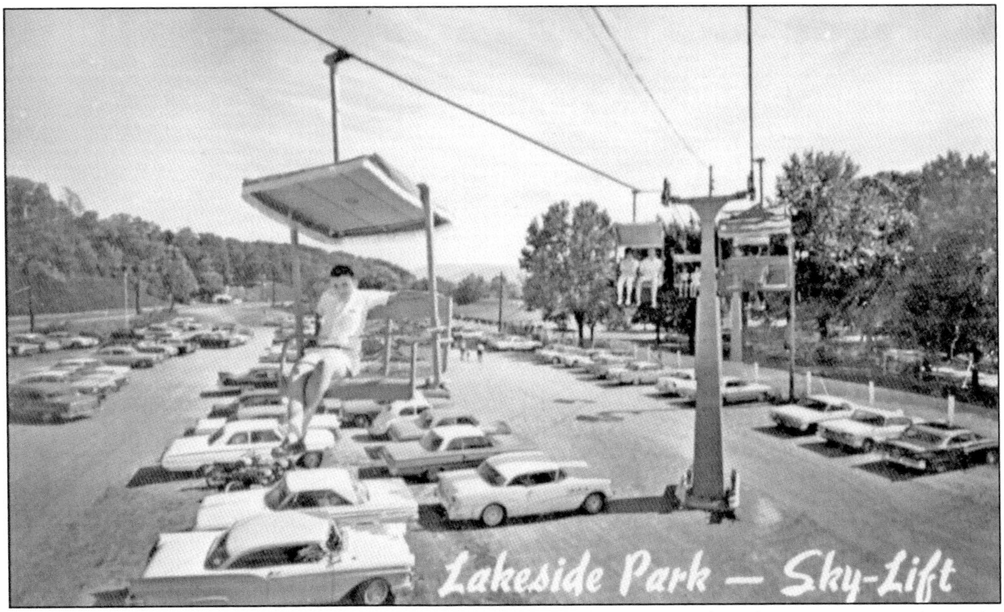

LAKESIDE PARK, *c.* 1960. Lakeside survived for over six decades, but the competition brought on by other major theme parks eventually took its toll. By 1983, the park was in financial trouble. Bought by Charles Fox in 1984, the park was struck by the flood of 1985. The flood seemed to seal the fate of the park. Lakeside's final day of operation was October 19, 1986. Today, the grounds of Lakeside are occupied by a strip mall.

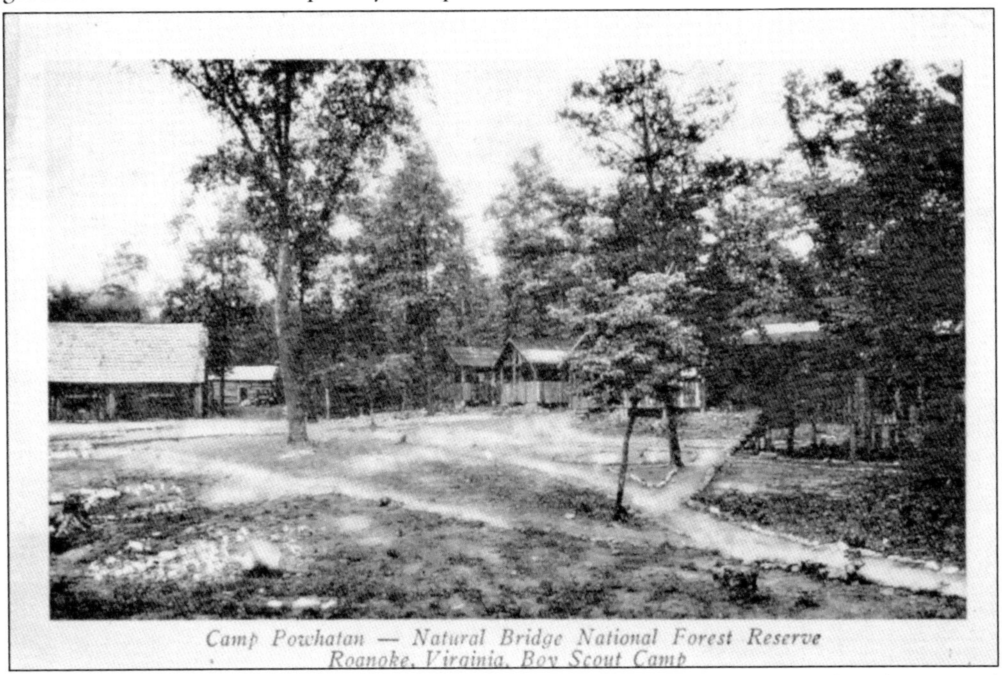

CAMP POWHATAN, BOY SCOUT CAMP, 1931. Camp Powhatan was located in the Natural Bridge National Forest Reserve. Scouting, having reached the United States in 1910, has a long history in Roanoke County. The Blue Ridge Mountains Council, No. 599, is headquartered in Roanoke County, having merged in 1972 with the Piedmont Council.

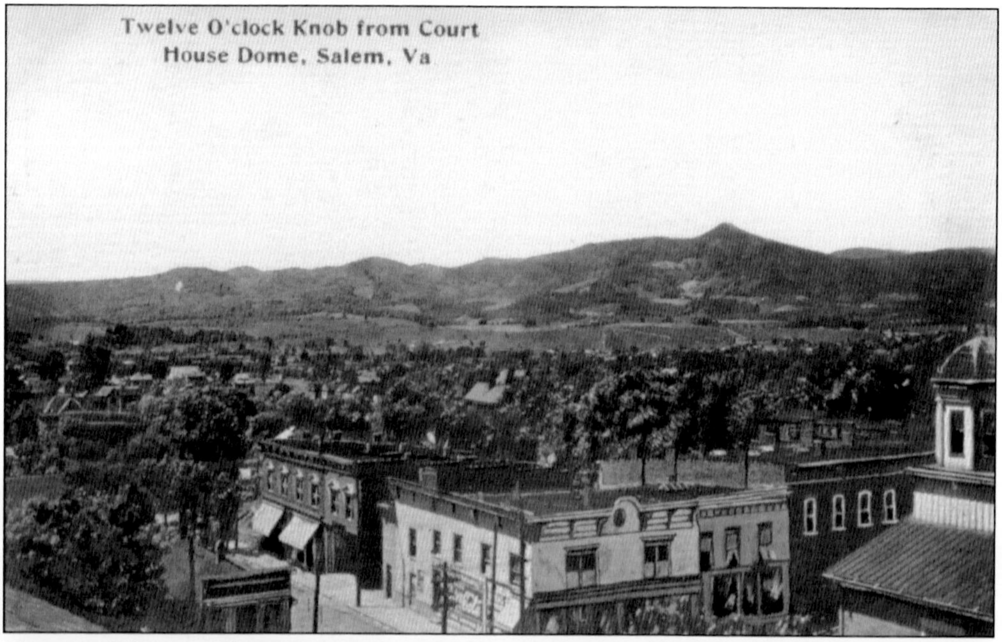

TWELVE O'CLOCK KNOB FROM COURT HOUSE DOME, SALEM, 1915. One of the most prominent geographical features in the Roanoke Valley is Twelve O'clock Knob, with an altitude of 2,707 feet. According to local tradition, the mountain received its name prior to the Civil War, when slaves, working west of Salem, determined it to be noon (and time for lunch) when the sun was just at a point directly over the mountain.

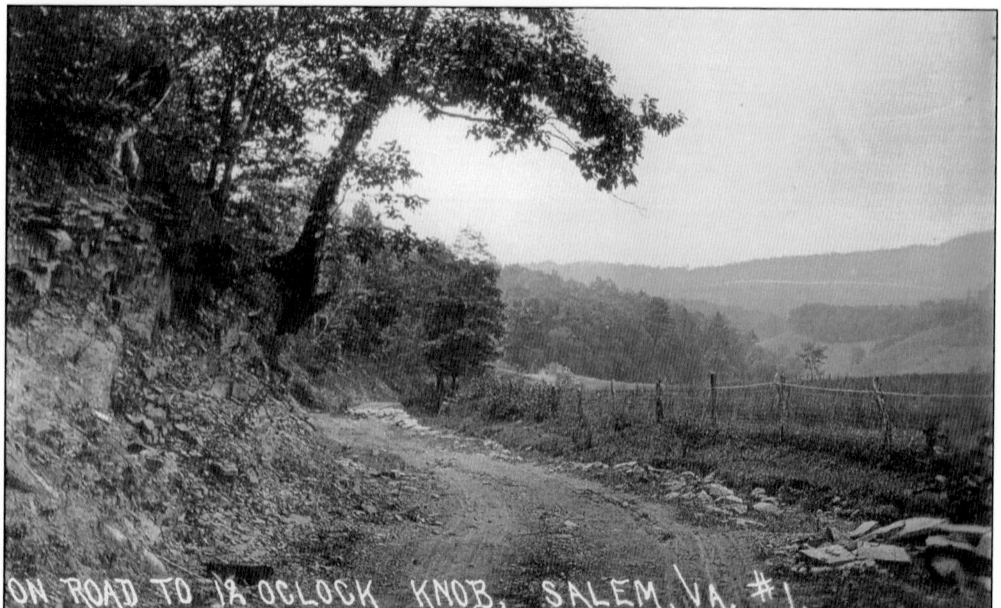

ON ROAD TO TWELVE O'CLOCK KNOB, SALEM, 1915. Exactly what road this might be cannot be determined. Historic records, however, show that interest in building a road from Salem across Twelve O'clock Knob to Back Creek, and then up Bent Mountain, dated back to 1840.

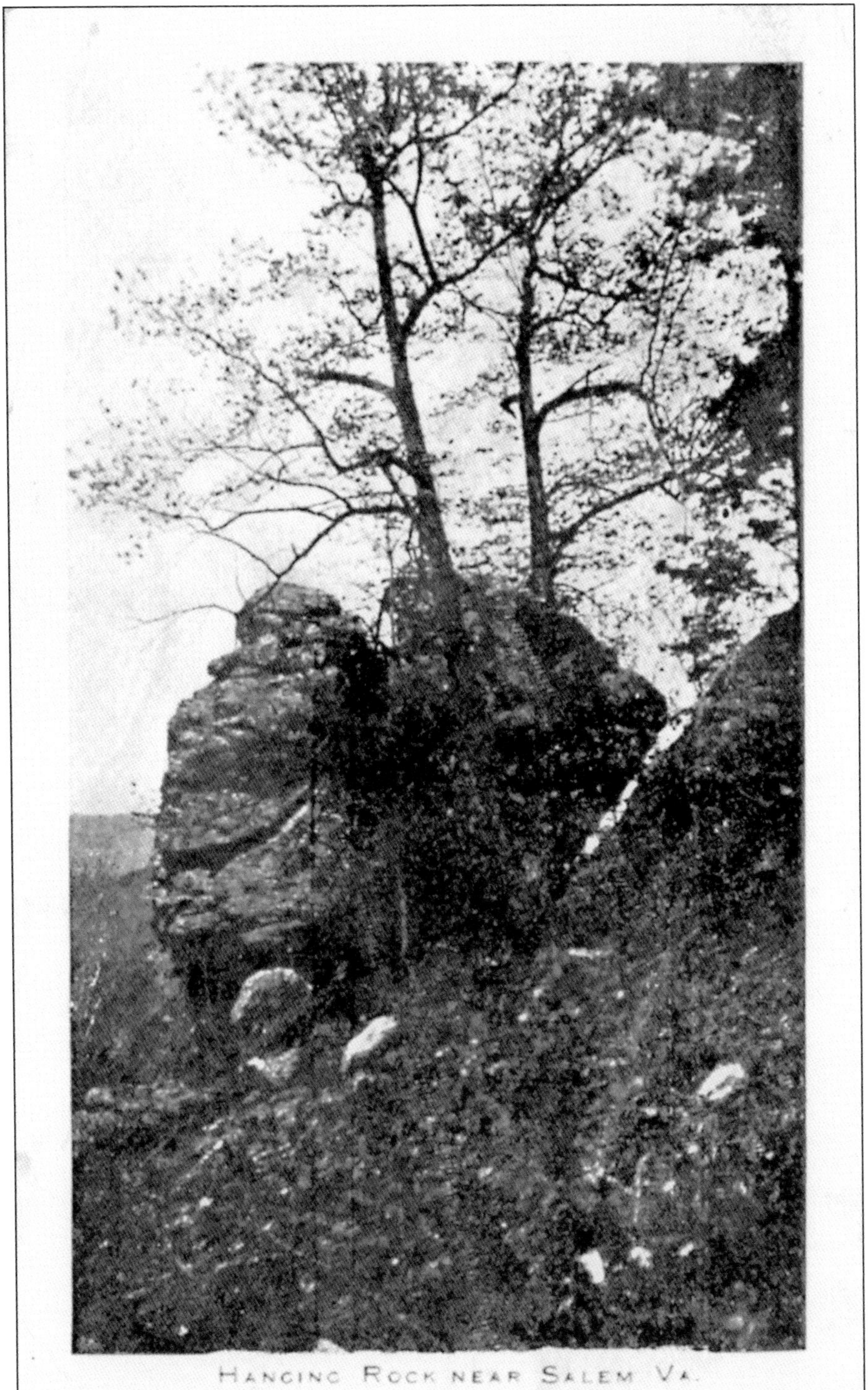

HANGING ROCK, NEAR SALEM, 1910. The name "Hanging Rock" was given due to the rock formation's appearance of projecting from the mountainside. The Battle of Hanging Rock was one of only two Civil War engagements within the bounds of Roanoke County.

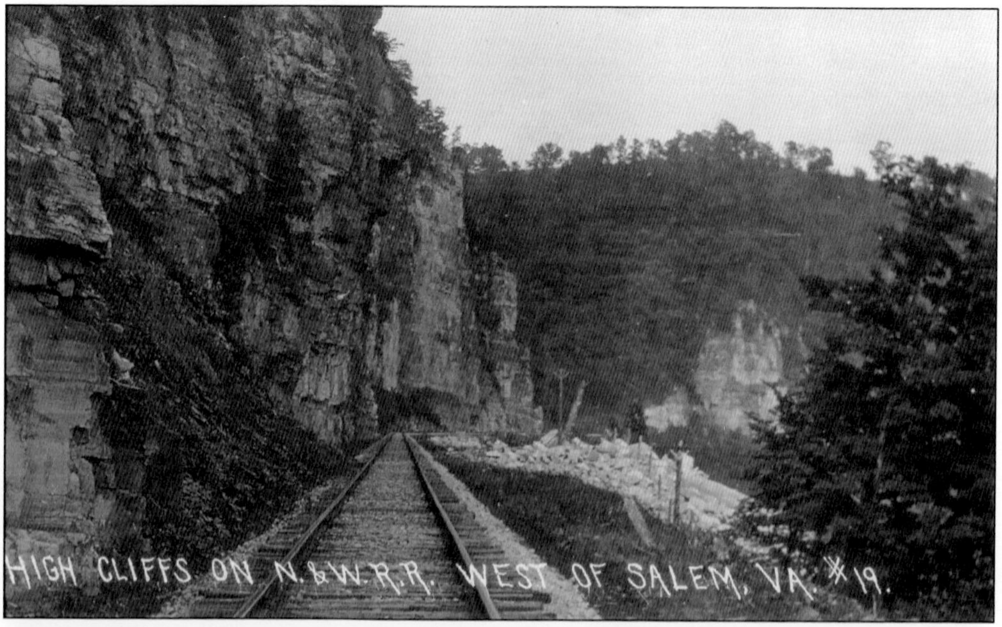

HIGH CLIFFS ON NORFOLK AND WESTERN RAILWAY WEST OF SALEM, 1915. The official arrival of the Norfolk and Western (N&W) Railroad (later Railway) into the Roanoke Valley occurred on June 18, 1882, when an N&W locomotive steamed into the newly-named town of Roanoke. With the coming of the railroad, the population and commercial activity of the Roanoke Valley began to boom.

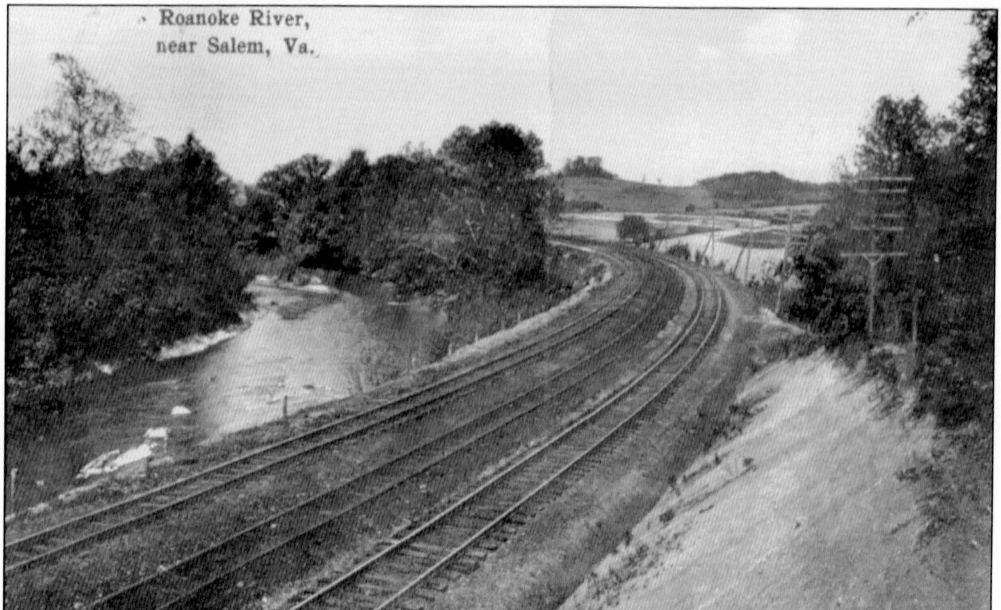

ROANOKE RIVER NEAR SALEM, 1915. The Roanoke River is approximately 337 miles long, moving west to east from North Carolina through Virginia. The Roanoke eventually flows into the Dan River and on to the Albermarle Sound. The river's original name was Sapony, after the Native Americans who lived along its banks. Later it became known as Goose Creek, and eventually the Roanoke, after its headwaters were determined.

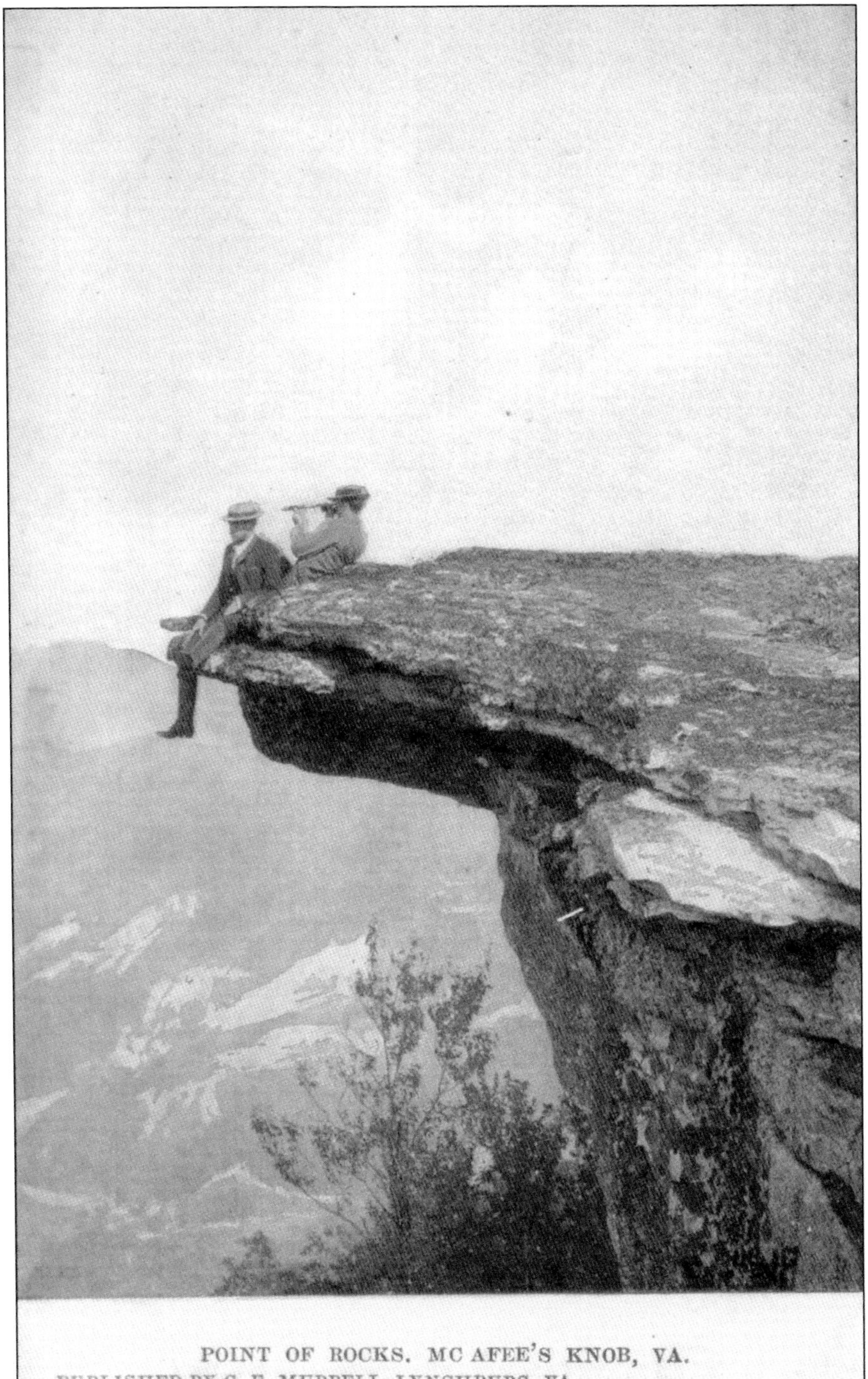

McAFEE'S KNOB, 1915. This postcard reads, "From the crest of McAfee's Knob, near Salem, at an altitude of 4,000 feet, and commanding a view of entrancing beauty. Point of Rocks projects over the valley far below. With nearly 2,000 feet of space beneath him, the visitor finds he does not have to travel thousands of miles to Yosemite Valley to grow dizzy on stupendous heights or to view men and horses dwarfed to pygmies in the depths below."

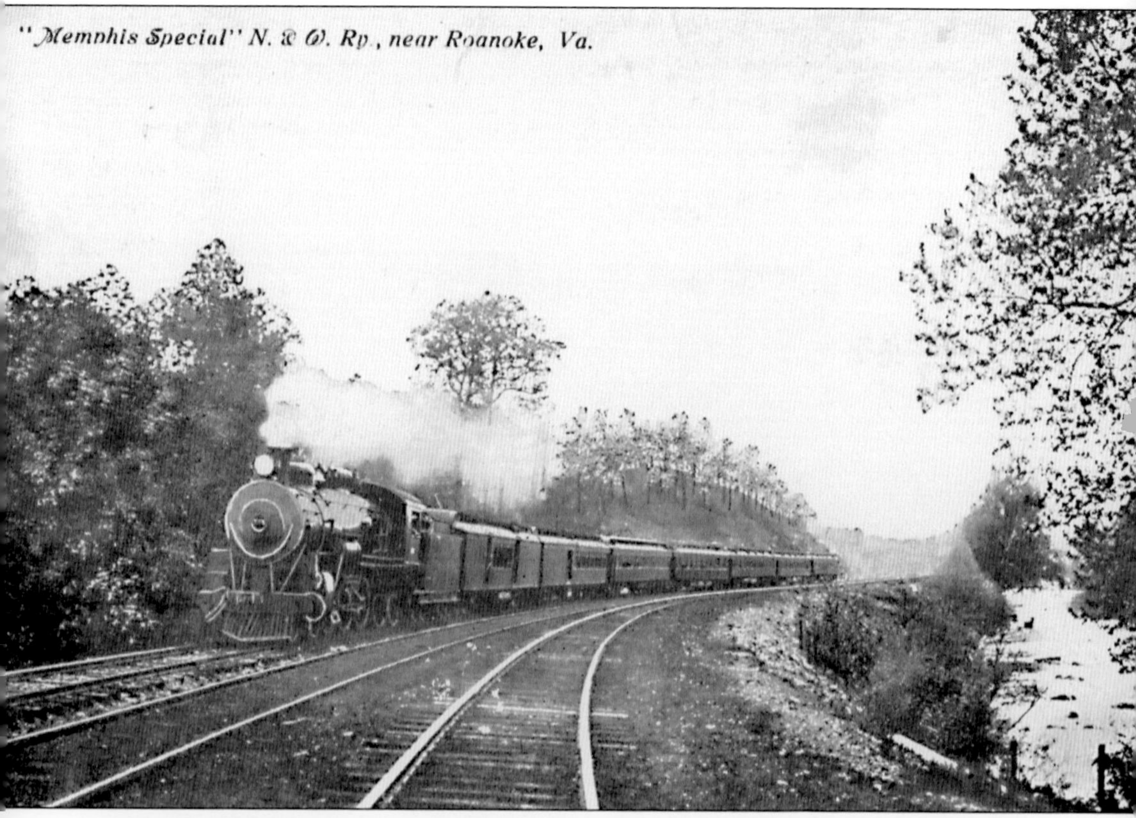

MEMPHIS SPECIAL TRAIN, SOMEWHERE NEAR ROANOKE, 1911. The Memphis Special made its debut through the Roanoke Valley on June 20, 1909, running between Memphis, Tennessee, and New York City. The Memphis Special remained a popular passenger train for years, being the fastest and most direct route to New York.

Seven

HEALTHCARE

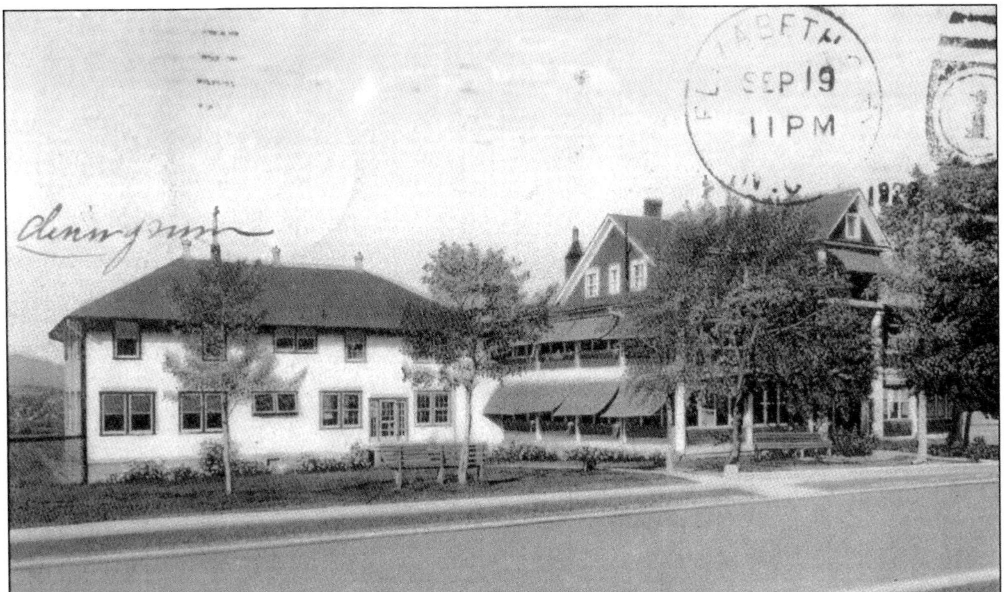

MOUNT REGIS SANATORIUM, *c.* 1920. The tuberculosis sanatorium was opened by a group of Roanoke doctors in 1914. This postcard depicts the main building and dining room of Mount Regis.

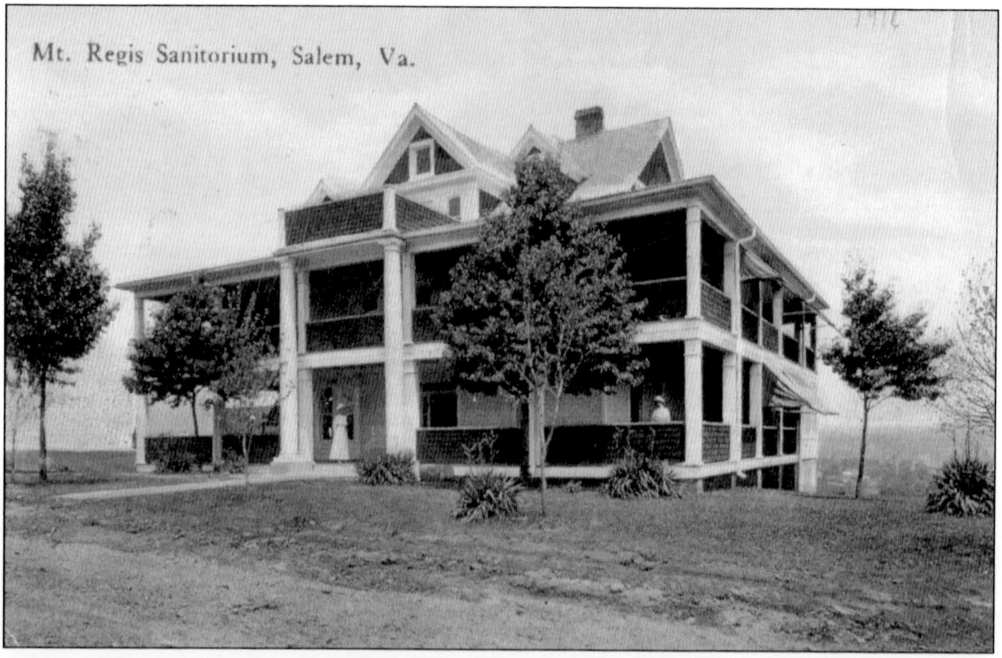

MOUNT REGIS SANATORIUM, 1916. Mount Regis was built on Development Hill in South Salem and closed its doors as a sanatorium in 1939. The building was then taken over by the Youth Administration to provide housing for nurses' aids in hospitals. After World War II, the White Cross Hospital, treating alcohol abuse, took over the facility.

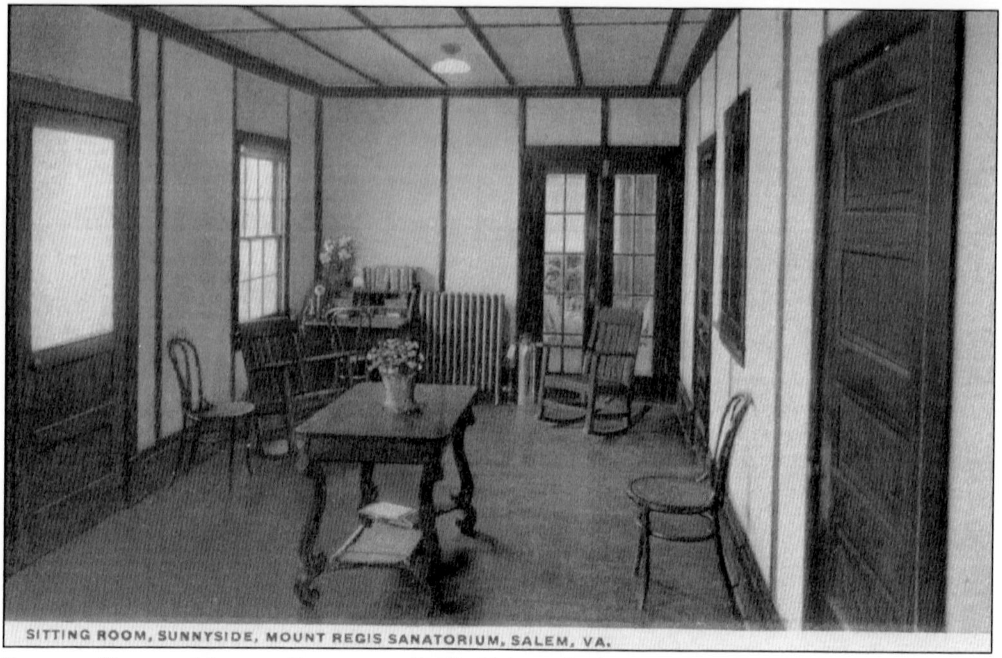

SITTING ROOM, MOUNT REGIS, *c.* 1920. Tuberculosis sanatoriums were numerous in the first half of the 20th century. By the late 1960s, tuberculosis was controllable, and facilities such as Mount Regis were converted to other uses, usually health related.

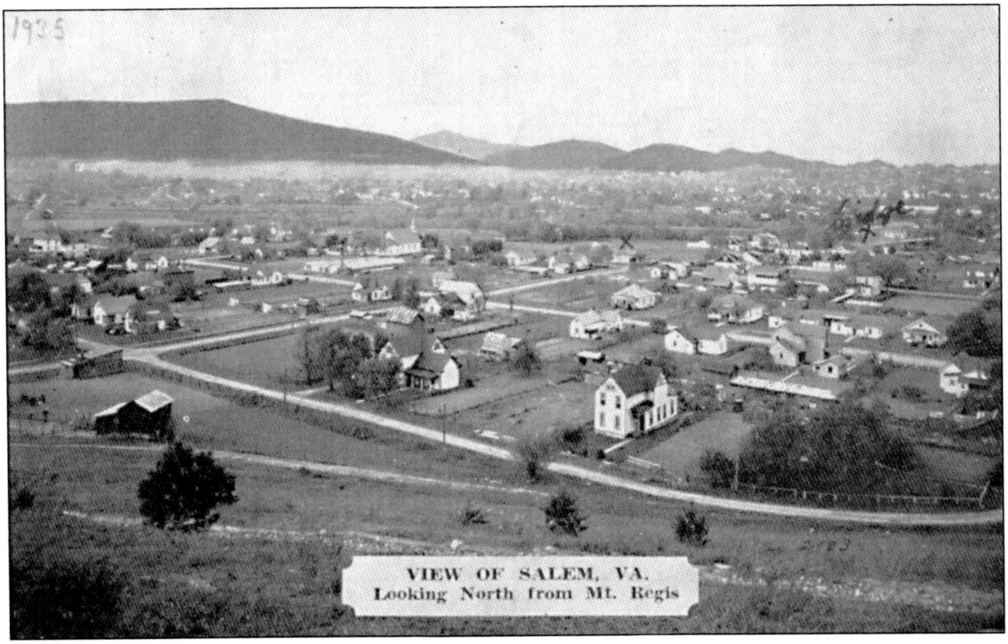

VIEW OF SALEM, LOOKING NORTH FROM MOUNT REGIS, 1935. In 1952, some residents of South Salem started a petition drive to incorporate a new town, Mount Regis. This was countered by other South Salem residents desiring annexation into Salem. With some legal maneuverings and posturing, the Mount Regis citizens settled down, acknowledging annexation was the predetermined outcome. Soon thereafter, Salem expanded its borders.

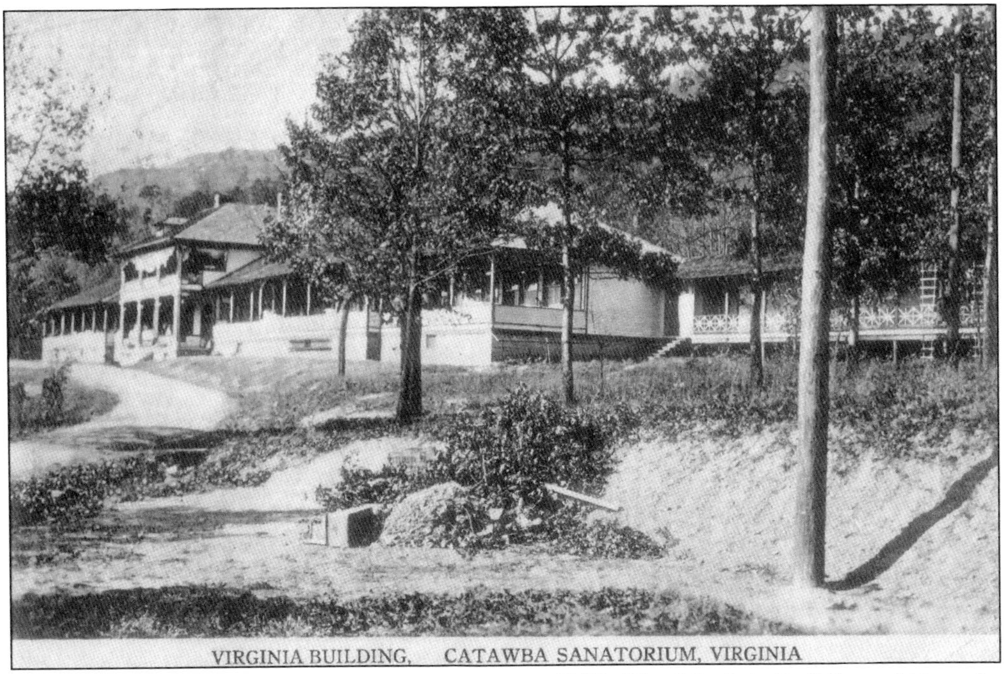

VIRGINIA BUILDING, CATAWBA SANATORIUM, 1915. The Virginia Building of Catawba Sanatorium was constructed in 1913, four years after the Catawba Sanatorium opened. The original property for the sanatorium had been the Red Sulphur Springs.

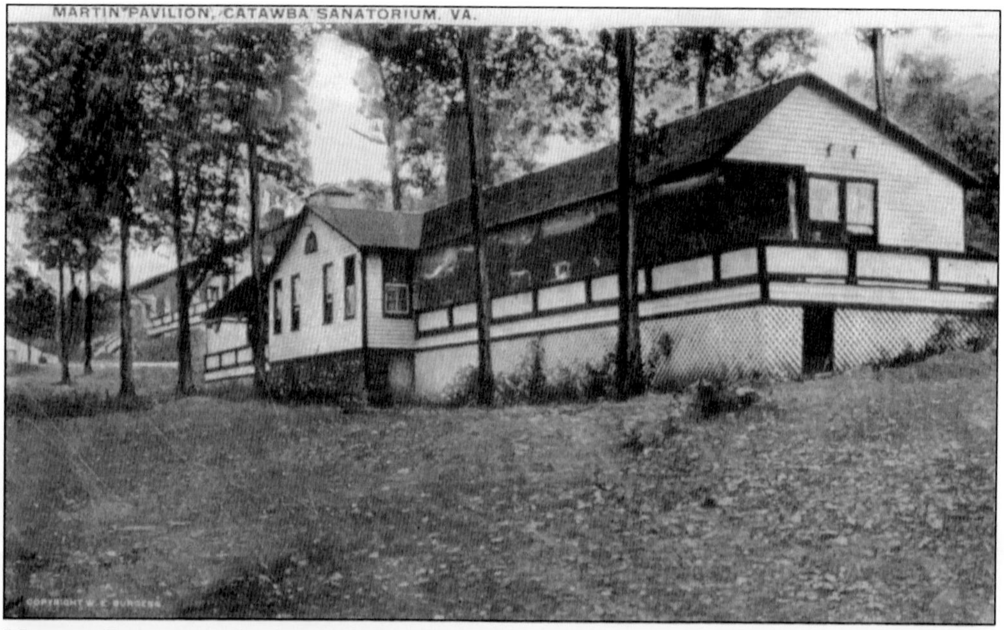

MARTIN PAVILION, CATAWBA SANATORIUM, *c.* 1920. When Catawba Sanatorium opened in 1909, it consisted of 42 beds located primarily in the old hotel that served the sulphur springs resort area. The sanatorium would expand significantly in both buildings and number of patients over the next few decades.

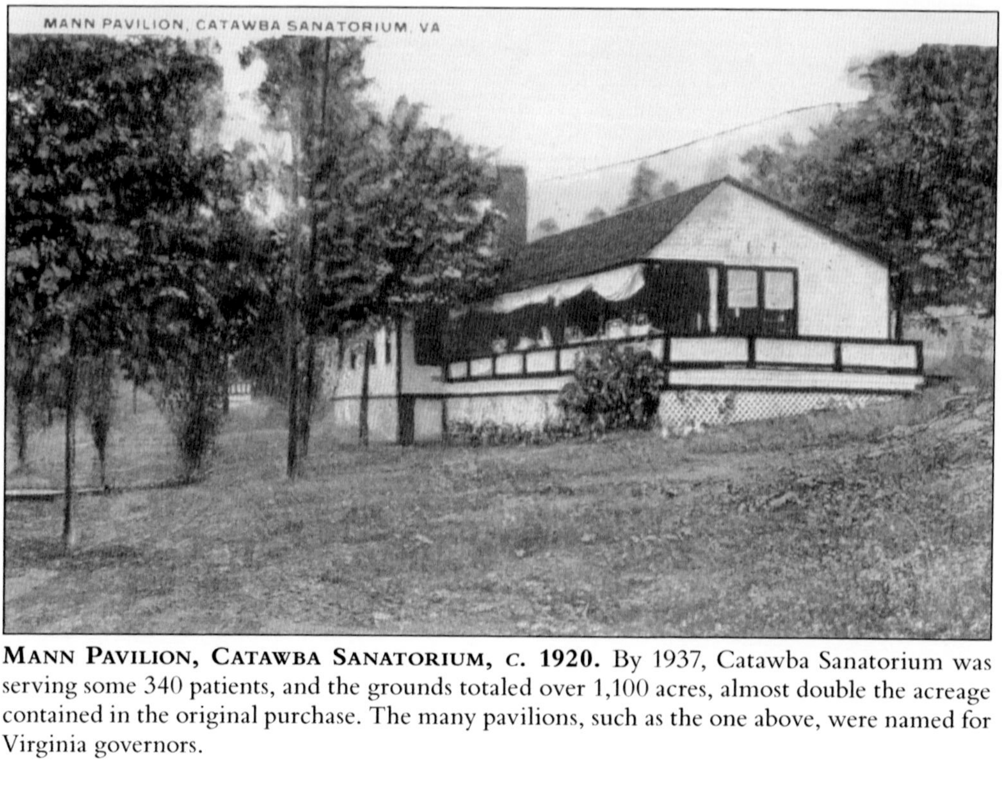

MANN PAVILION, CATAWBA SANATORIUM, *c.* 1920. By 1937, Catawba Sanatorium was serving some 340 patients, and the grounds totaled over 1,100 acres, almost double the acreage contained in the original purchase. The many pavilions, such as the one above, were named for Virginia governors.

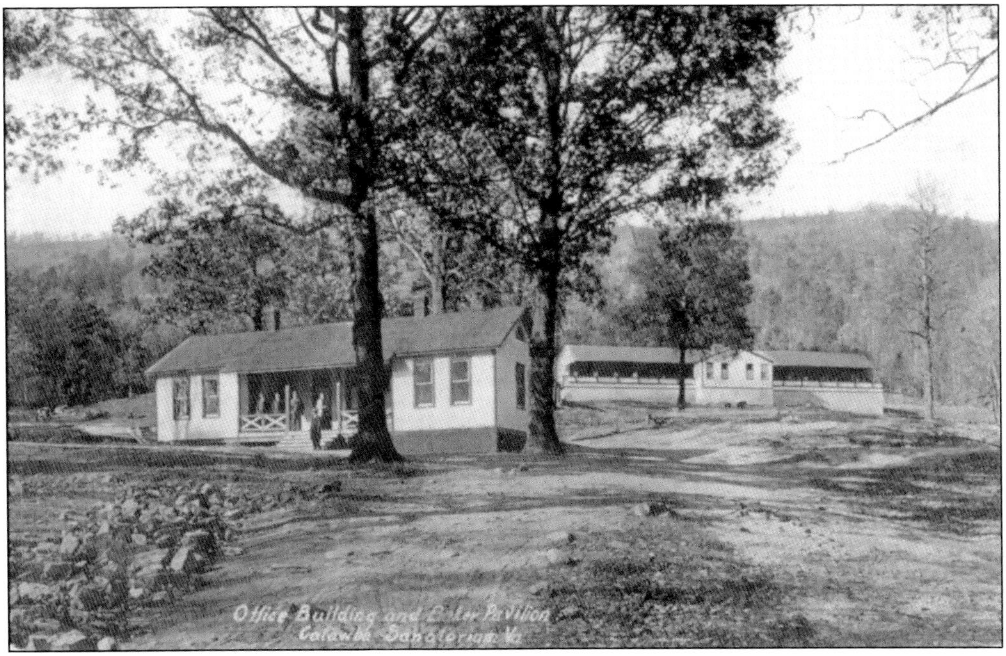

OFFICE BUILDING AND BAKER PAVILION. Catawba Sanatorium became, in many ways, a self-sustaining community. For many years, the sanatorium operated its own dairy farm. The number of patients and employees were such that the area soon had its own post office, school, chapel, and other amenities.

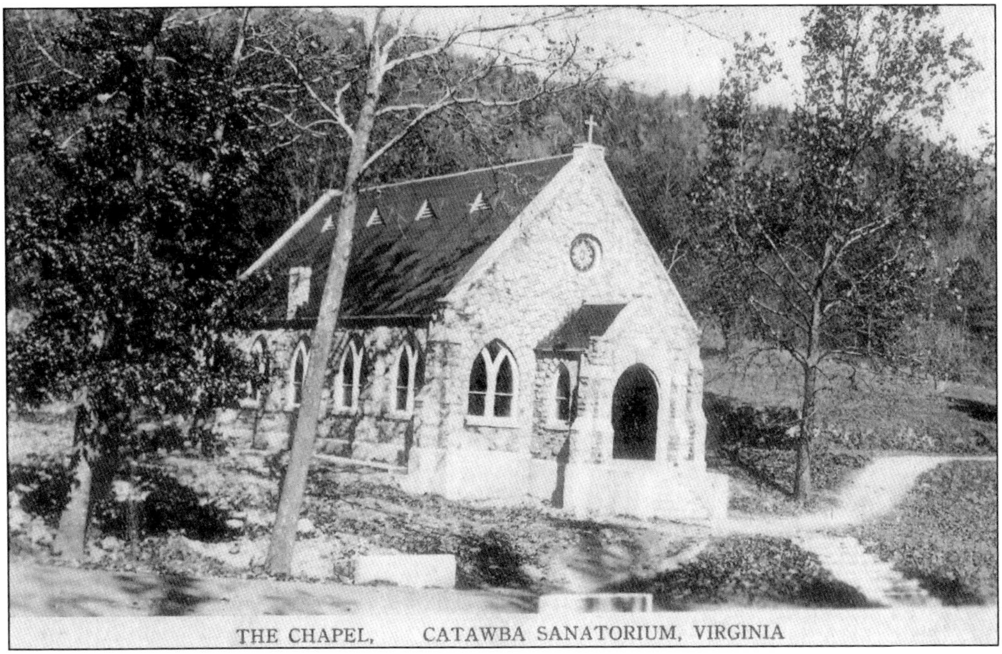

THE CHAPEL, CATAWBA SANATORIUM, C. 1920. The sanatorium's chapel was built in 1919. For the next 20 years, the sanatorium's campus developed to include nurses' quarters, a teachers' residence, an infirmary, a dining hall, and an administration building.

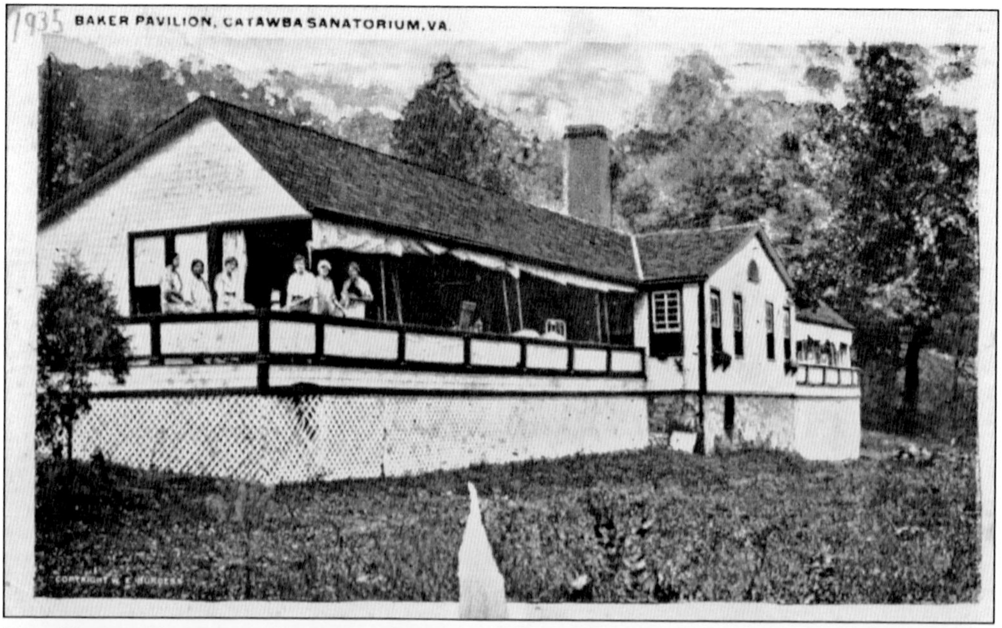

THE BAKER PAVILION, CATAWBA SANATORIUM, 1935. Catawba Sanatorium developed its own nursing school to train healthcare professionals in the treatment of tuberculosis. Between 1912 and 1954, the Catawba School of Nursing graduated 258 certified tuberculosis nurses.

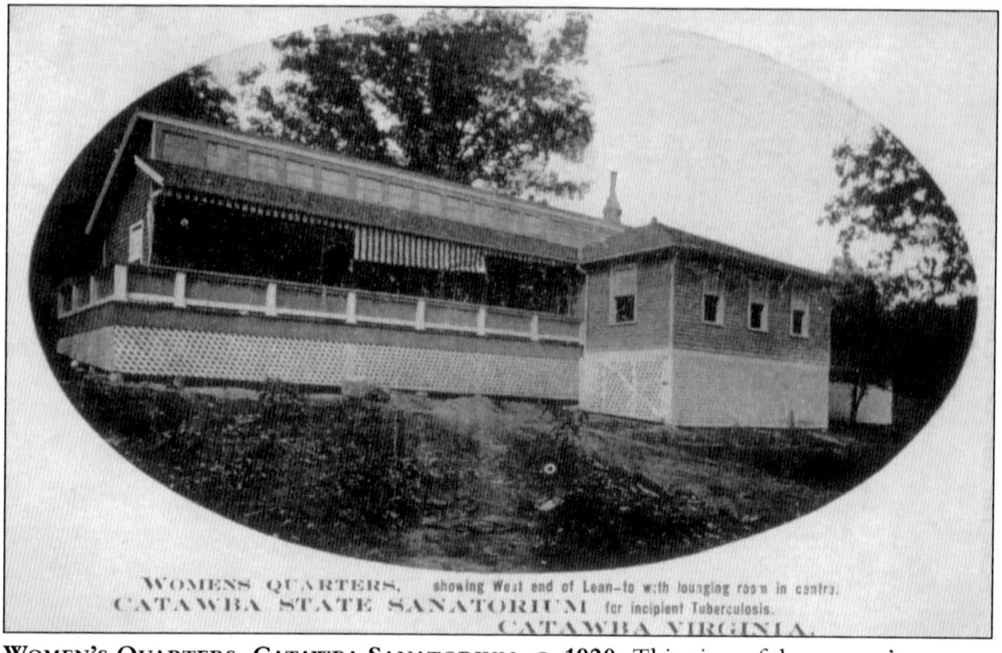

WOMEN'S QUARTERS, CATAWBA SANATORIUM, *c.* 1920. This view of the women's quarters shows the west end of the lean-to, with the lounging room in the center. Catawba ceased accepting tuberculosis patients on January 1, 1972. When it did, records indicated that some 25,000 tuberculosis patients had received treatment at Catawba Sanatorium during its 63 years of operation. Since 1972, Catawba Hospital has served patients with mental illnesses.

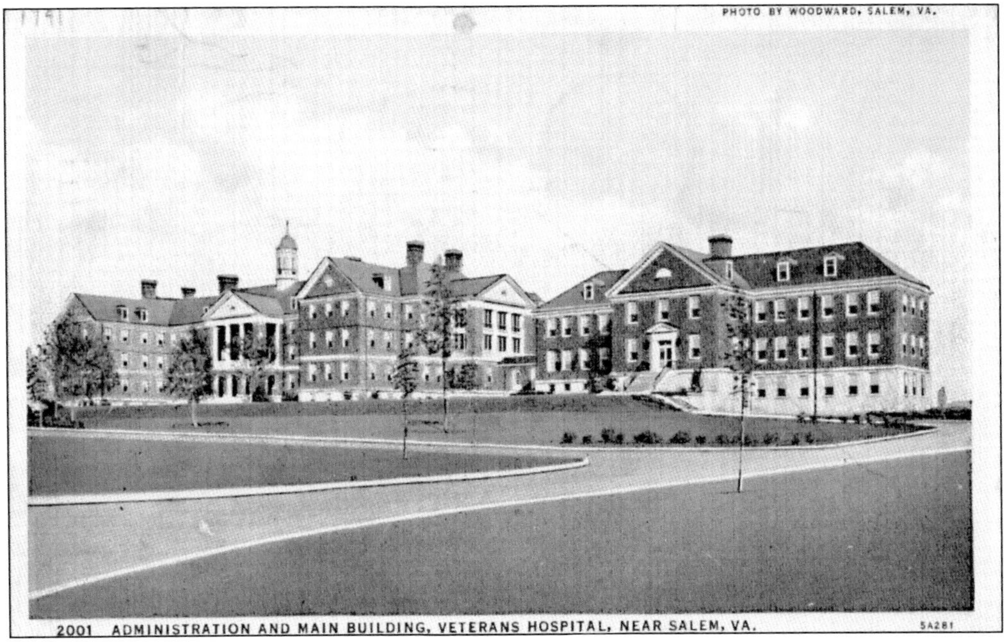

Administration and Main Building, Veterans Administration Hospital, 1941. The Veterans Administration Medical Center in Salem opened in 1934, with Pres. Franklin Roosevelt delivering the dedicatory speech to some 40,000 persons in attendance. The opening of the large medical center provided Salem with a needed boost during tough economic times.

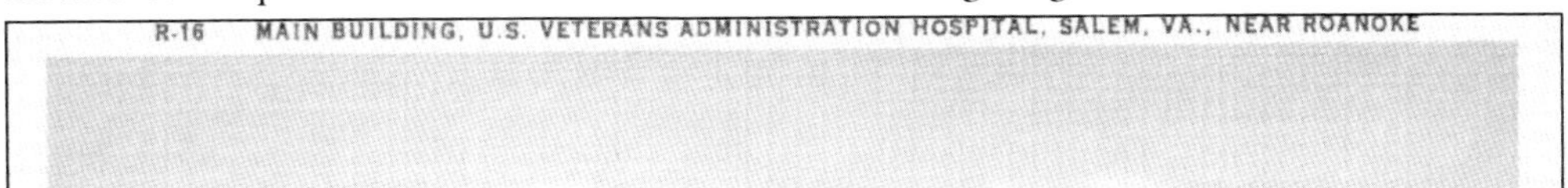

Main Building, Veterans Administration Hospital, 1940. When the Veterans Administration (VA) facility opened, it occupied a tract of land consisting of 445 acres. The total construction cost for the original facility was almost $1.8 million. The brick was provided by Salem's Old Virginia Brick Company, which complimented the Georgian Colonial–style architecture.

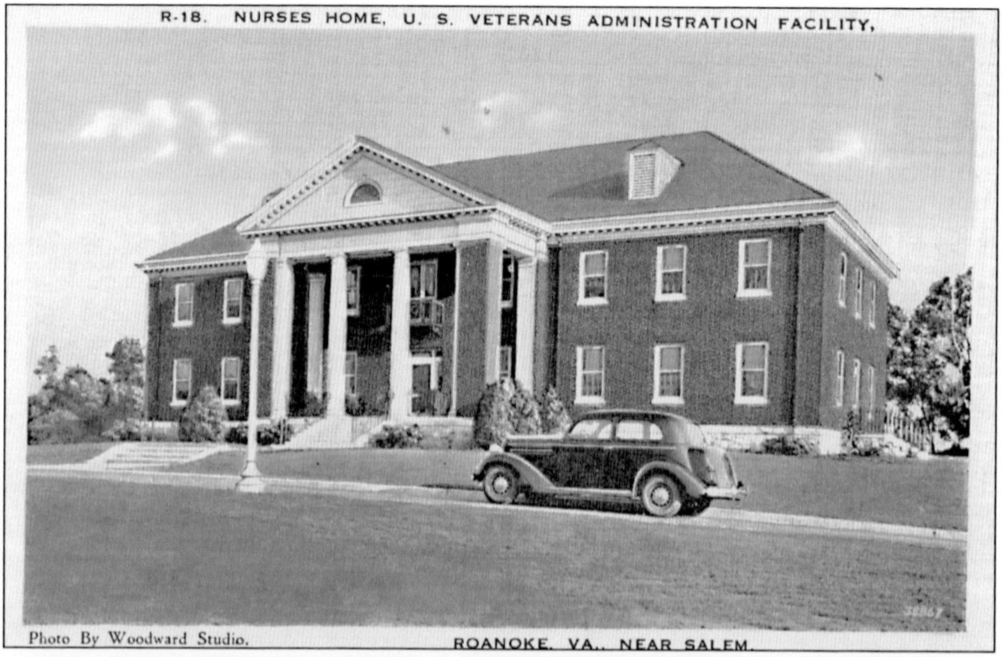

NURSES' HOME, VETERANS ADMINISTRATION HOSPITAL, 1940. The VA facility erected structures such as the nurses' home to house medical staff. The first patients were admitted to the facility on April 23, 1935. Some of the patients, as a form of therapy, actually conducted farming operations on the grounds of the facility, engaging in raising hogs and cattle.

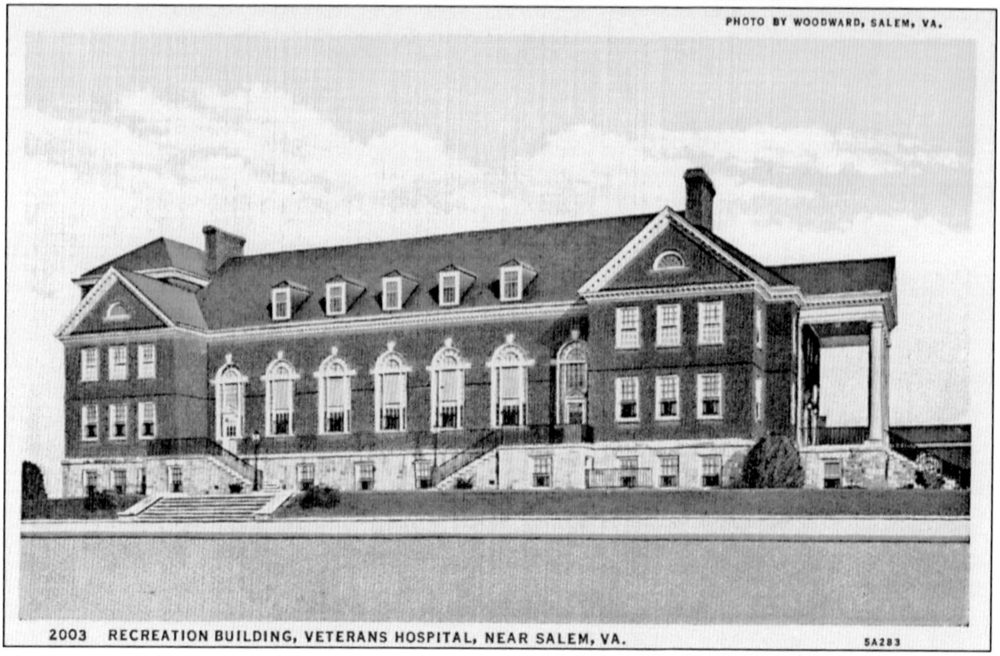

RECREATION BUILDING, VETERANS ADMINISTRATION HOSPITAL, 1940. A second wave of development occurred at the VA Hospital just after World War II to accommodate the influx of new patients. By 1949, the hospital was caring for some 2,000 veterans. Another distinguished visitor to grace the campus of the hospital was then-actor Ronald Reagan in 1957.

Eight

Route 11 and Connections

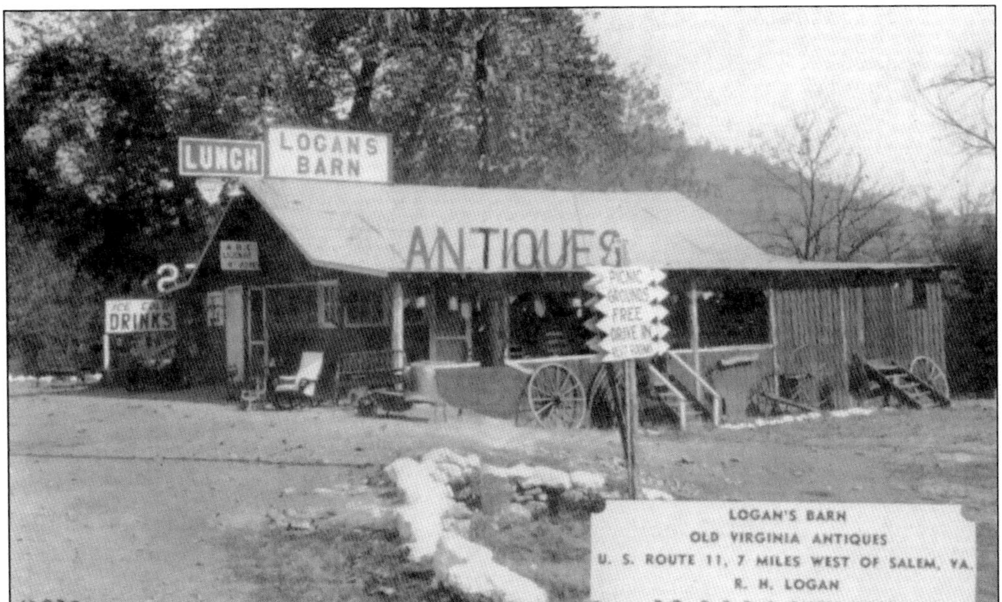

Logan's Barn Antiques, c. 1950. This card promoted the antique shop as "one of the largest and most interesting shops in the South." It was located five miles west of Salem, on Route 11/Route 460.

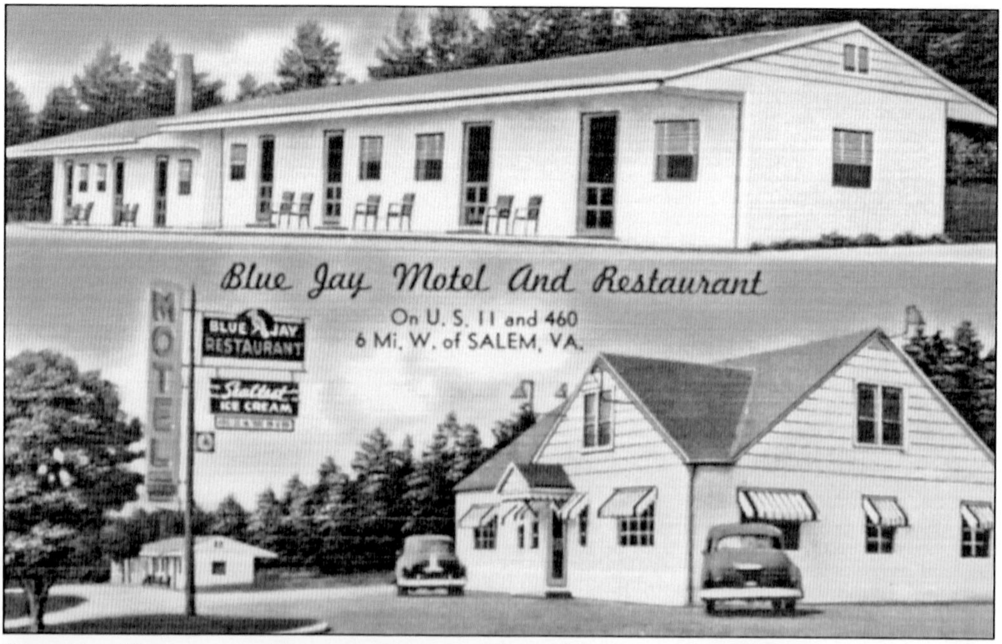

BLUE JAY MOTEL AND RESTAURANT, *c*. 1950. The Blue Jay Motel was located six miles west of Salem on Routes 11 and 460. Route 11, formerly known as the South Road, became an official state road in 1919.

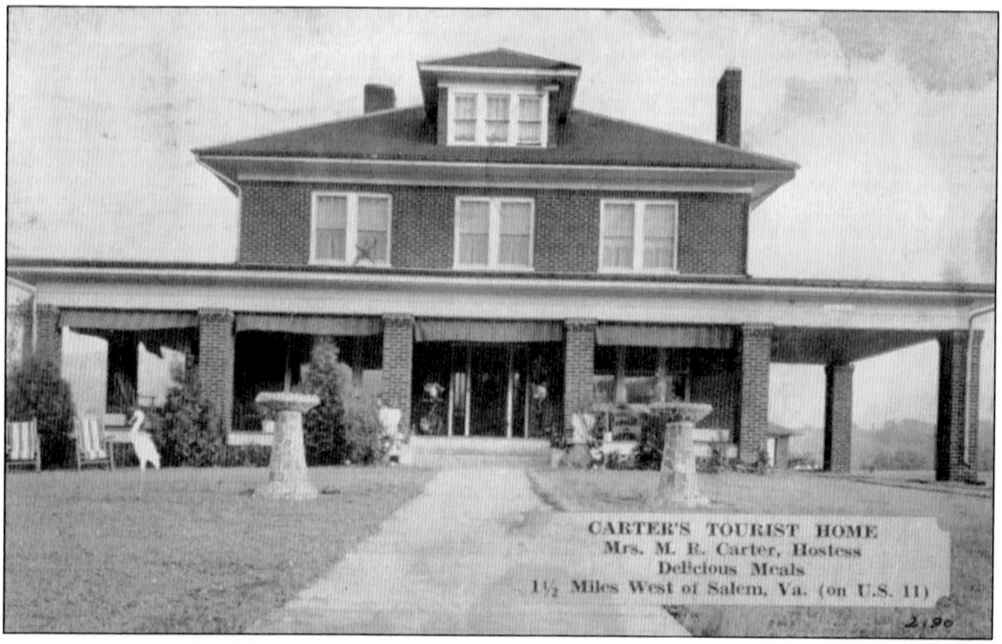

CARTER'S TOURIST HOME, 1935. Carter's Tourist Home was overseen by Mrs. M. R. Carter, hostess. This card promoted her establishment as offering "delicious meals." The tourist home was one and a half miles west of Salem on Route 11.

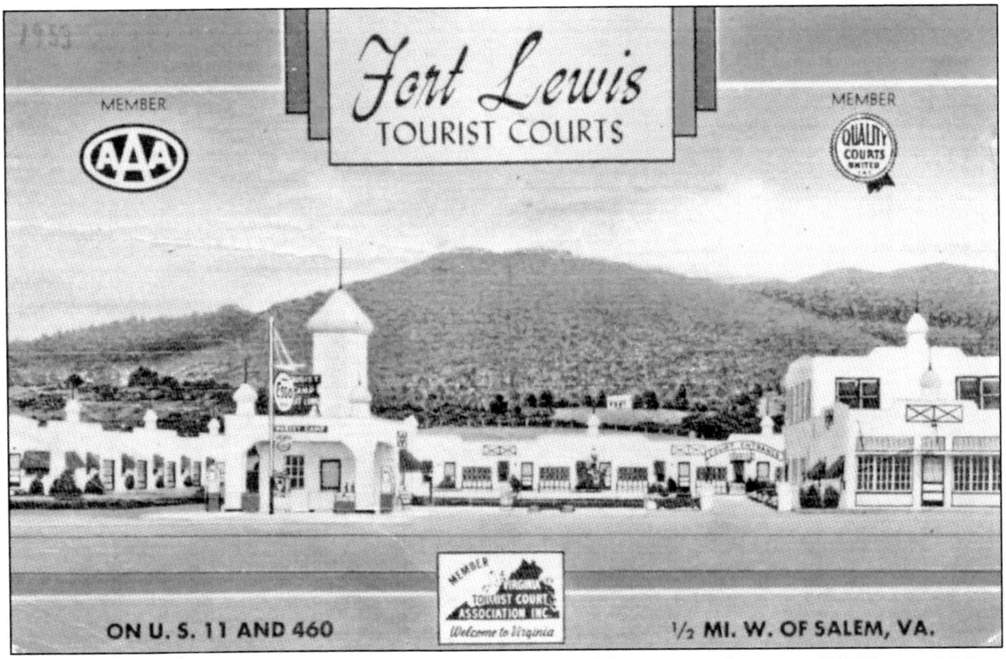

FORT LEWIS TOURIST COURTS, 1953. The sender of this postcard wrote, "Will spend New Years Eve here, rained all day, having a good time. This motel is very comfortable. See you in San Francisco." The Fort Lewis Tourist Courts were half a mile west of Salem on Route 11.

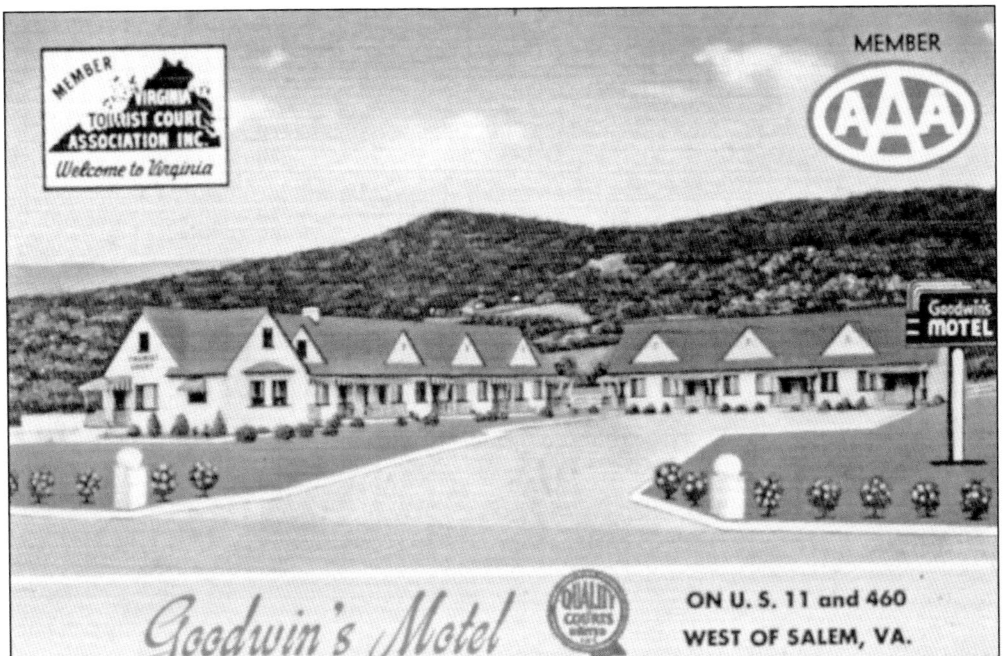

GOODWIN'S MOTEL, *C.* 1950. The Goodwin Motel's postcard boasted "approved drinking water." The motel was located west of Salem on Route 11, which served for many years as the modern-day equivalent of the interstate.

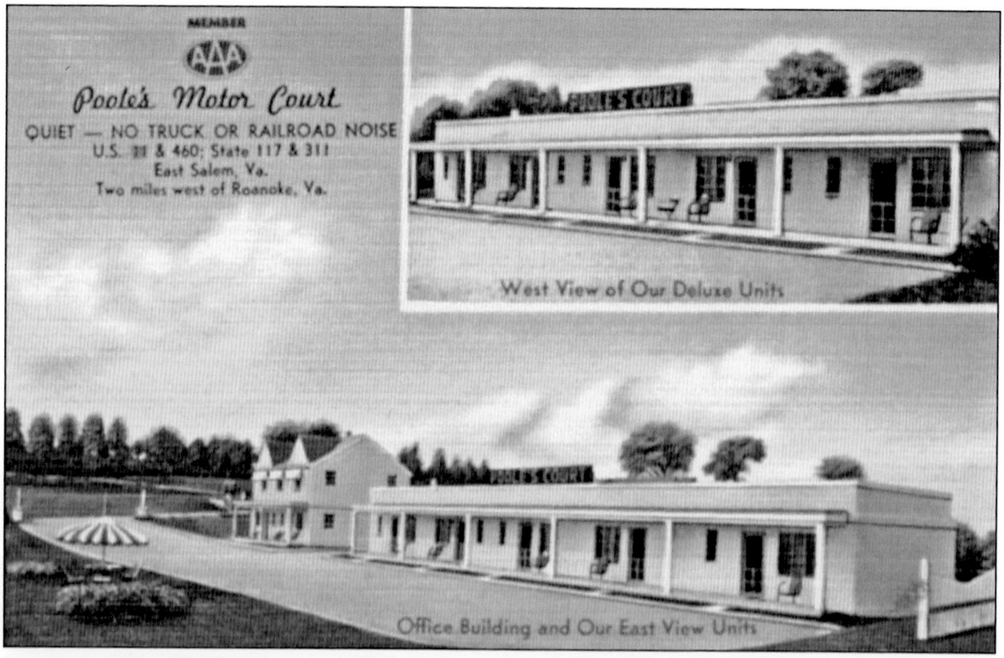

POOLE'S MOTOR COURT, *c.* 1950. This motor court was managed by H. R. Poole, who mailed this particular postcard to Joseph Lang of West Hempstead, New York, with the simple message, "You're welcome in Virginia." The establishment lured visitors by claiming "no truck or railroad noise." Its address was 811 East Main Street in Salem.

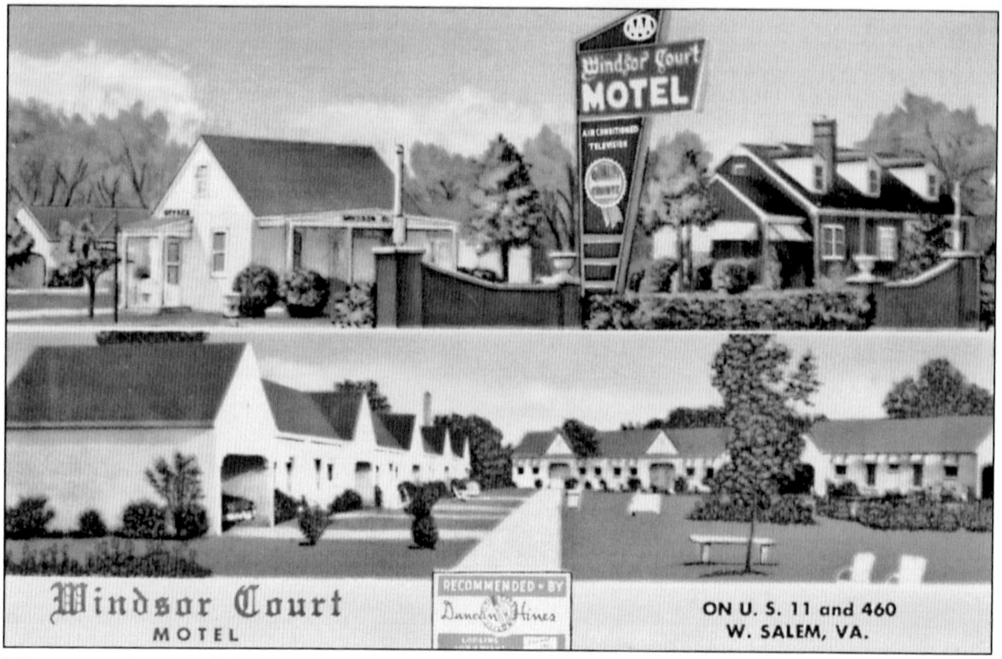

WINDSOR COURT MOTEL, *c.* 1950. Windsor Court Motel was at 1908 West Main Street, Salem. Effie Snead was the owner and, at the time the card was published, Charles Snead was the manager.

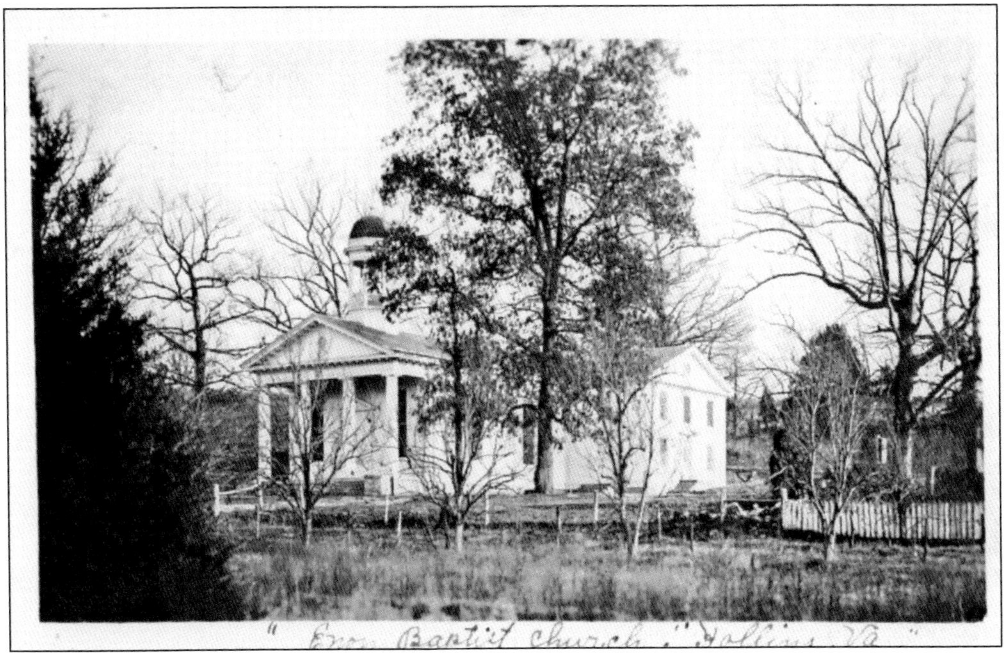

ENON BAPTIST CHURCH, HOLLINS, 1915. Enon Baptist Church is one of the oldest Baptist churches in the Roanoke Valley. Built across from the entrance of present-day Hollins University in 1855, the church was established by Charles Cocke, president of Hollins Institute.

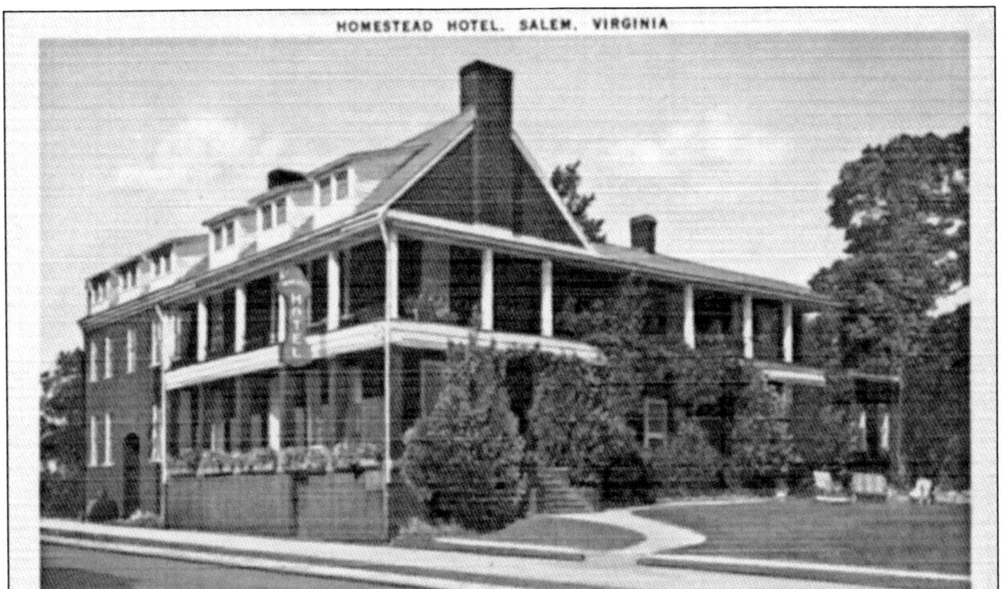

HOMESTEAD HOTEL, *C.* 1940. The Homestead Hotel has a long history. Built by David Wade in 1802, it was formerly known as the Old Globe Tavern and boasted five huge fireplaces and 27-inch-thick walls. At the time this card was published, it was the only original stagecoach tavern still open to the public on Route 11.

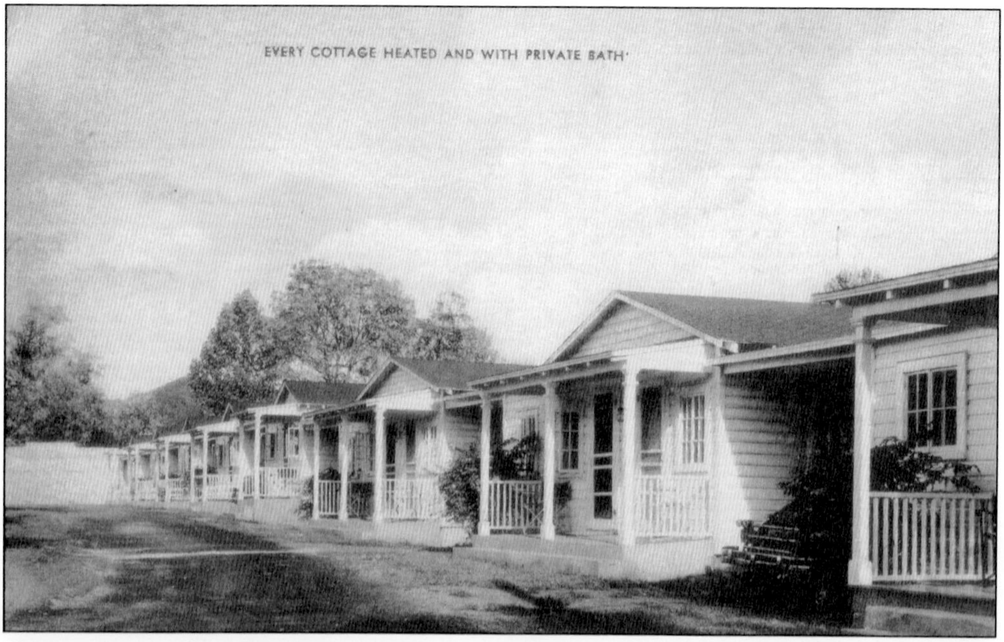

TRAVELTOWN, CLOVERDALE, NO DATE. Traveltown, located on Route 11 in Cloverdale, advertised "Every cottage heated with Private Bath." In the mid-1920s, Route 11 became a link in the Washington-to-San Diego Lee Highway, making it a part of the transcontinental highway system.

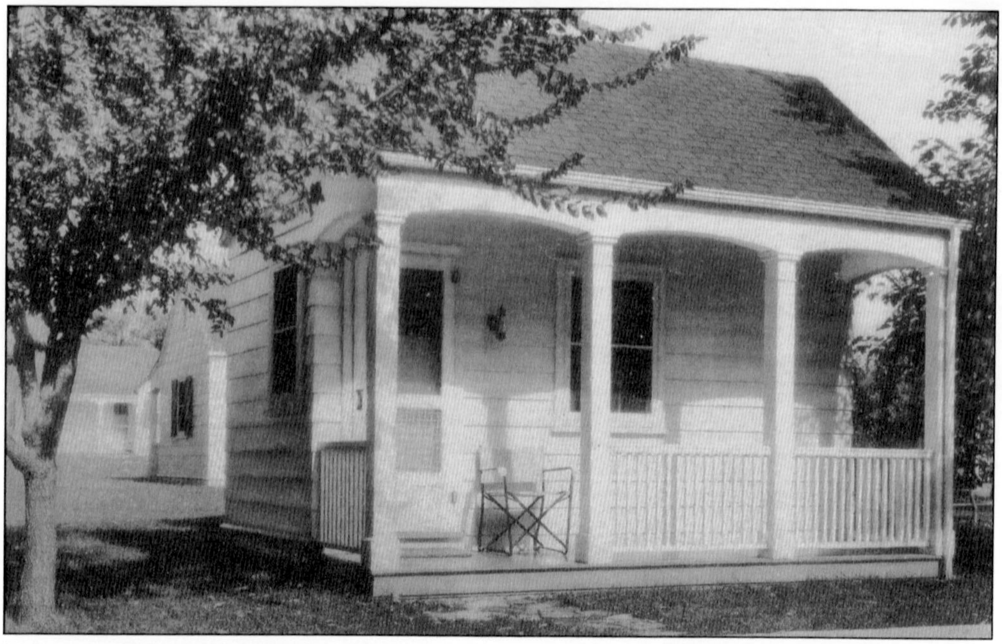

TRAVELTOWN, CLOVERDALE, NO DATE. The vast majority of tourist homes, motor courts, motels, and other tourist-related businesses dried up after the emergence of President Eisenhower's interstate highway system. Small towns were bypassed, and routes such as Route 11 were no longer used with any significance by destination travelers.

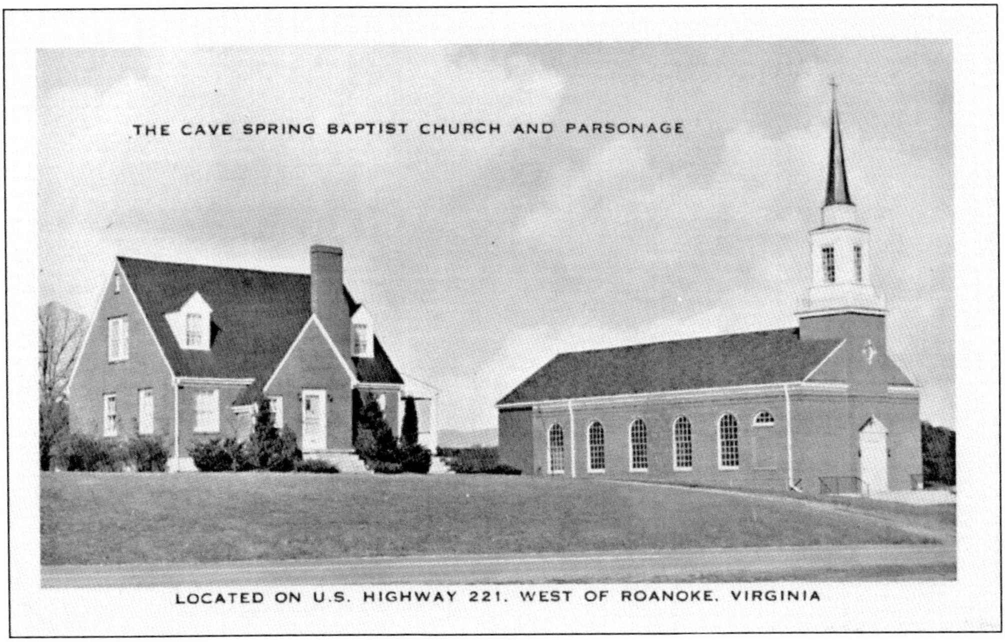

CAVE SPRING BAPTIST CHURCH AND PARSONAGE ON ROUTE 221, *C.* 1960. Route 221 connected with Route 11 and was another major road prior to the interstate system. Cave Spring Baptist Church in Roanoke County was organized in 1875. The sanctuary shown on this card was built in 1957.

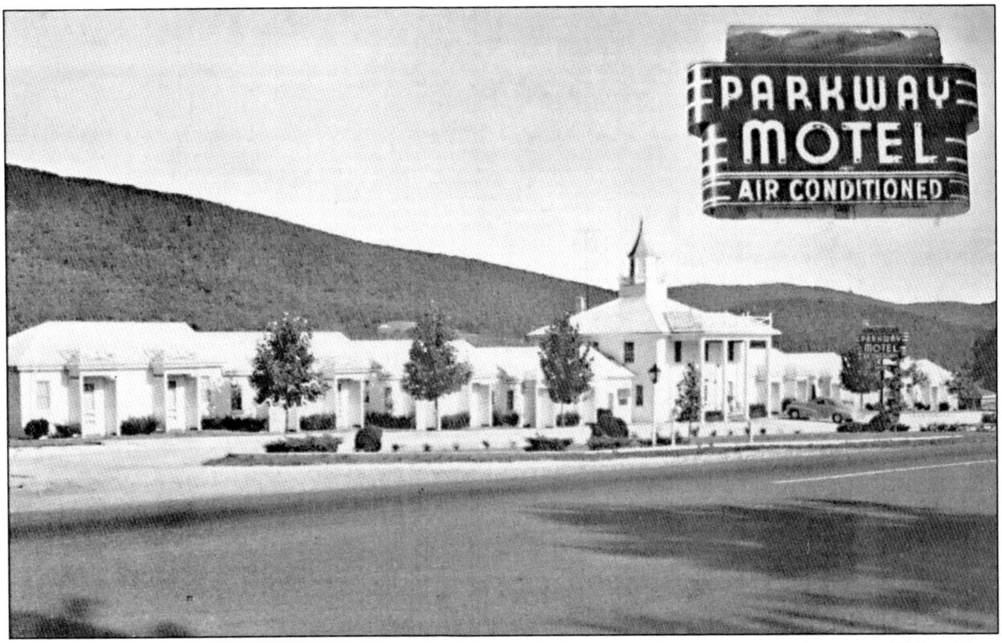

PARKWAY MOTEL, *C.* 1960. The Parkway Motel was located on Route 220 just off the Blue Ridge Parkway, three miles south of Roanoke. The card promoted the motel as having "room telephone, air conditioning, all tile baths, hot water heat, air foam mattresses." The motel was razed in the late 1990s.

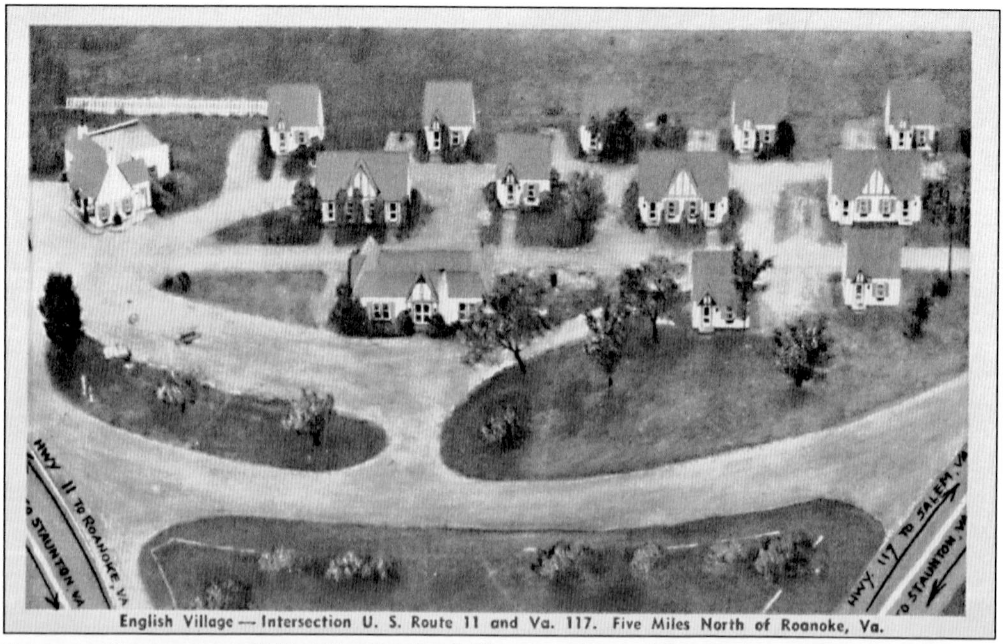

ENGLISH VILLAGE, C. 1940. The English Village was located five miles north of Roanoke, at the intersection of Route 11 and Virginia 117. The proprietor at the time this card was published was C. R. Davidson.

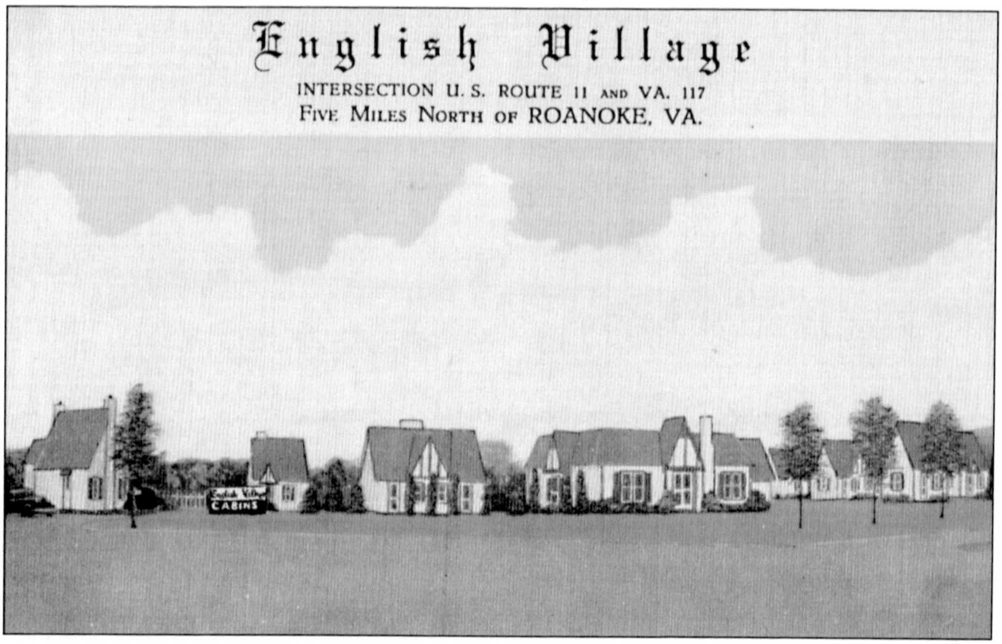

ENGLISH VILLAGE, C. 1940. The English Village claimed many fine amenities for its day, including heat, tile showers, toilets, and "complete Simmons furnishings."

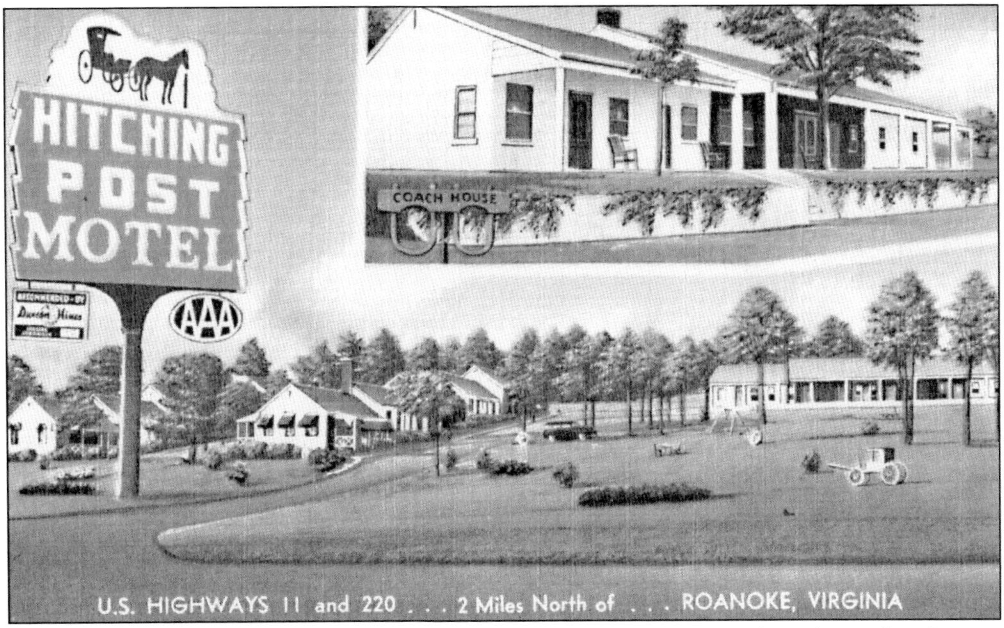

HITCHING POST MOTEL, HOLLINS, C. 1950. The Hitching Post Motel was located on Routes 11 and 220 between Roanoke City and Hollins College. At the time this card was produced, the managers and owners were Mr. and Mrs. Carl W. Windel.

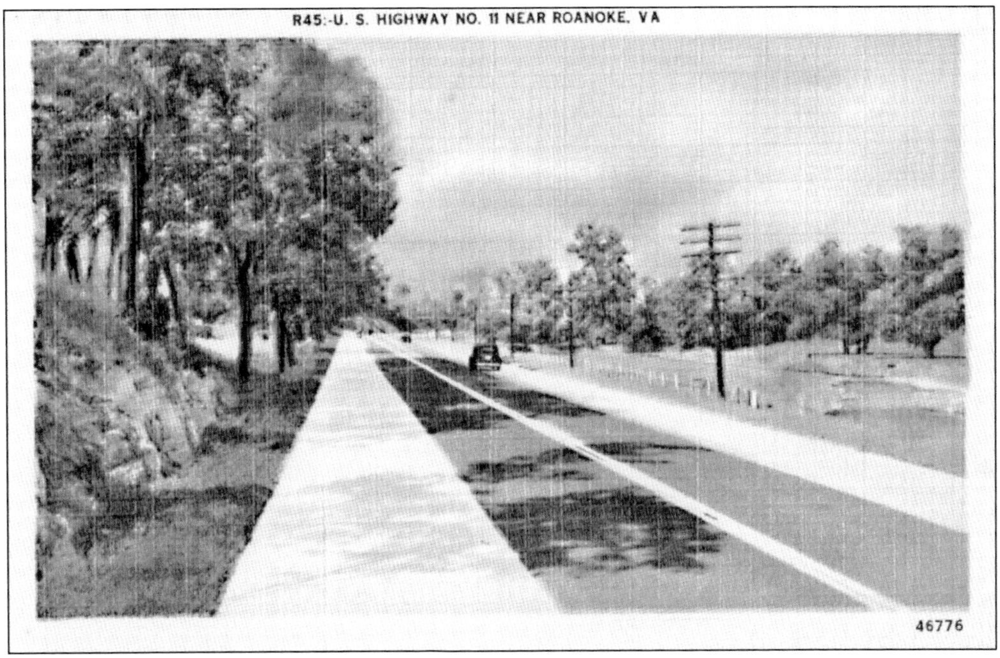

U.S. HIGHWAY 11, NEAR ROANOKE, 1945. Route 11, as far as the Roanoke Valley's segment, began in 1914 when a road and bridge were built that paralleled the railroad tracks, crossing the Roanoke River between Salem and Roanoke. In 1919, the state took over maintenance of the road, making it a part of the state system. By the next decade, Route 11 in the Roanoke Valley was part of a coast-to-coast network of roads.

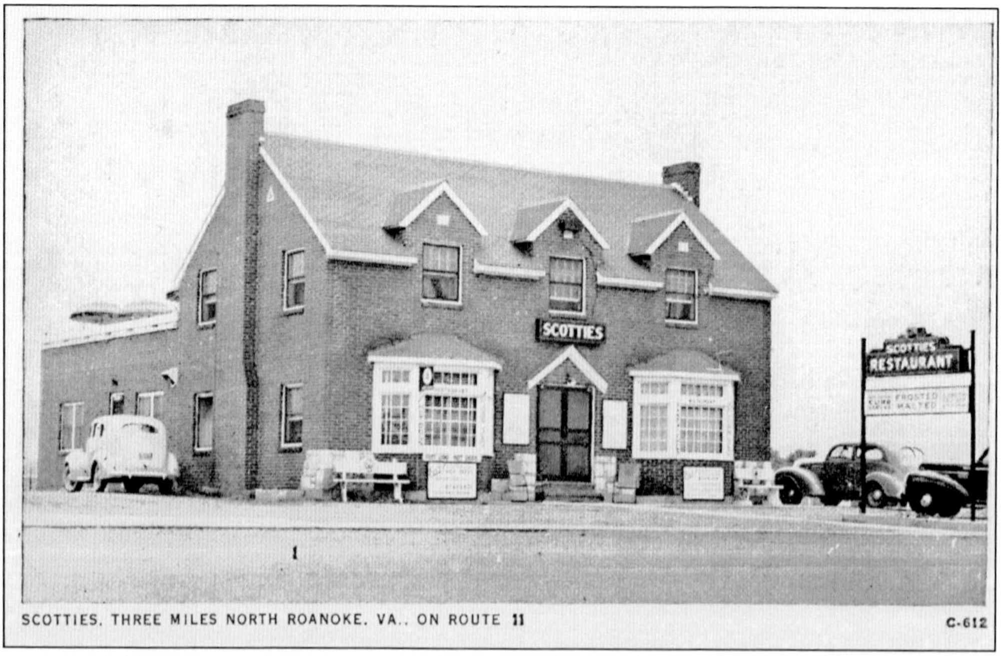

Scottie's Tavern, c. 1950. Scottie's Tavern was three miles north of Roanoke on Route 11 and specialized in country ham, chicken, and steak dinners. It even offered curb-side service. J. S. Scott was the manager.

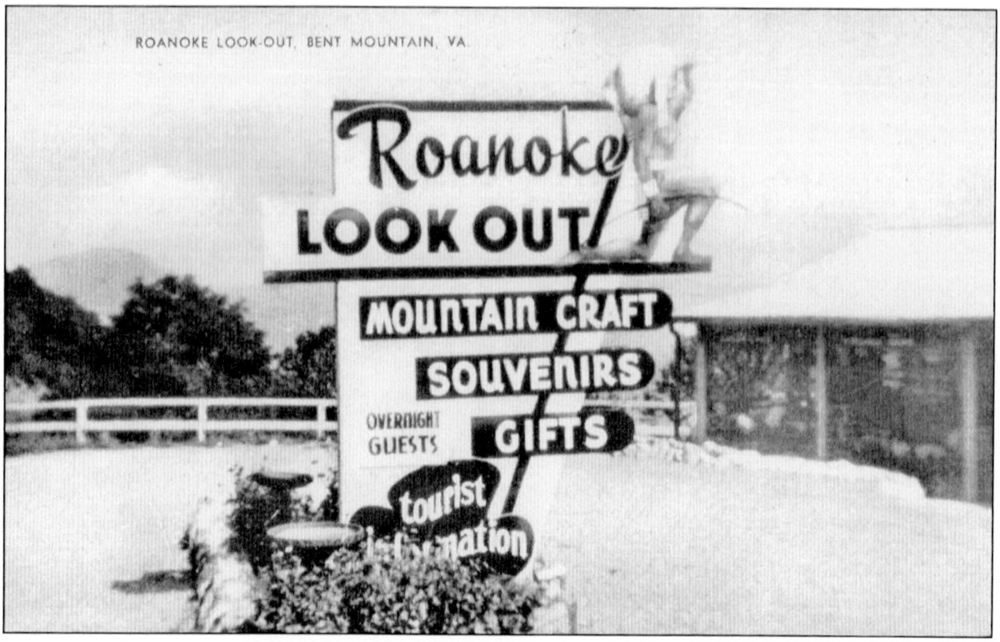

Roanoke Lookout, Bent Mountain, c. 1950. The gift shop at Roanoke Lookout offered hand-made baskets, pottery, windmills, rugs, and overnight accommodations. The gift shop was located on Route 221 at the top of Bent Mountain.

Nine

Roanoke City

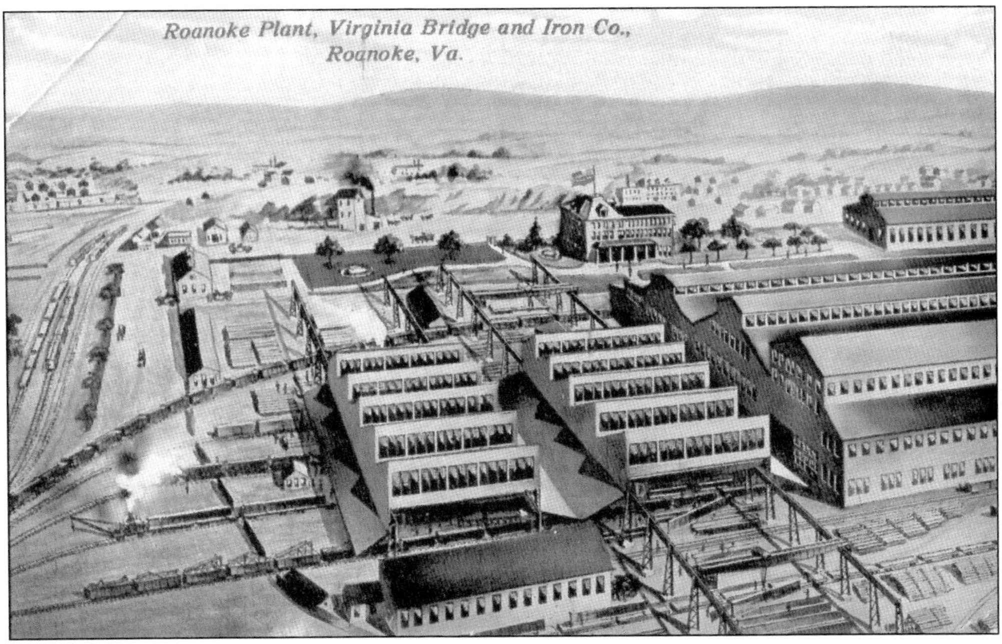

Roanoke Plant, Virginia Bridge and Iron Works, 1910. The Virginia Bridge and Iron Works began in 1888 as the American Bridge Works, changing its name in 1893. Other branch plants were located in Memphis, Tennessee, and Atlanta, Georgia. The Roanoke Branch was involved in hundreds of bridge projects throughout the state and some commercial buildings. After World War II, the plant was purchased by the American Steel Company. The plant closed in the early 1960s.

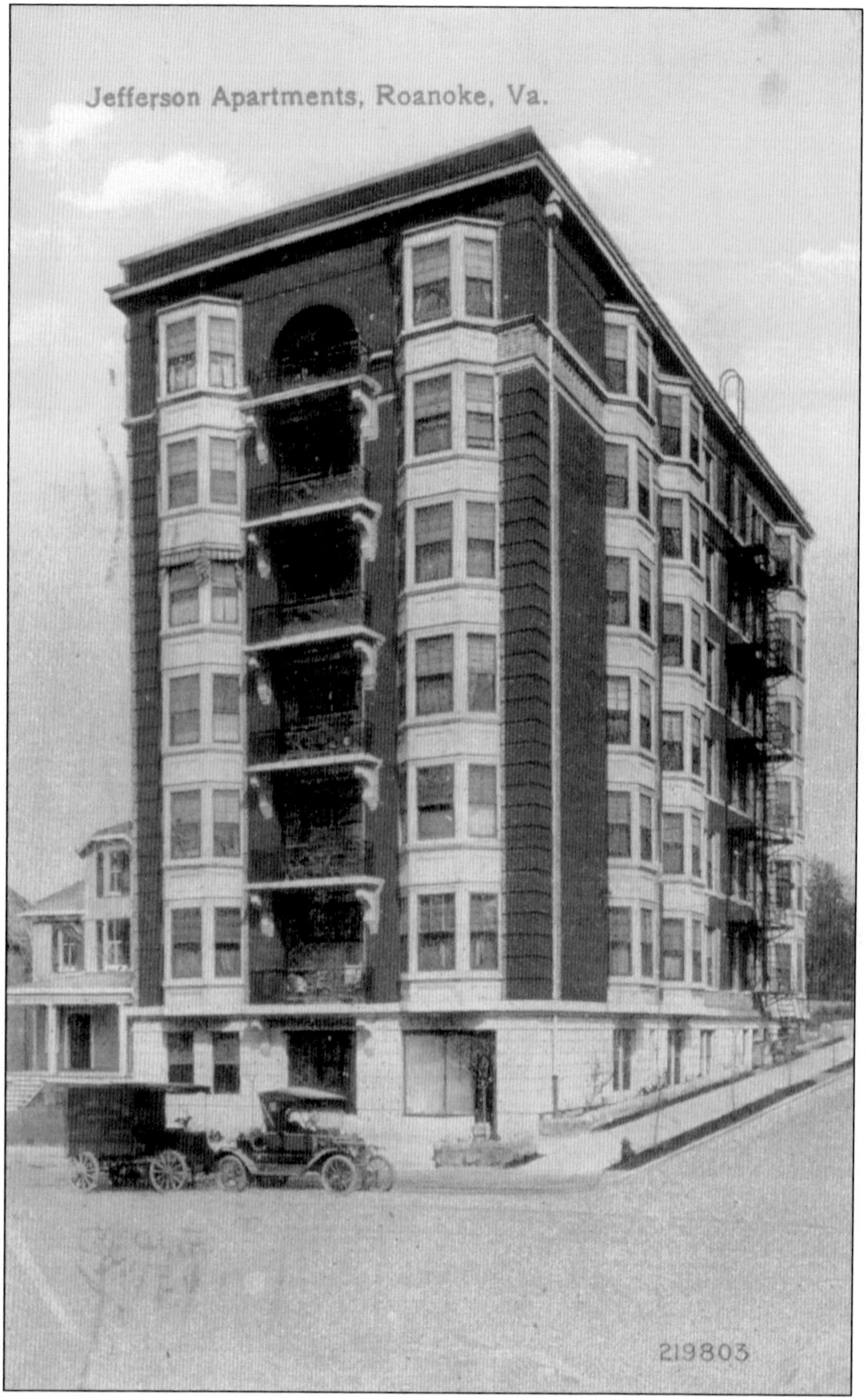

Jefferson Apartments, 1918. The Jefferson Apartments were built in 1912 on South Jefferson Street. The apartments existed for several decades before being razed in the late 1990s. The site was originally occupied by a house that was moved across Mountain Avenue to create the lot for the apartment building to be erected.

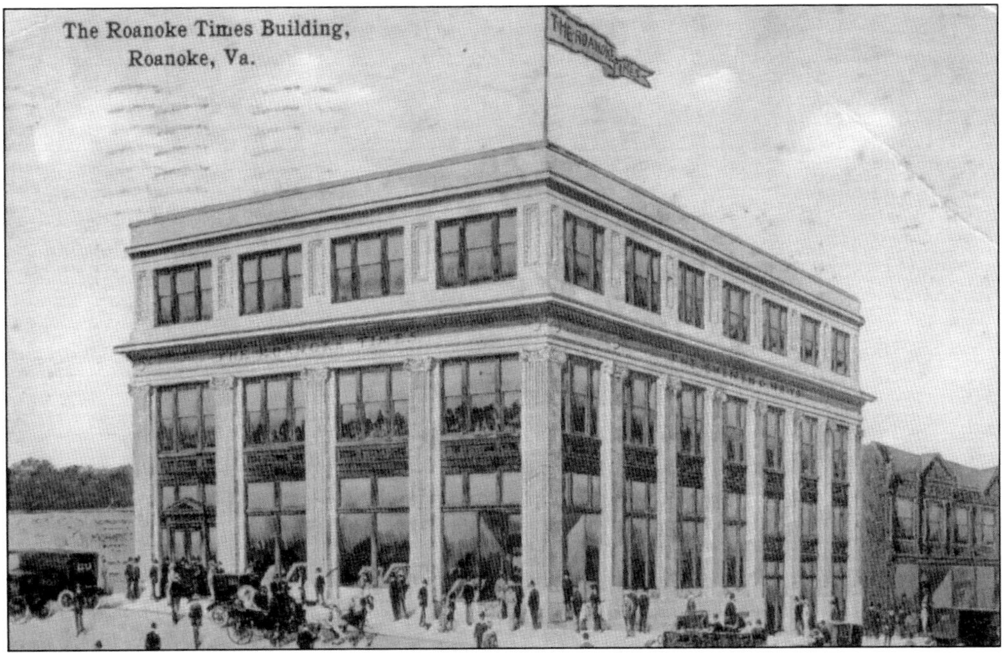

THE *ROANOKE TIMES* BUILDING, 1914. The *Roanoke Times* was the first daily paper in Roanoke, having been started by M. A. Claytor in 1886. In 1909, the *Times* was purchased by J. B. Fishburn, Edward L. Stone, and W. S. Battle and became the *Roanoke Times*, Incorporated. The *Times* building, shown here, was built in 1914.

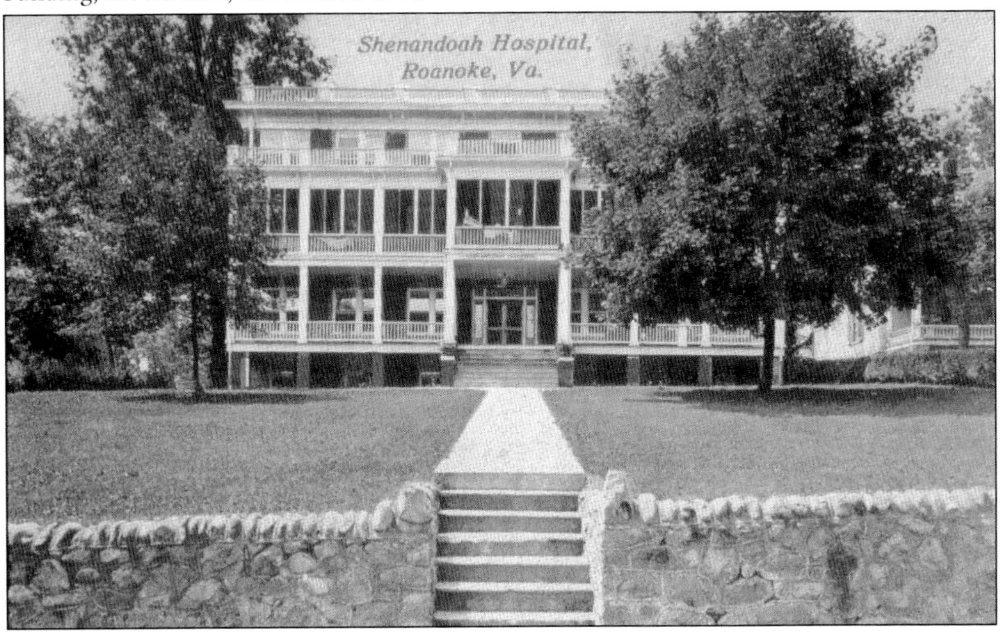

SHENANDOAH HOSPITAL, 1920. Construction of Shenandoah Hospital commenced in 1912, and the hospital opened the next year. The hospital was located on West Campbell Avenue between Seventh and Eighth Streets. Dr. J. H. Dunkley was president and was assisted by Dr. Ira Huff, Dr. W. S. Slicer, Dr. J. T. Hughes, and Dr. L. G. Richards. The hospital also had an 11-room house for nurses and doctors.

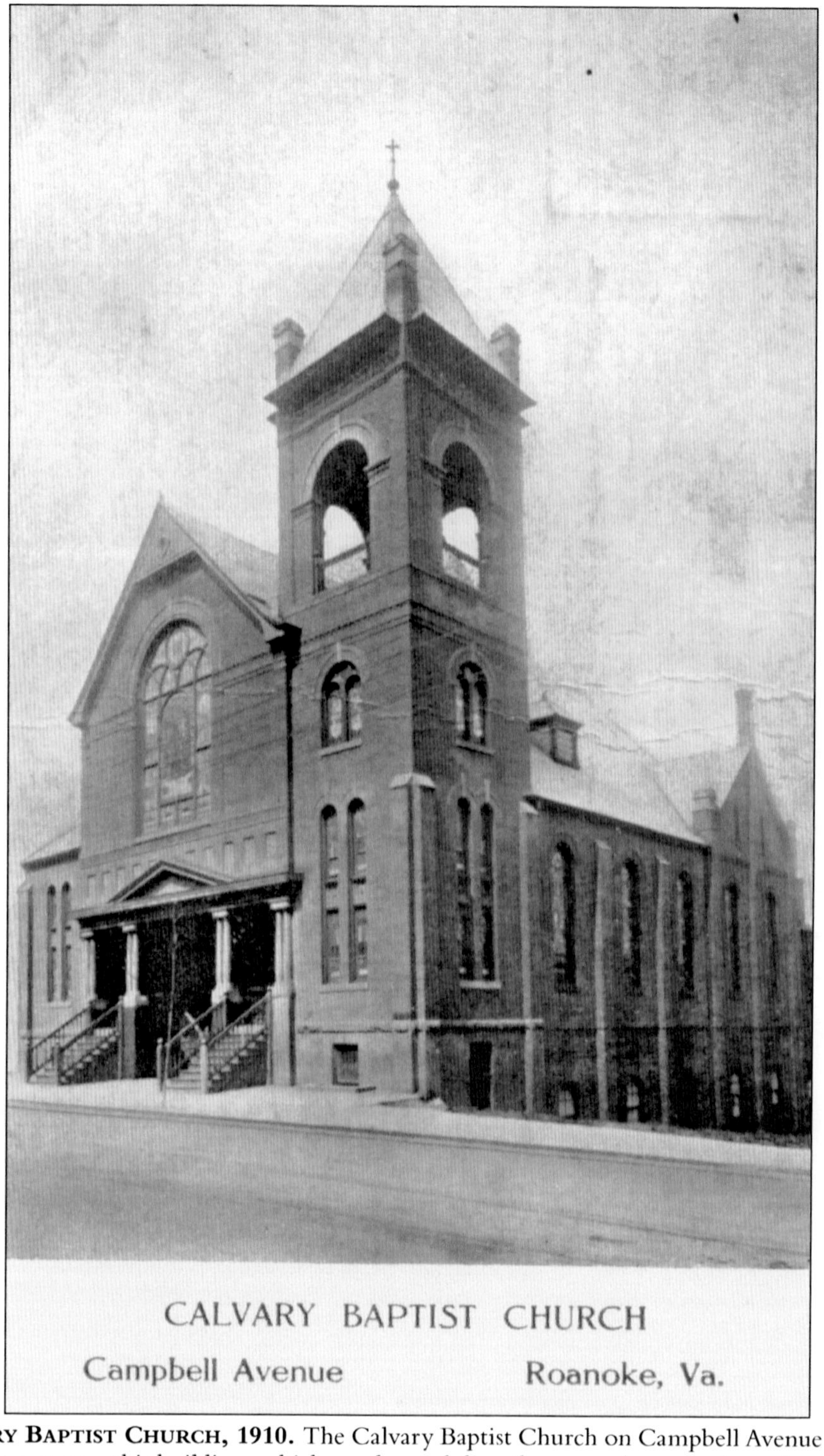

Calvary Baptist Church, 1910. The Calvary Baptist Church on Campbell Avenue had, as its early sanctuary, this building, which was located directly across the street from the present-day facility. Needing more space for the growing congregation and with the completion of the new sanctuary, this sanctuary (built in 1894) was razed in 1931.

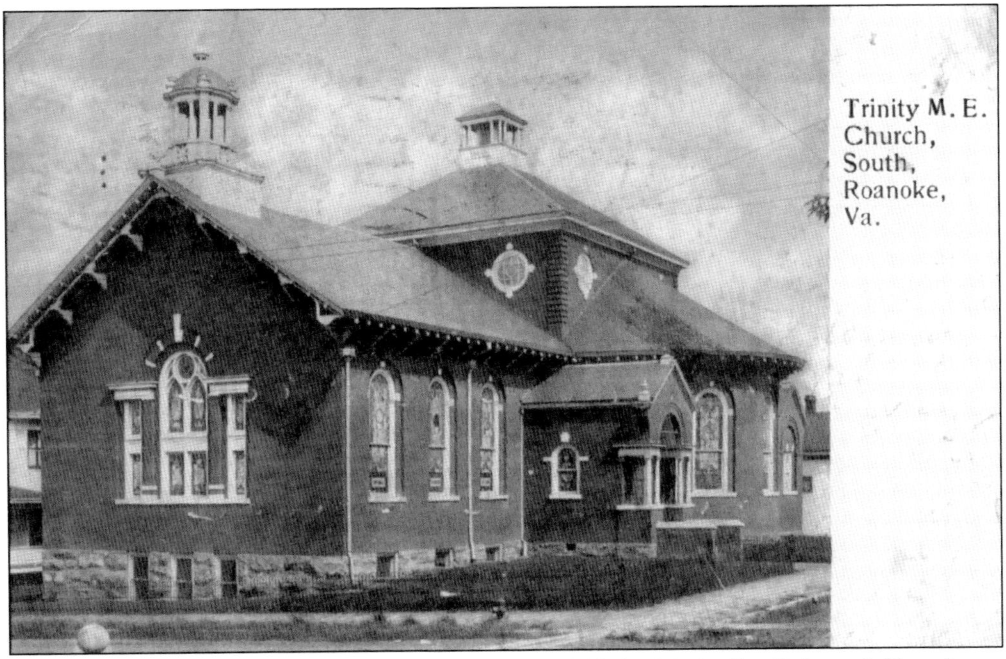

TRINITY METHODIST-EPISCOPAL CHURCH, 1906. Trinity Methodist-Episcopal Church was erected on the corner of Mountain Avenue and Third Street, SW, in 1902. The congregation had originally built a small structure on Kirk Avenue in 1891, near Jefferson Street. This sanctuary was officially dedicated on July 12, 1903.

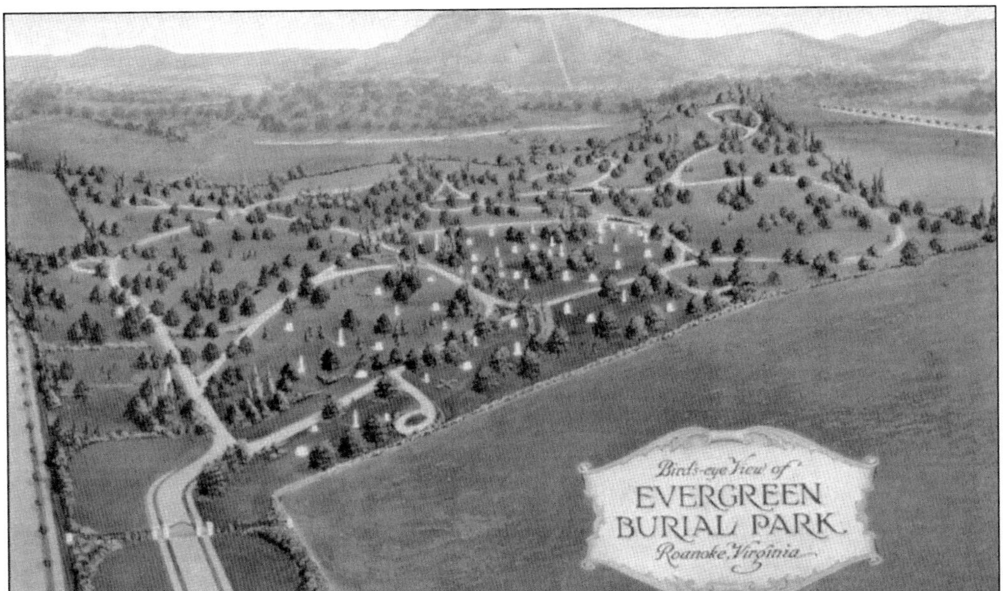

EVERGREEN BURIAL PARK, 1930. Evergreen Burial Park, located in the Raleigh Court section of Roanoke, was not officially annexed into the city limits until 1925 (along with other sections of Raleigh Court). One of the more prominent founders of the cemetery was Charles M. Armes, secretary of the Columbia Trust Company.

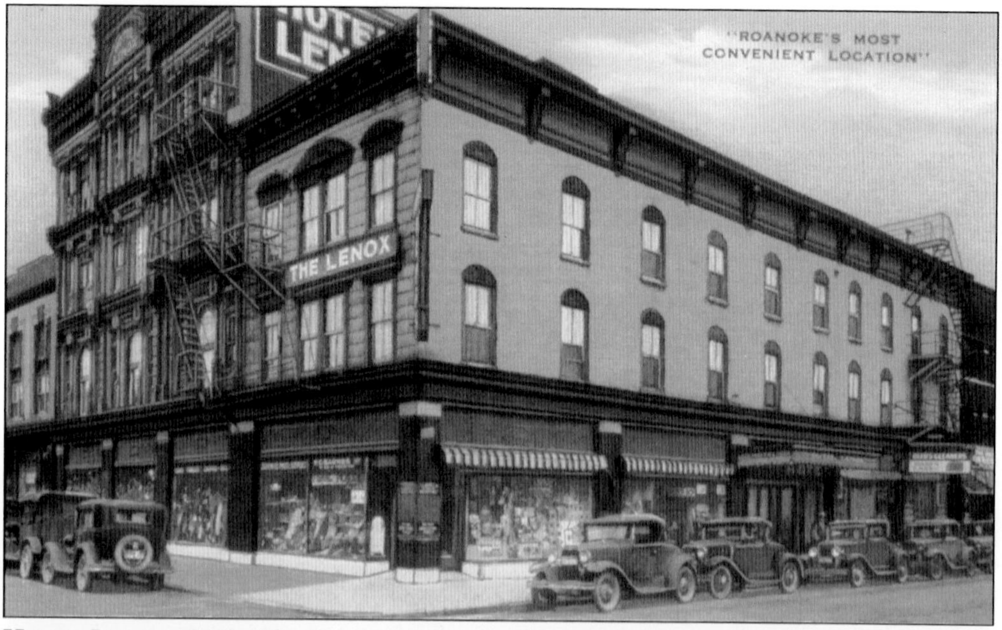

HOTEL LENOX, 1920. The Hotel Lenox opened in 1923, much to the pleasure of Roanoke businessmen who thought the city lacked quality rooms. During World War II, the facility was rented by the Milner hotel chain and became the Lenox-Milner Hotel, taking in the old St. James Hotel at that time. The structure was razed in the 1950s to make room for the Hunter Viaduct.

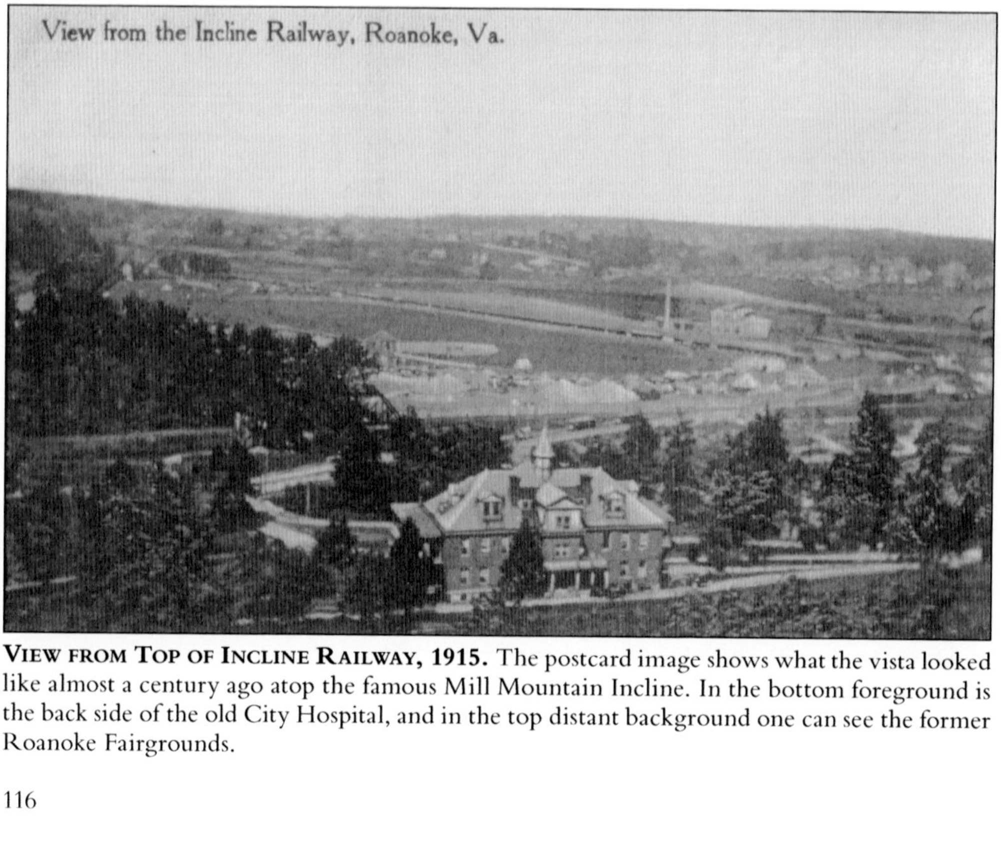

VIEW FROM TOP OF INCLINE RAILWAY, 1915. The postcard image shows what the vista looked like almost a century ago atop the famous Mill Mountain Incline. In the bottom foreground is the back side of the old City Hospital, and in the top distant background one can see the former Roanoke Fairgrounds.

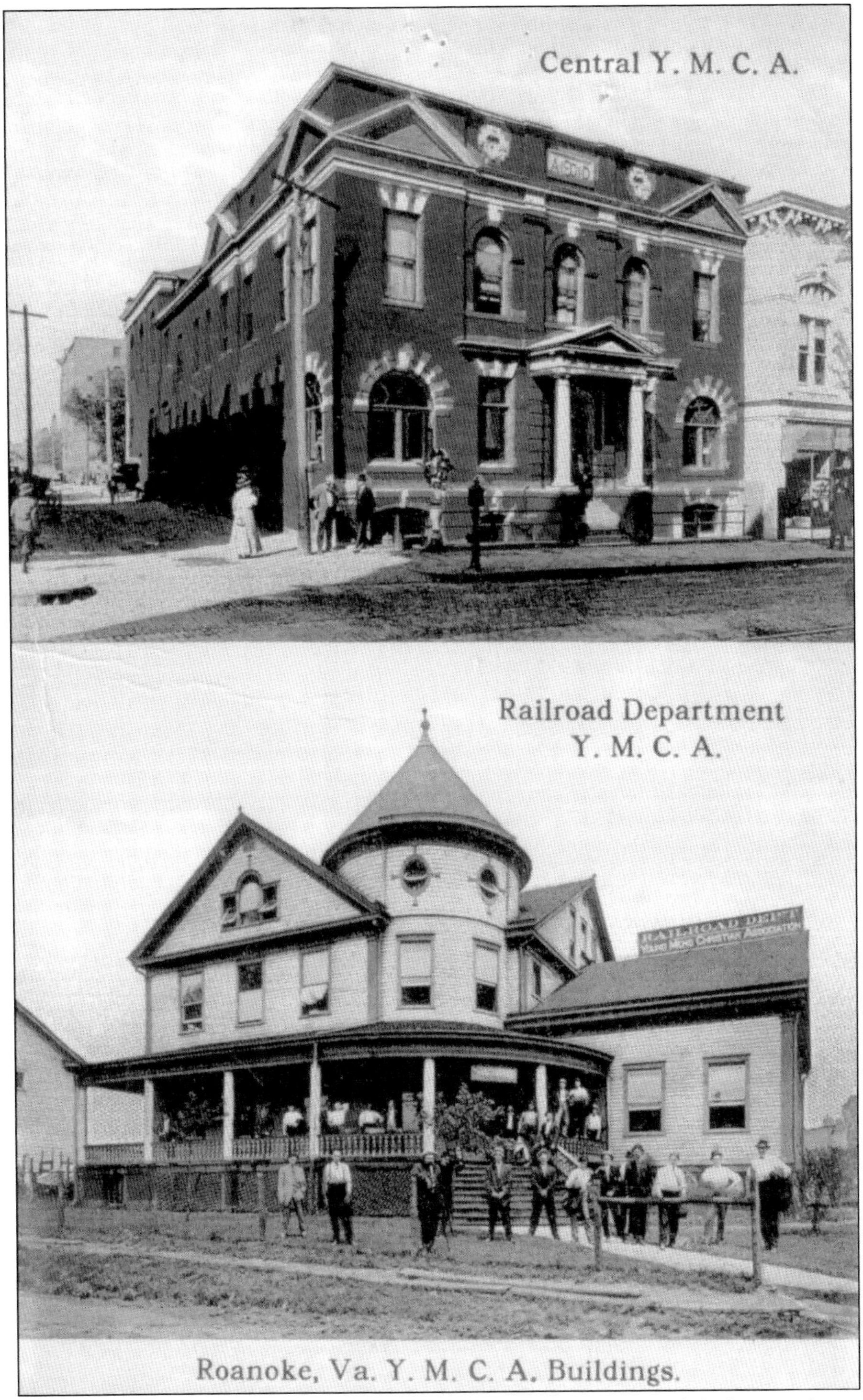

YMCA Buildings, 1915. The top image is of the Central YMCA, and the bottom image is of the Railroad Department YMCA. The Railroad YMCA opened on November 10, 1903. The Young Men's Christian Association arrived in Roanoke in 1883.

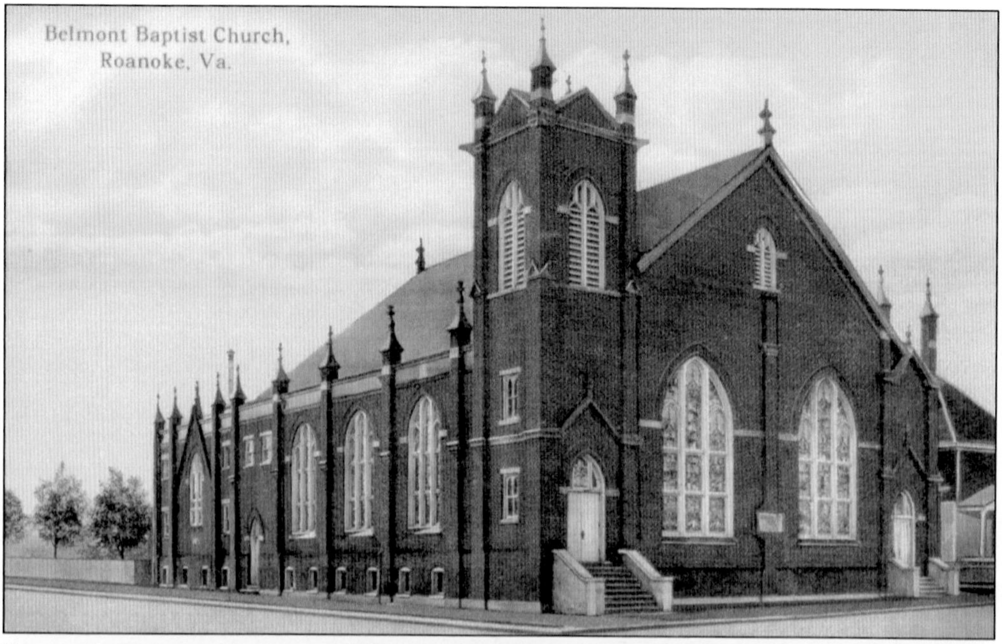

BELMONT BAPTIST CHURCH, 1915. Belmont Baptist Church was organized on October 17, 1901. They dedicated their first sanctuary in Southeast Roanoke in 1904. Belmont Baptist continues to worship in the sanctuary depicted on this card.

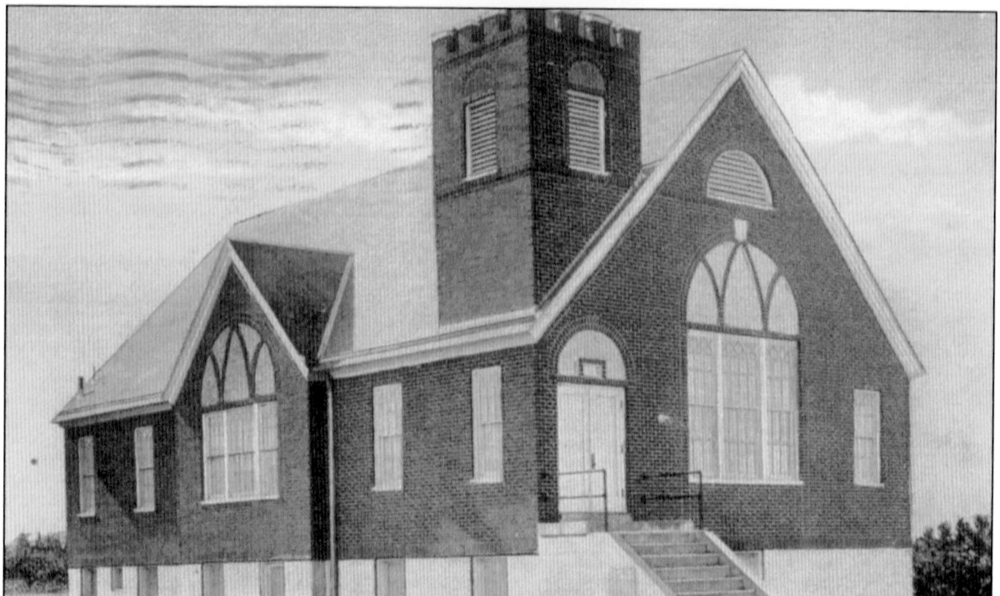

BELMONT CHRISTIAN CHURCH, 1918. The Belmont section of Roanoke, long-served by the Christian Church there, began as a 40-home development around 1889. The Belmont School opened in 1893. Soon to follow were a street car service (1905), the city's first automobile fire steamer (1911), and jitney buses (1921).

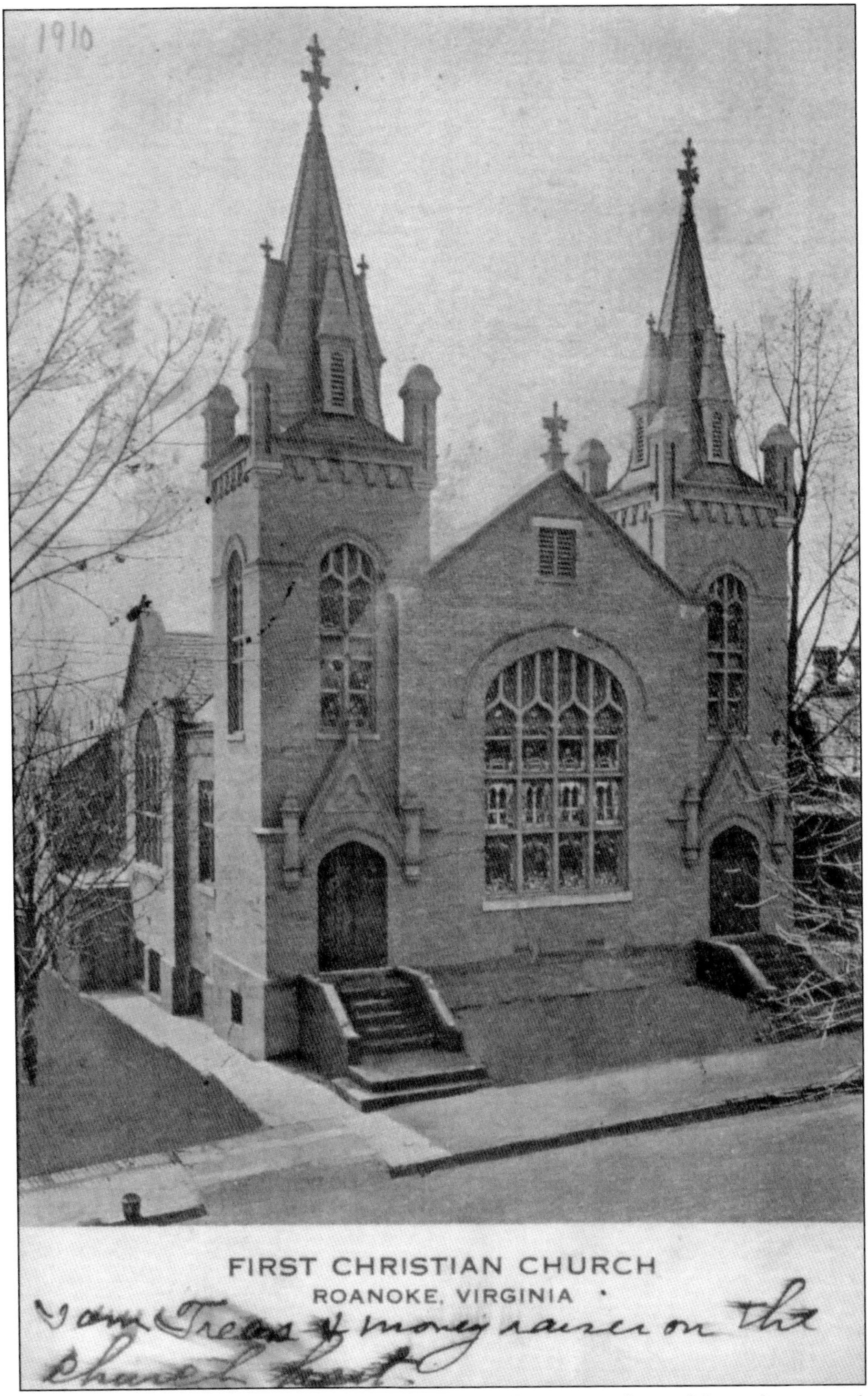

FIRST CHRISTIAN CHURCH, 1910. A member used this postcard to celebrate her new church sanctuary: "Our new church cost $15,000, pipe organ $2,650, pews $1,100. Expect to dedicate third Sunday in April." The church was badly damaged by a fire in 1917, but it eventually recovered.

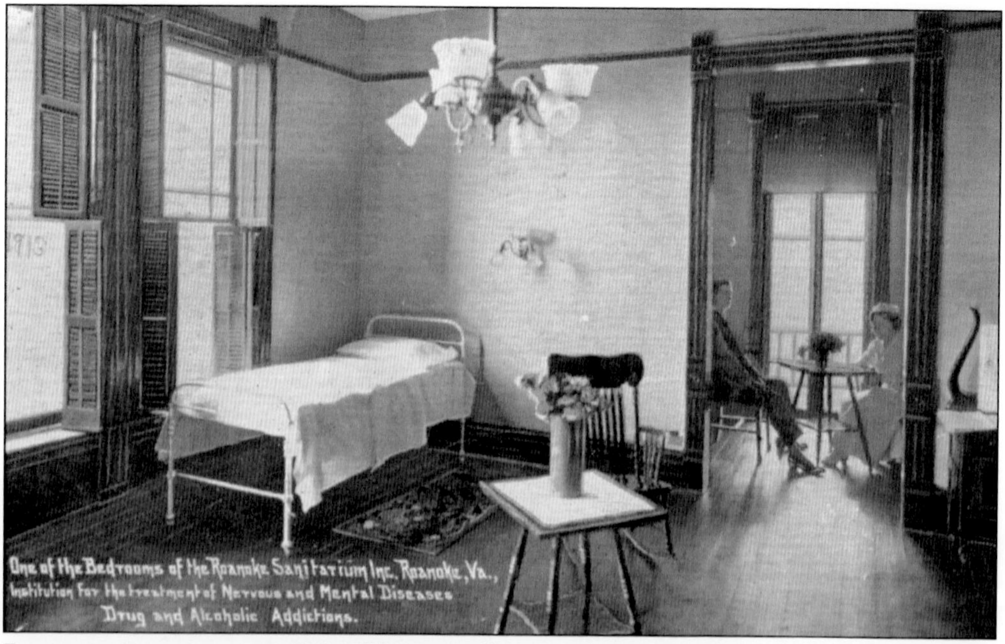

ROANOKE SANATORIUM, 1913. This postcard's description reads, "One of the bedrooms of the Roanoke Sanatorium Inc. Roanoke, VA., Institution for the treatment of Nervous and Mental Diseases, Drug and Alcoholic Addictions."

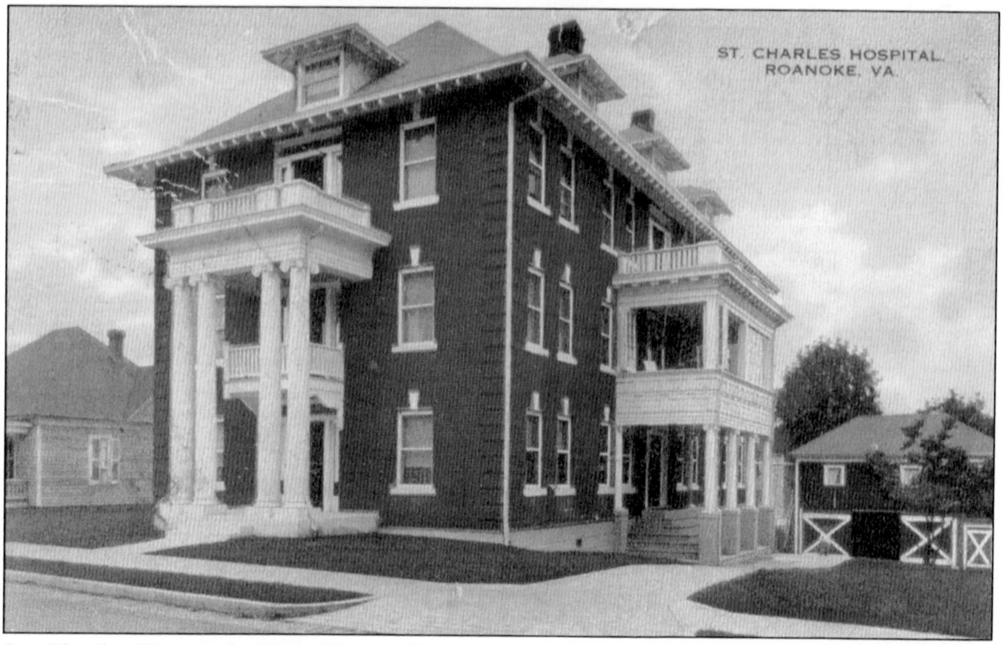

St. Charles Hospital, 1916. The St. Charles Hospital was located at 533 Mountain Avenue. It opened in March 1913 under the direction of Dr. J. C. Burke. The hospital closed in 1934, and the building was converted into apartments.

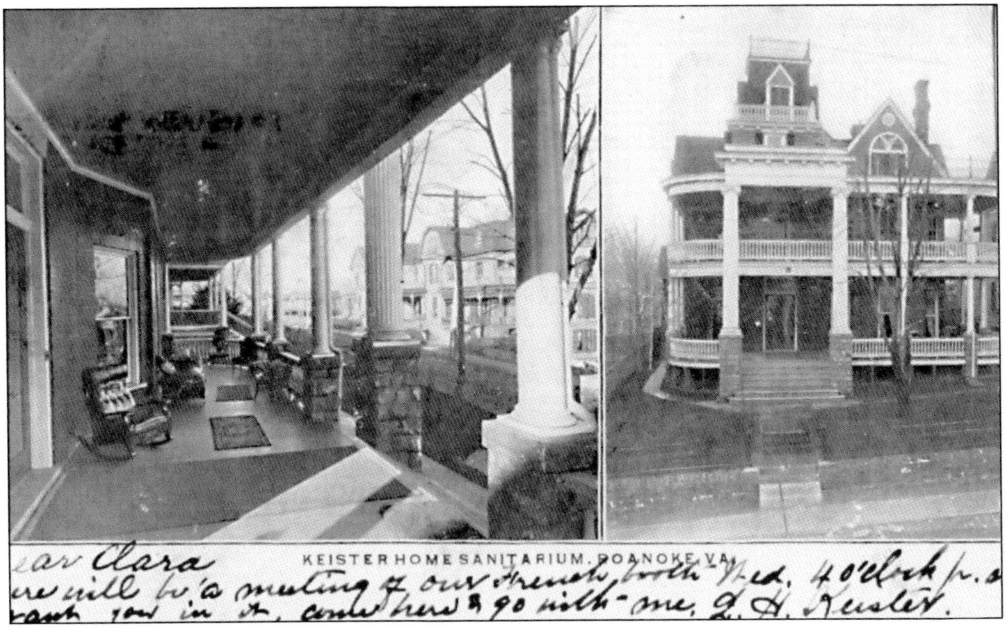

KEISTER HOME SANATORIUM, 1907. Sanatoriums were popular at the turn of the 20th century for the care and treatment of tuberculosis patients. Often doctors or others in the healthcare profession would establish homes and other institutions with such a purpose. Tuberculosis often wiped out entire families in the city at the turn of the century.

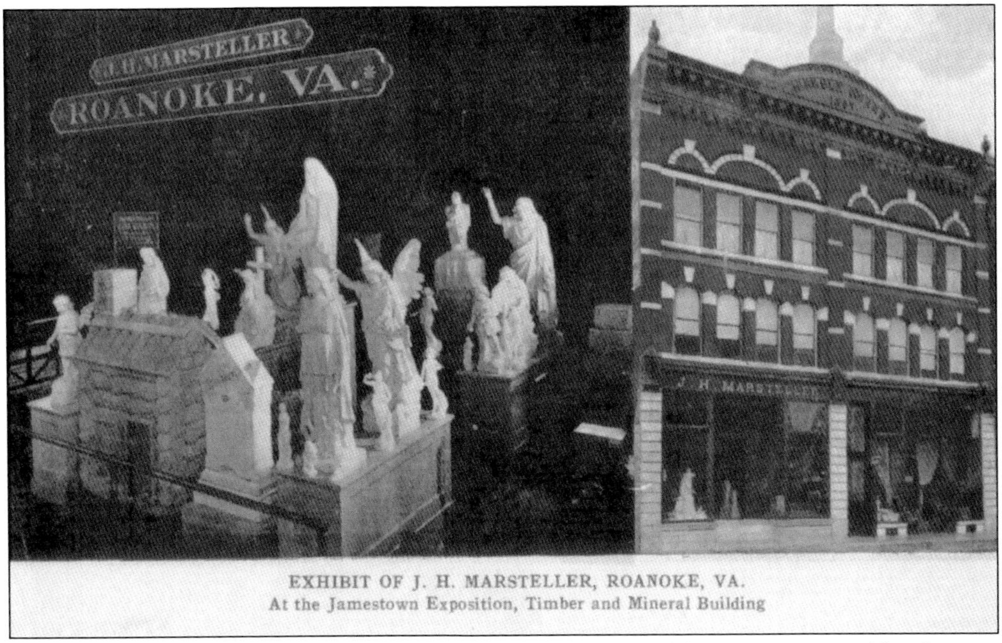

J. H. MARSTELLER, 1908. J. H. Marsteller created ornate marble monuments and headstones. This card was produced for Marsteller in 1907, showing on the left the exhibit of Marsteller at the 1907 Jamestown Exhibition's Timber and Mineral Building. The image on the right shows Marsteller's place of business in Roanoke, which was built on Campbell Avenue in 1897.

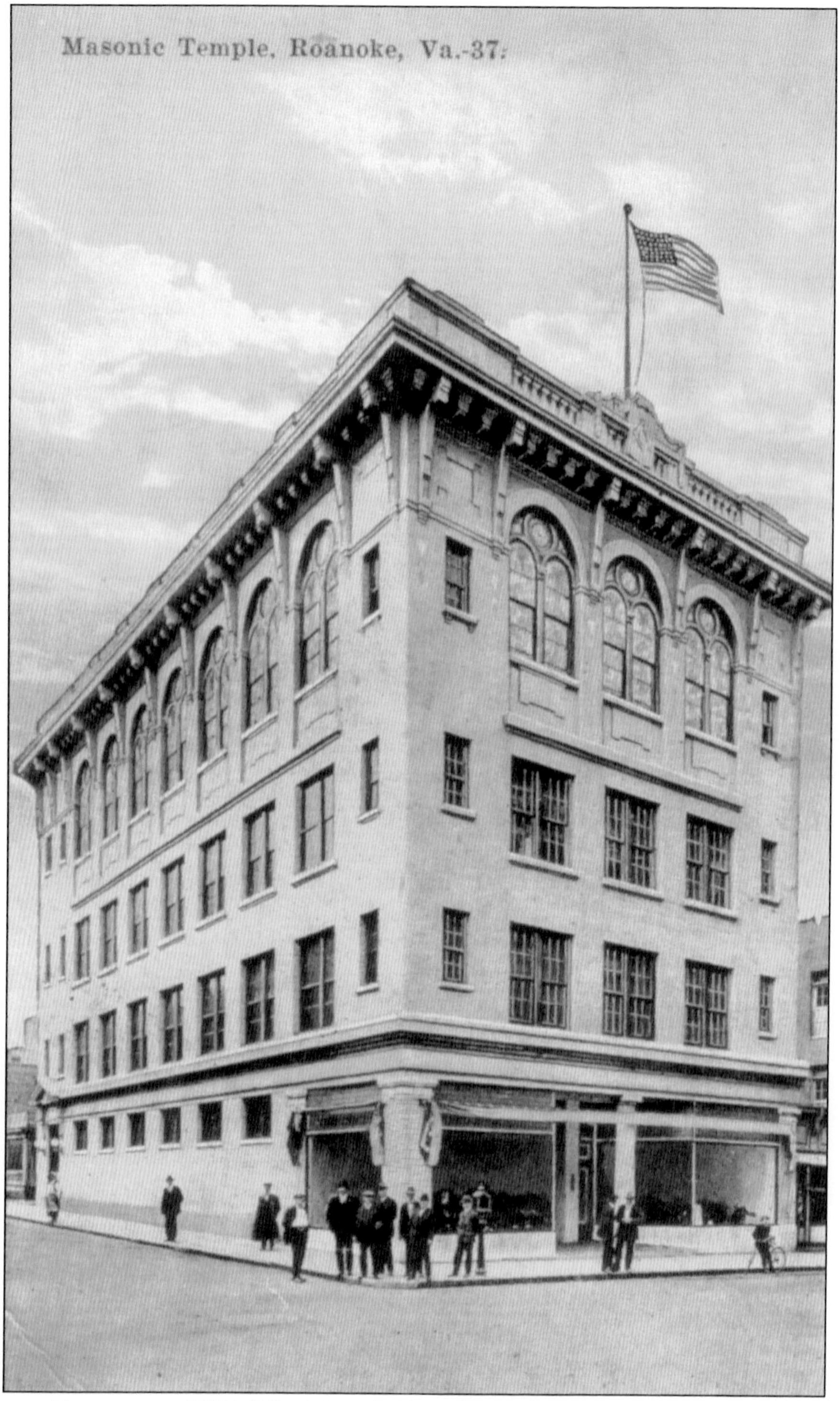

MASONIC TEMPLE, C. 1920. The Masonic Temple was located on the northwest corner of First and Kirk Streets. In 1915, the street level was occupied by Reams, Jones, and Blankenship furniture store. The store's slogan was "Marry the girl, we'll furnish the home."

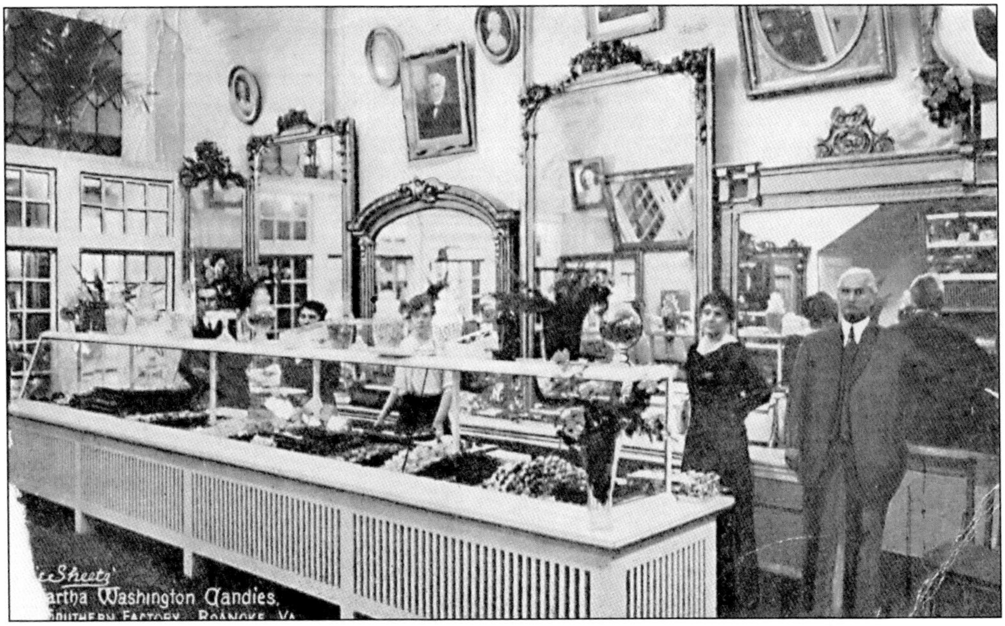

Martha Washington Candies, 1916. This interior view of the Martha Washington Candies store shows what the company considered its Southern factory. Martha Washington Candies Roanoke franchise was started by W. G. Baldwin at 310 South Jefferson Street in 1914. Baldwin was of the famed Baldwin-Felts Detective Agency.

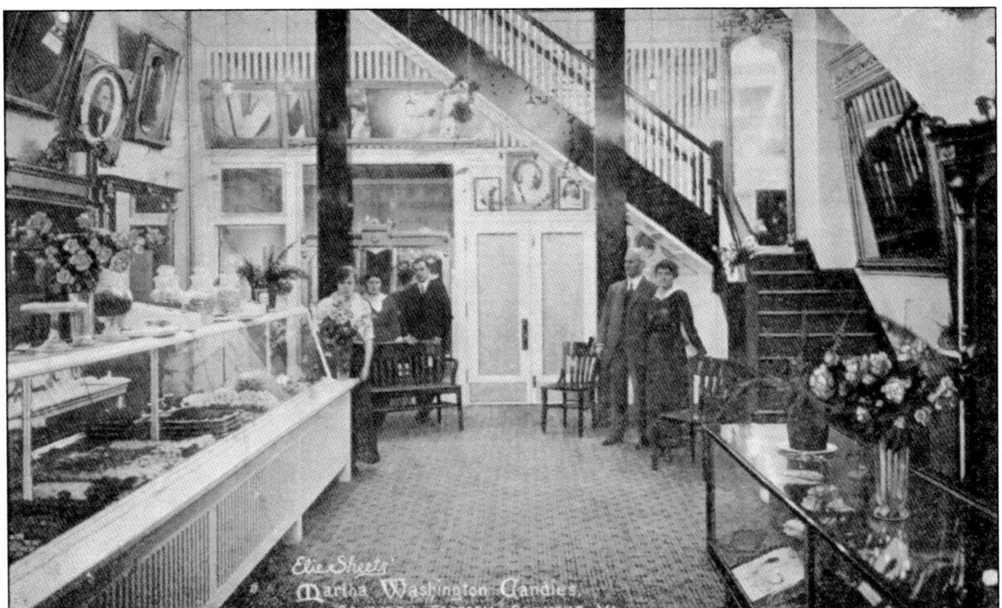

Martha Washington Candies, 1915. W. G. Baldwin had a successful candy business. One year after acquiring the Roanoke franchise, Baldwin announced that he controlled five other factories and 57 stores with headquarters in Roanoke. Baldwin died in 1936.

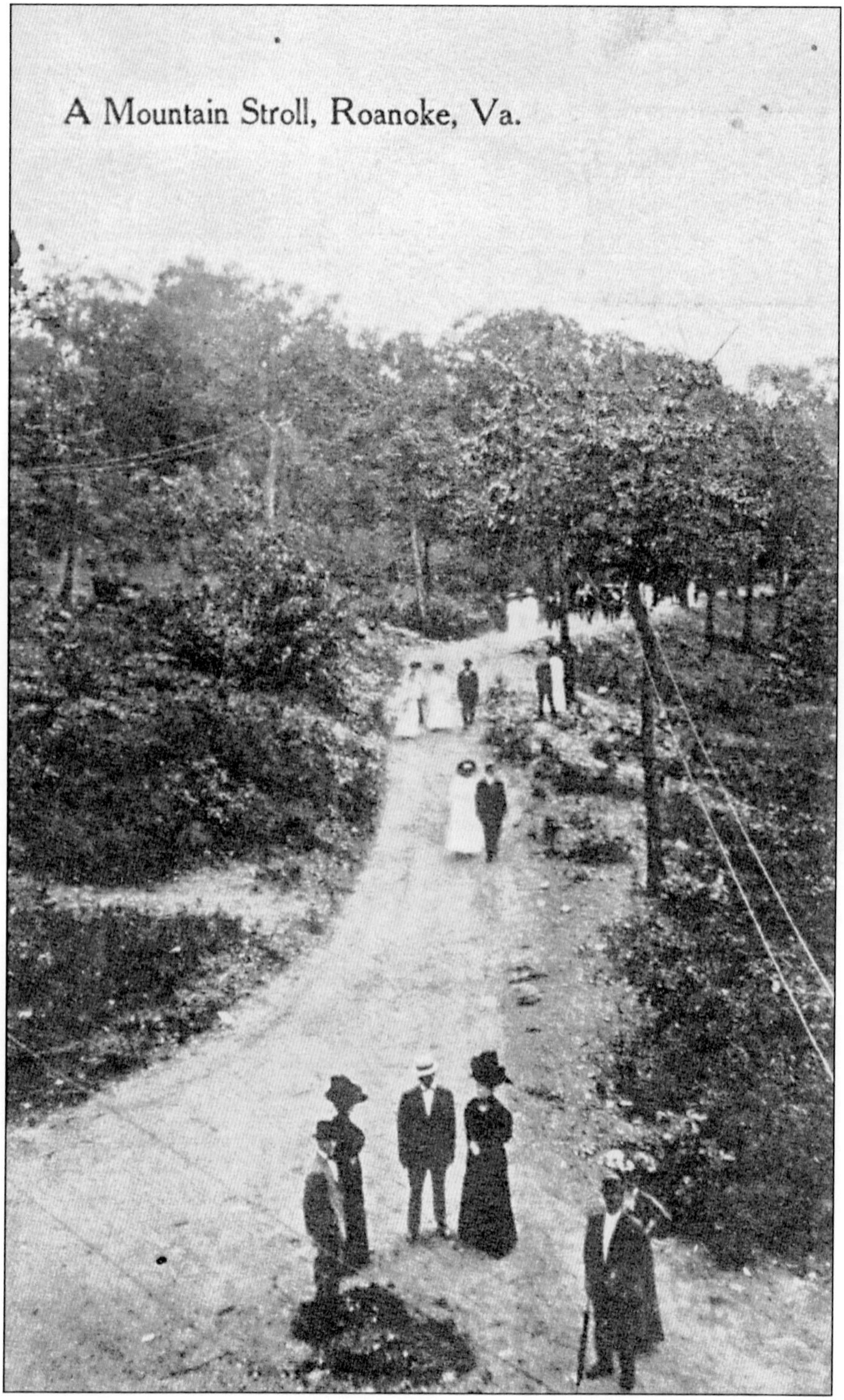

A MOUNTAIN STROLL, 1920. This view shows strollers atop Mill Mountain. The top of the mountain had park grounds and trails. The incline and the watch tower made it a popular destination.

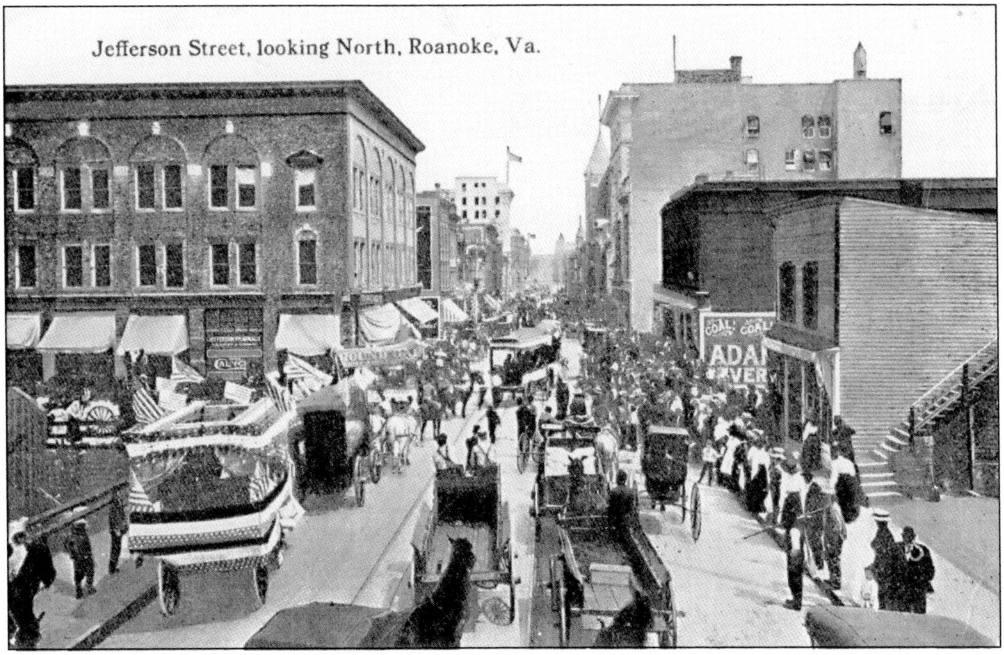

Jefferson Street, Looking North, 1912. This view of Jefferson Street shows one of the main streets in Downtown Roanoke as it looked nearly a century ago. Based on the bunting-covered wagons in the forefront, the card appears to depict a parade

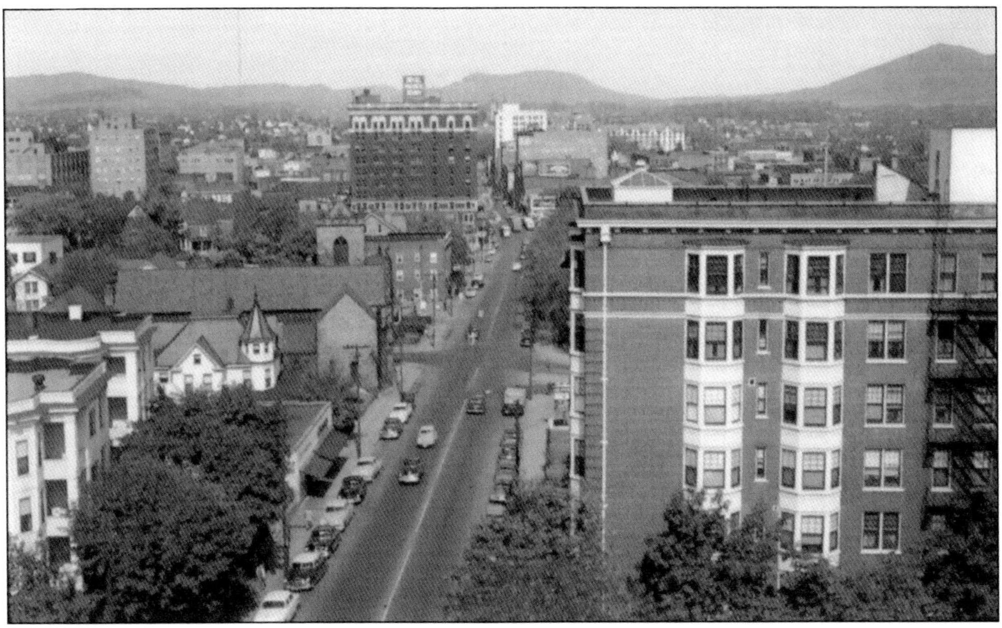

Jefferson Street, Looking North, *c.* 1960. In contrast with the above postcard, this photograph shows how Jefferson Street had changed in 50 years. This view looks north down Jefferson Street from Mountain Avenue, showing a variety of commercial buildings, apartments, and hotels.

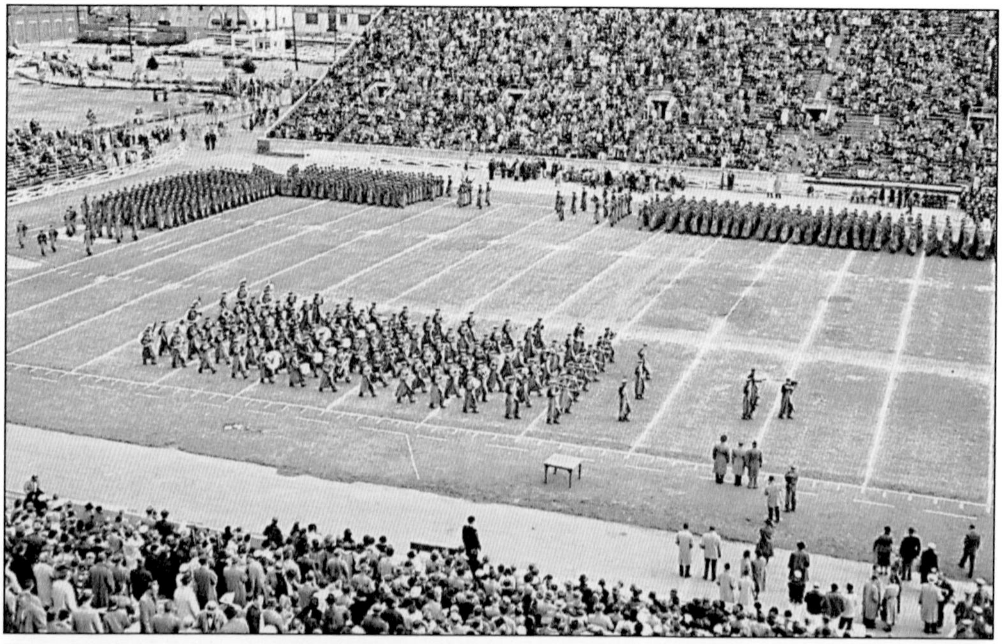

Victory Stadium, c. 1960. Victory Stadium was dedicated in 1942, named in anticipation of an Allied victory during World War II. This card shows some of the Virginia Military Institute (VMI) cadets on the field as part of a football game being played between VMI and VPI (Virginia Polytechnic Institute, or Virginia Tech), a Thanksgiving Day tradition in Roanoke for many years.

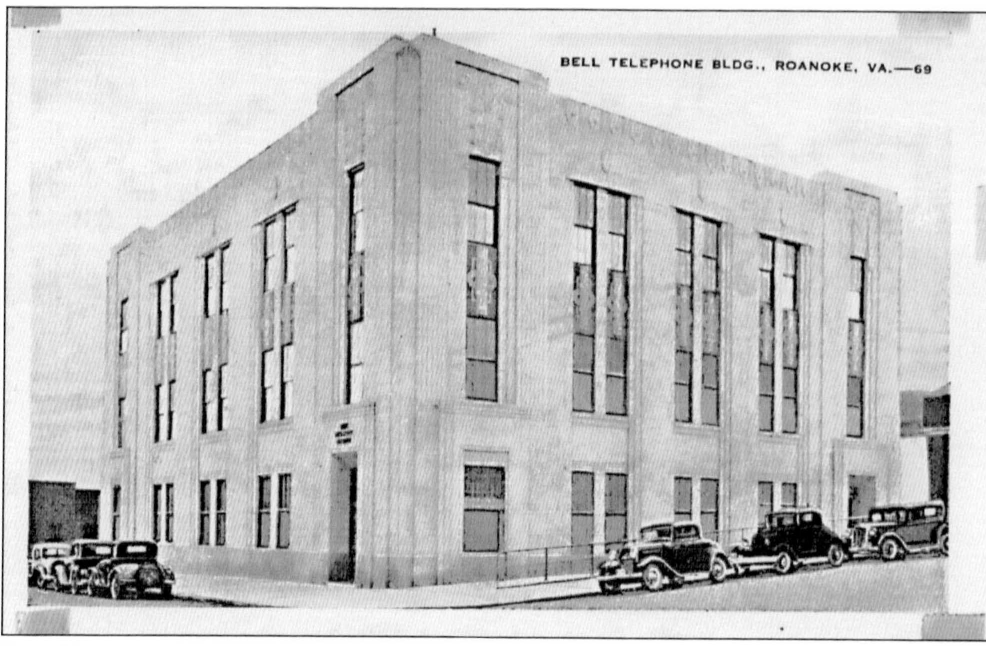

Bell Telephone Building, c. 1940. The Bell Telephone Company began service in Roanoke on May 19, 1884. In 1895, Bell Telephone introduced long-distance service. That year, Roanokers could call Bedford, Lynchburg, and Danville.

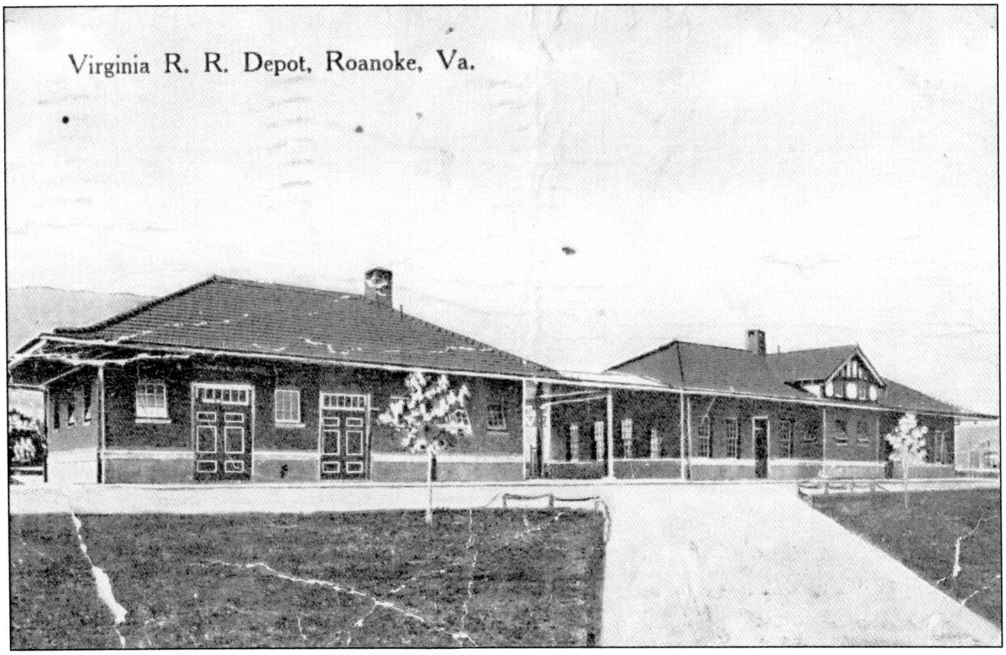

VIRGINIAN RAILROAD DEPOT, 1914. The Virginian Railroad Depot was constructed in 1909. The building's original design was 162 feet long and 32 feet wide, with waiting rooms on one end and baggage and express on the other. Today, the depot is owned by the Roanoke chapter of the National Railway Historical Society, and funds are being raised for its restoration.

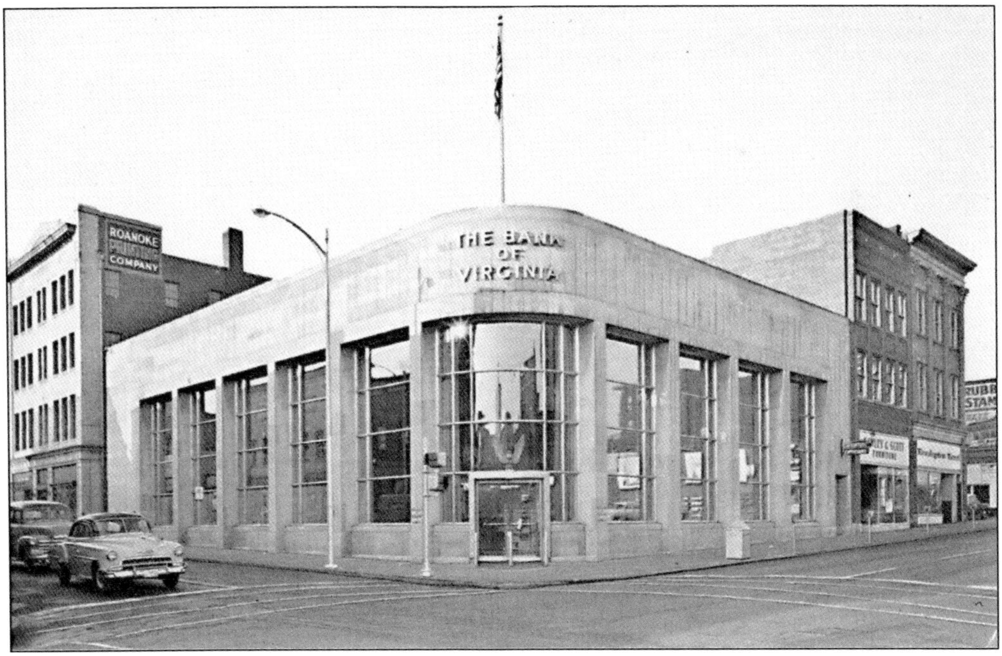

THE BANK OF VIRGINIA, *c.* 1960. The Bank of Virginia was located for many years at the corner of First Street and Church Avenue. The bank was one of a number of local and regional banks that served the downtown area back in the 1960s and 1970s, before mergers became so predominant. The building was razed many years ago.

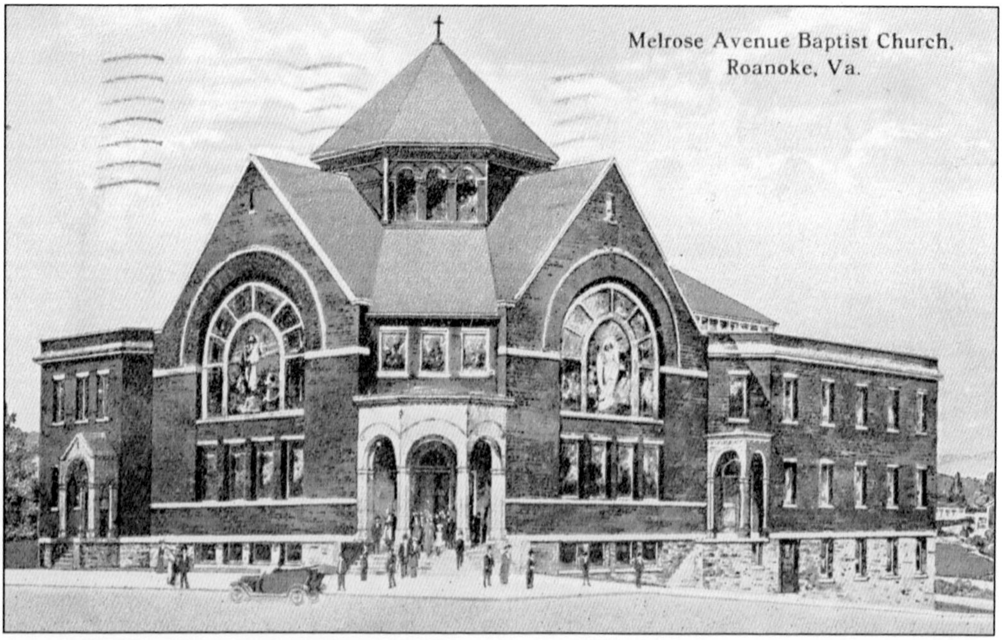

MELROSE AVENUE BAPTIST CHURCH, 1917. This rendering of Melrose Avenue Baptist Church was a bit overdone, as the sanctuary originally built in the early 1920s was not quite as ornate (but nonetheless a beautiful, dignified structure). The congregation eventually moved off of Melrose Avenue to its present location on Peters Creek Road.

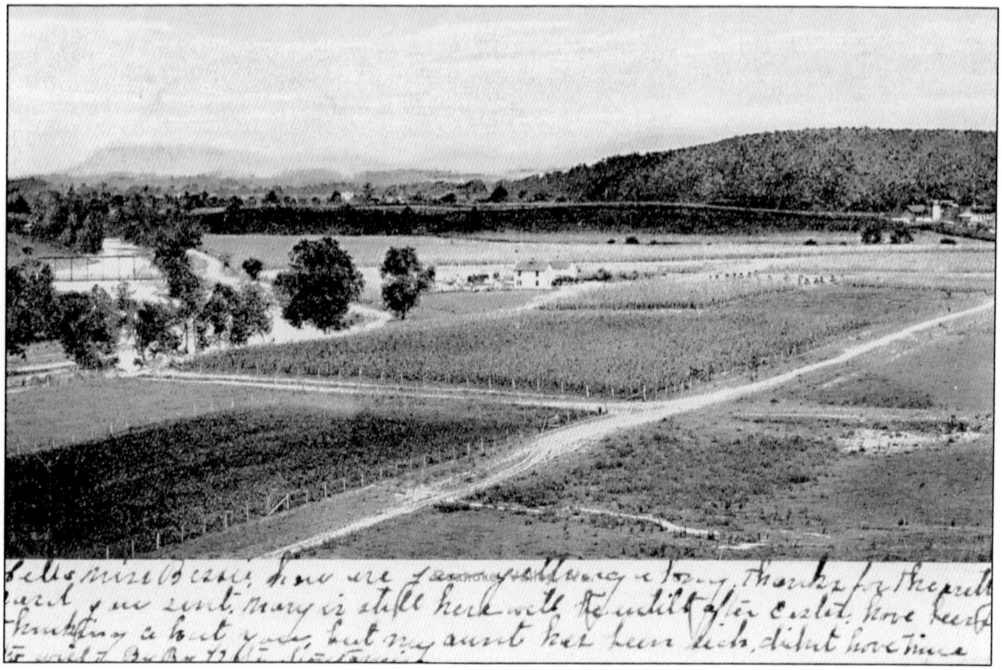

ROANOKE VALLEY, 1907. This pastoral scene shows an undetermined location in the Roanoke Valley along the Roanoke River. Wherever the landscape shown here is, it almost certainly has been altered by a century of valley growth and development.